of Tokhat Matthew, Solomon Caesar Malan

The Life and times of S. Gregory the Illuminator the founder and patron saint of the Armenian Church

of Tokhat Matthew, Solomon Caesar Malan

The Life and times of S. Gregory the Illuminator the founder and patron saint of the Armenian Church

ISBN/EAN: 9783741163920

Manufactured in Europe, USA, Canada, Australia, Japa

Cover: Foto ©Andreas Hilbeck / pixelio.de

Manufactured and distributed by brebook publishing software (www.brebook.com)

of Tokhat Matthew, Solomon Caesar Malan

The Life and times of S. Gregory the Illuminator the founder and patron saint of the Armenian Church

Harvard College Library

BOUGHT FROM THE
GRANT WALKER
BEQUEST

THE LIFE AND TIMES

OF

S. GREGORY THE ILLUMINATOR.

RIVINGTONS

LONDON	*Waterloo Place*
OXFORD	*High Street*
CAMBRIDGE	*Trinity Street*

THE LIFE AND TIMES
OF
S. GREGORY THE ILLUMINATOR,

The Founder and Patron Saint

OF THE ARMENIAN CHURCH.

TRANSLATED FROM THE ARMENIAN.

BY

THE REV. S. C. MALAN, M.A.

VICAR OF BROADWINDSOR.

RIVINGTONS,
London, Oxford, and Cambridge.
1868.

PREFACE.

THE question, asked some time ago,—whether or not, "holy" stands before "Catholic Church," in the Armenian version of the Nicene Creed—led me to think that a few authentic documents in connexion with the Armenian Church, might prove acceptable to those who take interest in more than one branch of Christ's holy Catholic Church on earth.

I therefore gathered together and translated the following:—

I. *A short Summary of the Armenian Church and Nation*, which is a reprint in a separate form from the Minutes of Home Administration in Russia, for the year 1843. The copy kindly lent me on this occasion by the Rev. R. W. Blackmore, Rector of Donhead S. Mary, Wilts, was given him in 1843, by Nerses V., who was then Patriarch elect of Armenia, and was afterwards visited at Etchmiadzin by Muravieff, as mentioned by him in his travels. So that the information contained in this summary may be relied on as correct, so far as it goes.

II. *The Acts and Martyrdom of S. Thaddeus and of S. Bartholomew, the Apostles of Armenia.* These are translated from the Armenian, and give the traditions on the subject commonly believed in the Armenian Church.

III. *The Life and Times of S. Gregory the Illuminator, the Founder and Patron Saint of the Armenian Church.* The translation here given is from the original by the Vartabed Matthew (of Tokat ?), published at Venice in 1749.

In preparing this, I had the choice of two things— either to select my own materials, and, acting as critic, to write a history of S. Gregory; or to translate one already written from the best, if not the only available, authorities, namely, Agathangelos and Simeon Metaphrastes, by an Armenian, with Armenian sympathies for "the Sun of Armenia," as S. Gregory is called among his own people. I chose the latter course as preferable; my object in this case being, not so much to sever truth from fiction, or, at least, probable facts from mere legends, as to put into English the history of the first Patriarch and Patron Saint of Armenia, as it is commonly received in his Church, without any comment of my own, beyond an occasional word or note by way of explanation, always enclosed within brackets. I therefore aimed only at giving a grammatical translation, purposely leaving the idiom thereof such as to remind the reader that both the original and the translation of it give other men's thoughts, and not my own.

IV. *The Confession of Faith of the Armenian Church.* I first began the translation of this treatise from the Russian work of Joseph, once Patriarch of Armenia and Prince Dolgorucki, published at S. Petersburg in 1799, which is yet spoken of among Russian Armenians as the standard book on the subject. Although it professes to be translated from the Armenian, as stated on the title-page, I yet soon found that it is almost word for word the translation of Schrœder's *Confessio Fidei Armenicæ Ecclesiæ*, written by himself with notes of his own, and found in his *Thesaurus Linguæ Armenicæ*, pp. 249—298. I then translated it from his copy, and the authorities given, from the Armenian; comparing Schrœder's original with the Russian translation, which is tolerably correct; except that it omits all the bits of scholarship or of close criticism given by the learned German.

Lest, however, I should make a mistake, I wrote to S. Petersburg; and through the kind offices of his Excellency Mr. De Golovnine, late Minister of Public Instruction, I ascertained from Mr. Delianoff, an Armenian, who is Senator, Secretary of State, attached to the Ministry of Public Instruction, and Director of the Imperial Library, that there exists no Armenian original of this Russian translation by the Patriarch Joseph; so, that we may look upon Schrœder's treatise as the true expression of the Armenian faith. For the Patriarch calls God and men to witness that it is so; and challenges the latter to find aught amiss in it.

We may therefore rely on the authenticity thereof; bearing in mind, however, that as it is the Confession of Faith of the Armenian Church, by which is always understood the Armeno-Gregorian, or Armenian Church of S. Gregory, this Confession is always placed at the beginning of the Common Prayer Book (*Jamakirk*) of that Church; whence, therefore, it is with sundry prayers, removed, in the editions of that book published by schismatic or Romish Armenians. It is not found in the *Jamakirk* I have, published at Venice in 1837, while it forms, so to speak, the preface to the one I brought from Constantinople, published by Gregorian Armenians.

V. *The Order of Holy Baptism in the Armenian Church.* I translated this from that order, as it is given in the *Medz Mashdots,* or Armenian Ritual: comparing it with the Russian translation thereof by the Patriarch Joseph, and with the Order of Baptism given me at Jerusalem by the Armenian Archbishop, and published by his authority.

VI. *The Office of the Divine Liturgy of the Armenian Church.* This is translated from an original

Preface. vii

I bought at Constantinople, and compared with the translation by the Patriarch Joseph, with the Romish Armenian Liturgy published at Venice, and with the French translation by Dulaurier. The differences between all these are given in notes.

VII. *Instruction in the Christian Faith of the Armenian Church*, by the Vartabed Mser, and published in Armenian at Moscow in 1850, under the auspices of the Patriarch Nerses V., already mentioned. It is an important treatise for the knowledge of the Armenian faith, inasmuch as it gives native authorities for every point of doctrine put forward.

VIII. *The Differences between the Armenian and the Greek Churches.* This is an interesting and well written account by Muravieff, not only of the differences in doctrine that sever the Armenian Church from the Greek, but also of all the efforts at re-union between the two Churches, made chiefly by S. Nerses of Cla or Hromgla, and the Archbishop of Lampron. This account is translated from the Russian of Muravieff's Travels, vol. ii. pp. 206—257.

Of these several treatises, all prepared for the press at the same time, only the first three are now published. The small interest still taken in such matters, in spite of a great deal of desultory talk about "the re-union of Christendom," does not justify the publishers in attempting more at present.

Yet, as the portion of the work left out is by far the most important as regards doctrine and matter of fact in Church history, should any encouragement be given to the publication of the treatises now omitted, they may see the light at some future day. Church folk, however, are now so taken up with silks, lace, candles at noon-day, and other questions equally frivolous,—very much like children playing at dolls while their house is on fire,—that more solid lore and better sense meet with little or no favour.

In sooth, the only inducement to an honest workman to toil at an irksome task of this kind is assuredly not held out to him by man. But the labour is for Christ and for His Church; and this of itself is the greatest reward.

S. C. MALAN.

BROADWINDSOR,
June 13, 1868.

CONTENTS.

INTRODUCTION.

A SHORT SUMMARY OF THE ARMENIAN CHURCH AND PEOPLE.

	PAGE
I. Of the Armenian Kingdom and Nation	3
II. Of the Armenian Church	22
III. Of the Armenian Hierarchy	50

INTRODUCTION OF CHRISTIANITY INTO ARMENIA.

I. The Acts and Martyrdom of the Holy Apostle Thaddeus	66
II. The Acts and Martyrdom of the Holy Apostle Bartholomew	99

HISTORY OF THE LIFE AND TIMES OF S. GREGORY THE ILLUMINATOR.

CHAPTER I.

Of the time and place of his birth 107

INTRODUCTION.

A SHORT SUMMARY OF THE ARMENIAN CHURCH AND PEOPLE [1].

I. *Of the Armenian Kingdom and Nation.*

AMONG the many and various nationalities of the Russian Empire at present gathered by Providence into one body, there is found in the Armenian people, also called Haïks or Haïkans, the remnant of one of the oldest stocks or types of the human race. In spite of endless vicissitudes and revolutions during a long line of centuries, this people alone, among Eastern nations, still retains its peculiar features with, as it were, stubborn constancy and exclusiveness. It still cherishes its original customs, manners, and habits, together with the associations and ideas inherited from a high ancestry, not only wherever it is scattered over the whole earth, but especially at home, in the land of its once powerful and glorious existence; where it now lingers among the ruins of its ancient cities, and the crumbling monuments of its great men of old. Yet in no respects is the Armenian people so whole and united

[1] Translated from Russian State Papers. See Preface.

as in matters of faith drawn from the first at the spring of Eastern light, through the preaching of Christ's Gospel, which, owing to peculiar circumstances, has caused a singular exception in the Christian world[1]—namely, the isolated individual community called the Armenian Church.

Armenians themselves, relying on traditions still preserved among them, trace their origin up to Haïk, a grandson of Japhet, who lived at the time of the Tower of Babel, and took part in it; and who, after the confusion of tongues and the dispersion of peoples that happened there, left the plains of Shinar for the foot of Ararat, that second cradle of the human race[2]. There he established himself and his family,

[1] [This, from a Greek point of view, means only the Orthodox or Greek Church, from which that of Rome is excluded; wherefore are Latins rebaptized by the Greek Church. Ἡ τῶν Λατίνων διαφορὰ (as regards Baptism) λέγει ὁ μέγας ἐκκλησιάρχης Σίλβεστρος (τμ. θ΄. κφ. ε΄.) αἵρεσίς ἐστι, καὶ οὕτως εἶχον αὐτὴν οἱ πρὸ ἡμῶν. "The Latins then," continues the Greek commentator, "are heretics from olden time, and as such, they are unbaptized;—they are laics, and besides being cut off from the Orthodox Church, have none of the graces whereby the priests of the Orthodox Church administer the holy mysteries." Κανὼν. μς΄. τῶν. ἁγ. Ἀπ. ἑρμην. p. 31, and Καν. ζ. τῆς β΄ οἰκ. Συν. p. 92.]

[2] There are still found around Mount Ararat not only oral traditions of the Ark, but also traces of the Universal Deluge as it is described in Holy Scripture, preserved in the names of several places. Thus the name of the town of "Nakhitshevan" means "the first descent"—of course, from the Ark; likewise the name of the small place called "Ag'ori" signifies, "he (that is, Noah) planted the vine;" and the name of the district of "Ar'noyudui," means "at Noah's feet."

[The name *Ararat*, mentioned for the first time in Gen. viii. 4, where it is said, not of a particular mountain but of the mountains of Armenia, is of native origin, and, according to Moses of

the parent stock of the people that called themselves
Haïkans, after him their ancestor, and gave the
name of Haïzdan or Haïkstan to the land in which
they first settled. The sixth descendant in a
straight line from Haïk, by name Aram, a cotemporary and ally of the great Assyrian Ninus, distinguished himself in so many ways, but especially
by conquests and victories, that ever since, the sur-
rounding nations called all Haïkans Armenians, and
their land, the land of Haïk, Armenia. Any how,

Chorene (lib. i. 14), was given to the first province of Armenia,
on account of the defeat sustained there by Arai, son of Aram,
against whom Semiramis made war; Ararat being, according to
this etymology, *Arayi-arat*, the blot or disgrace of Arai. Mount
Masis (Mount Ararat), on which Armenians say the Ark rested,
is situated in the province of *Ararat*, or *Airarat* as it is sometimes
written; hence its name. The tradition, however, that makes
the Ark to have rested on the hills of Cardu (Cordyæni Montes),
mentioned in the Targums, the Syriac version, and the Coran,
is far more probable. Those mountains rise on the north of the
plains of Shinar in Mesopotamia, and were also reckoned to *Ararat*
or *Armenia*. As to *Nakhitshevan*, in the province of Vasburagan,
it is variously written *Nakhdjavan*, *Nakhstchavan*, *Nakhstchevan*,
and *Nakhtschuvan*. The word thus written will not bear the
meaning of "first abode or settlement" or "first descent" given
to it by European travellers; it must be made into *Nakhig-avan*
or *Nakhig-itchevan*, as Indjidjean remarks (Anc. Geogr. of Armenia, p. 219), giving this etymology, as if it were of European
invention and new to Armenian writers. Akonz Köver also does
not mention it in his history of Genesis. As to the name *Aghori*,
the connexion between it and "planting the vine" does not
appear. And as to *Arhnwodu* or *Arnodu*, a small town of the
same province of Vasburagan, no mention is made in the work
above quoted of the etymology here given by the Russian
writer, but it is sometimes written *Odn-arnu*. Indjidj. p. 162.
St.-Martin (Mém. Armen. p. 267) however gives pretended
etymologies for these words from other authors.]

the name of Armenia, variously written, appears from time immemorial and every where as the proper name of the land which, from the first, was called by its own people Haïstan, and is so called unto this day[4].

[4] It is called "Armenia" by Greeks, Romans, and Syrians; "Arminiakh" by Arabs, and "Armen" by Persians. In the ancient sacred books of Persia, attributed to Zerdhust, a tract of country corresponding to Armenia is there called *Yeremeno* or *Eeremeno*, which is the same name; due allowance being made for the changes of letters peculiar to the Zend language. It is most probable that this name is connected in more ways than one, or than that of syllables alone, with the name of "Aram," given in the Old Testament to the countries called by the Greeks Syria and Mesopotamia, on the borders of Armenia. In the books of the Old Testament, Armenia is properly called Ararat (Gen. viii. 4. 11. 2 Kings xix. 37. Isa. xxxvii. 38). Besides, in these same regions may one remark the biblical names "Ashkenaz" (Jer. li. 27) and "Togarmah" (Ezek. xxvii. 14; xxxviii. 6). In consequence of this, Armenian writers call themselves Ashkenazians and Togarmians.

[Without dwelling on the fact that these appellations are claimed by other nations of Europe and of Asia, we may notice that our author omits the word in Jer. li. 27, which is most to the point, namely, *Meni* or *Mini*, whence the etymology proposed by Bochart (Geogr. Sacr. col. 20) and others, *Ar-meni*, the Mount-Meni, rendered by J. Bryant the "Mount of the Moon," meni, μὴν, being the well-known name for the moon, with which he connected the worship of the Ark. Be this as it may, we can but notice, in addition to what they say, this passage of Eustathius, in his commentary on Dionys. Perieg. l. 694, ἀπ' οὔρεος Ἀρμενίοιο—ὅτι τὸ Ἀρμένιον ὄρος—ἀπόσπασμα εἶναι τοῦ Ταύρου, παρατείνον ἕως καὶ εἰς Ἀρμενίαν τὴν οὕτω κληθεῖσαν ἢ ἀπὸ τοῦ ῥηθέντος Ἀρμενίου ὄρους, ἢ ἀπό τινος Ἀρμένου Ῥοδίου ἀνδρός—that this Ar-meni, or Mountain of Armenia, is a branch of the Taurus that extends into Armenia, thus called, either from that mountain, or from a certain Armenus, a native of Rhodes, who is said to have gone thither with Jason. Strabo, however (lib. xi. c. 14. § 12 ; c. 4. § 8), makes this Armenus a native of a town of that name in Thessaly, on the authority of Cyrsilus Pharsalius, who followed Alexander the Great in

There was a time when the frontiers of Armenia or Haïstan extended far and wide. They embraced his expedition; adding, in proof of it, the similarity there was between the Armenian and the Thessalian dresses. This "Mount Armenios" is mentioned by Armenian writers on the authority of Steph. Byz. and other Greek writers (Indjidj. Antiq. i. p. 94). Josephus, Ant. i. 4, quotes Nicolas of Damascus about τὸ ὑπὲρ τὴν Μινυάδα μέγα ὄρος κατὰ τὴν Ἀρμενίαν, Βάρις λεγόμενον, wherein we find Meni, Minyas, in connexion with this mountain, in which some will see the Ark (Baris), thus alluded to by Berosus (lib. ii. p. 57, ed. R.), προσοκείλαν τὸ πλοῖον ὄρει τινὶ—καὶ ὅπου εἰσὶν (Xisuthrus and his family) ἡ χώρα Ἀρμενίας ἐστίν. Something also is made of Amos iv. 3, where ha-harmona, translated "the palace" in the Authorized Version, is rendered τὸ ὄρος τὸ Ῥομμάν in the LXX., and written "the mountain of Remana" in the Armenian Version; but in Targ. Jonathan and the Syrian Version, "beyond the mountains of Armenia;" which the Arabic Version reads "on the mountain of Rama;" and the Vulgate, "in mount Armen." One would naturally look for this Ar-meni in Pehlevi, and for hara-meni or for some such compound word in Zend, as one finds Ar-burg and hara-berezaiti for Alborz, the highest summit of the Iberian and of the Bactrian Caucasus; but no such term occurs, nor yet Eermeno, as said by our author, either in Pehlevi or in Zend, so far at least as I know. But this subject would carry us too far. The fact remains, that, as Indjidjean says, whereas the terms "Armenian" and "Armenia" are never once used by Armenians themselves, the terms Haïk and Haïstan, by which they name themselves and their country, are not once heard of in ancient historians of other countries. The family of Togarmah, as it is given by Georgian and Armenian writers, viz. Haïk, the eldest son, then Karthlos, who gave his name to Georgia (Karthli), and Partos, Movgan, Legan, Keros, Govgas, Ekres, rests on local traditions. The son of Haïk was Armenak; and from a passage in Moses of Chorene (lib. i. c. 11), where Armenak is said to have settled in a plain at the foot of the Aragadz mountains, to the north of the province of Ararat, it is not impossible that the name of Armenia may have come from him, the second king of the country. See Tchamitch, Hist. of Arm., vol. i. c. 3, and Hist. of Orpel. ch. 1, cet. For, as regards Eermeno, as St.-Martin gives it from Anquetil's Avesta (Mém. Armen. p. 269), it is a myth. The real word is airyaman, first and foremost the high table-land crowned by the hills of Ararat, which, spreading in the form of a triangle, between the chains of the Caucasus and Taurus, reached unto three inland seas, the Black Sea, the Caspian, and the Mediterranean, where this forms the Bay of Alexandretta. There lay the original kernel of the Armenian nation, which, in after time, developed itself so far, as to be no longer held within the ranges of the Caucasus and of Mt. Taurus, but to be thus obliged to push into Asia Minor on the one side, and on the other as far as the mountains of Iran. But the ancient land of Armenia, properly so called, was bounded on the east by the lake of Urmiah, and the course of the rivers Kur and Araxes; on the west by the sources of the Kizil-Irmak, the classic Halys; on the north by the upper courses of the Kur and Chorok; and on the south by the high chain of the Kurdish Taurus, divided asunder by the rivers Euphrates and Tigris.

Formerly Armenia was divided by geographers and historians into Greater and Lesser; being parted the one from the other by the Euphrates, that takes its source in the interior of Armenia proper; Greater Armenia being on the left bank or eastern side of the river, and Lesser Armenia on the western side of it.

"obedient," also "prayer" and "the Genius of prayer" (see Spiegel Vendid. xxxii. Farg. tr. note), and not the name of a country; though it be derived from *Airya*, "noble, true, loyal;" also an Arian, an inhabitant of Aryana, or Iran. Neither has the name of a city or country "Irman," mentioned in the Shah-nameh, any thing to do with it.]

Greater Armenia was then divided into the following fifteen provinces:—I. Pardzr-Haïk, or upper Armenia; II. Daïk, afterwards called Akhaltzik; III. Kukar, the Gogarene of the Ancients, now called Somkhet; IV. Udi, formerly called Otena, now Shaki; V. Charrod-Haïk, or fourth Armenia, on the borders of the Sophene of Greek and Latin writers; VI. Duruperan, or Taron of the ancients; VII. Ararat, the heart of Armenia; VIII. Vasburagan, called Aspuragan and Vasparagan by Byzantine historians; IX. Siunik, otherwise called Sisagan, probably the Sacasene of classic authors; X. Artsak, now Karaban; XI. Pkhaidagaran, to which belongs the present Shirwan, called by Armenian writers Khorin-Haïk, that is, Inner Armenia; XII. Agtsnik, otherwise Agtsen, the Arzana and Arzanena of Byzantine writers; XIII. Mokk, probably the classic Moxoene; XIV. Gord-Haïk, that is, Kurdish-Armenia, the Gordene or Cordiene of Greek and Latin authors; and lastly, XV. Parska-Haïk, the Persian Armenia of classic authors.

Lesser Armenia, on the other hand, on the western side of the Euphrates, contained only five provinces, which were:—I. Aratchin-Haïk, or First Armenia; II. Ergrort-Haïk, or Second Armenia; III. Errort-Haïk, or Third Armenia; IV. Euphratesia, called Comagene by ancient writers; and V. Cilicia, otherwise Zemlia-Sisskaia (the Land of Sis) and Tsogr-Alshan, or Cœle-Syria [5].

[5] Armenians attribute the subdivision of Armenia into Greater and Lesser, as well as into First, Second, Third, &c., to Aram

According to home traditions, almost the whole of this region was under the descendants of Haïk, who governed it at times as independent rulers, and at others, as more or less dependent on their powerful neighbours of Assyria, Persia, or Media, until the dismemberment of ancient Asia, wrought by the conquests of Alexander the Great. The last king of the race and dynasty of Haïk was Baghe, who perished, they say, while fighting against the Macedonian conqueror, as ally of the ill-fated Darius Codomannus (B.C. 328)[e].

From that time Armenia has been a prey to the troubles that convulsed Western Asia in consequence of the utter extinction of her line of native kings. After the death of Alexander, Armenia,

himself, from whom the country received the name of Armenia. It is however most probable, that at least the numerical division into First, Second, &c., belongs to the Roman period. [From the expression used in Jer. li. 27, "the kingdoms of Ararat," or of Armenia, it would seem that the country was subdivided at a comparatively early period.]

[e] During the whole reign of the Haïkan dynasty, the seat of the Armenian government was at Armavir on the Araxes, in the province of Ararat, now only an insignificant village, called Surmeli by the Turks. The most celebrated of the Sovereigns of the race of Haïk was Digran or Tigranes I., a cotemporary of Cyrus, and it would seem also an ally of his in his wars with Astyages the Mede, who, according to Armenian traditions, perished on the field of battle by the hand of Tigranes himself. This same Tigranes is also said to have founded the city of Tigranocerte, now called Amid or Diarbekr by the Turks. [Sert, near the Murad Chaï, situated on a high table-land, difficult of approach, and commanding a magnificent view of the high hills of Armenia, is also by some supposed to be the Tigranocerta of olden times.]

which then stood in the position of a conquered province, endeavoured in vain to recover her former independent state. For the Seleucidæ, who helped themselves to all the lands brought by Alexander under his own dominion, were not disposed to keep their hands off Armenia; but they obliged her to be governed by rulers of their own choice.

Under Antiochus the Great, however, two native Armenians, Artaxias and Zadriad, who had been appointed by the Seleucidæ governors of Greater and of Lesser Armenia respectively, took advantage of the defeat of Antiochus by the Roman army (B.C. 199), and proclaimed once more their native land independent; each of them continuing ruler of his own division of the country. Zadriad, who governed Lesser Armenia, handed down his throne to his descendants, whose rule continued until the final overthrow of North-western Asia by Mithridates the Great, king of Pontus. Then, after various changes, this part of Armenia was added to the Roman Empire under Vespasian. But Greater Armenia, no later than in the days of Artabazd[1], son of Artaxias, surrendered herself willingly into the hands of Arsaces VI. (or Mithri-

[1] According to Greek historians, the celebrated Hannibal, when obliged by the Romans to seek refuge at the court of Antiochus the Great, fled to Artaxias, and built for him in the province of Ararat, on the Araxes, the city of Artaxata (in Armenian Ardashad or Ardashar), which was for some time after that the capital of the Armenian kingdom. There now remains of it nothing but somewhat remarkable ruins in the neighbourhood of Erivan.

dates I.), king of Parthia, surnamed Arsaces the Great, who then made his own brother king over her, and after him his son Valarsaces, called Vologeses in classic authors, who founded his own new dynasty of Armenian kings that retained the title of Arsacidæ, as well as that of kings of Parthia.

The rule of the Arsacidæ continued in Armenia for nearly six centuries, from B.C. 149 to A.D. 428. The beginnings thereof were both the happiest and brightest times for Armenia. But when Mithridates the Great fell, and the barrier that kept off the Romans from North-western Asia was thus thrown down, Armenia, that lay on the road to Parthia, became the scene of the most bloody contests and of disastrous wars, between those two European and Asiatic Empires, struggling with each other on that field of battle for the sovereignty of the then known world. Affinity of blood and of nation, however, led Armenia to side with the Parthians, with whom she found a natural protection against the Romans; a boon which had to be purchased at a high price by submission on the part of the younger Armenian Arsacidæ to the elder Parthian branch of the same dynasty. But when the elder Arsacidæ were put down by Ardashir or Artaxerxes, who restored the Persian Monarchy in the centre of Asia, for the sake of the Sassanidian dynasty which he founded, this new dynasty brought to bear all the hereditary and family jealousies of the elder Parthian Arsacidæ, upon the younger Armenian branch of that same family, and for this reason it tried to put them under the dependency of Rome.

When, however, the seat of the Roman Empire was brought to the Bosphorus, on the borders of Asia, the nearer approach of the Roman armies to those of Persia, which had taken up the place, and acted the part of Parthia in the East, only tended to increase their mutual jealousy. Then did Armenia fare still worse. She had to suffer not only from every encounter of these formidable neighbours, but also from others; until the end of it was, that the Byzantine Emperor Theodosius the Great and the Persian Shah Shapur III. (A.D. 387) parted that unfortunate country between themselves. The Arsacidæ continued yet a little while among the faded remains of their ancestry, with a mere shadow of power, as vassals both of Emperors and of Shahs. Then came a moment when one of these, Chosroes III., gathered once more the whole of the former kingdom of Armenia under his rule, proclaiming himself tributary both of Byzantium and of Iran. This, however, did not last long. For Shah Behram V. deposed Ardashes IV., the successor of Chosroes, thus putting an end to the power of the Armenian Arsacidæ, and, withal, effacing in Armenia the faintest trace of her independent existence[a].

[a] During the reign of the Arsacidæ, the central power of Armenia removed towards the south, to the banks of the Tigris, in the province of Agtsnik, where the kings then fixed their residence, at first at Nisibis, in Armenian, Metsbin (B.C. 149 to A.D. 14); then they went to Edessa, in Armenian, Oorfa or Oorha (A.D. 14—55); then back again to Nisibis (A.D. 55—79); and

After this, and for about two hundred years (A.D. 428—632), the greater portion of Armenia continued under the rule of the Persian Shahs, being governed by men of their own choice, called "Marzbans." Meanwhile the Byzantine Emperors who had possession of sundry fragments of the Armenian kingdom, would not give up their pretensions to the whole. In time, however, the Sassanidian monarchy fell during the political convulsions caused in the very heart of Asia by the religion of Mahomet and the conquests of the Caliphs (A.D. 632). And then, Armenia, groaning under the Arab yoke, gave herself up of her own accord to the Emperor Heraclius, who made for her a new order of rulers, with the Byzantine title of "Patricians" or "Curopalates." These Curopalates and Patricians were in general

thence the Arsacide Sanadrug returned to reside at Armavir, the ancient capital of the Haïkan kings. But his successor, who was not of the Arsacidæ, Erovant II., lived (A.D. 58—78) in the city of Erovantashad, built by himself in the province of Ararat, near the confluence of the Akhurean with the Araxes. Then Erovant's successor, a son of Sanadrug, Ardashes III. (A.D. 78—120), rebuilt Artaxata or Ardashad, an ancient city in those parts [built by Hannibal; see note above, p. 11], and in it fixed the seat of his kingdom, which continued there until Vagharsh, or Valarsaces, a nephew of Ardashes (A.D. 178—198) brought it to the city of Valarshabad, which he rebuilt, and where it remained for nearly a century and a half, until A.D. 344. Valarshabad was abandoned by Chosroes II., who, at first, went thence to Ardashad, and then to the new city of Tovin or Tevin, built by himself (A.D. 350). From that time Tovin, or Tevin, became the residence of the Arsacidæ until their downfall; but a part at least of this, the capital city of Armenia, continued to subsist some time later, even in the tenth century.

chosen from native Armenians, as the Marzbans had also been chosen by the Persian Shahs[*].

But the Caliphs who had inherited the power of the Sassanidæ, received also with it all their pretensions to the land of Armenia. They soon, therefore, shared with the Cæsars the right of government in Armenia; but later, having succeeded in bringing the whole country under their sole dominion, they set over it Governors of their own, called "Osdigans."

This state of things lasted about two centuries (A.D. 693—859), during which Armenia was a prey to continual revolutions and domestic troubles, caused on the one hand by the fanaticism and the despotism of Mahomedan princes, and on the other hand, also, by remnants of national vanity and self-love, fed and flattered by powerful native families accustomed to lord it over their own race with the titles of Marzbans, Patricians, or Curopalates[1].

[*] Among the Marzbans, Armenian historians particularly notice Vakhan-Medz, or Vakhan the Great, of the Mamagonian race, who governed Armenia under the Shahs Balash and Kobad (A.D. 485—511); and of the Curopalates and Patricians, the most noteworthy belong also to the same race, Khamasasb (A.D. 654) and Gregory (A.D. 659—683). The latter perished in battle against the Khazars, who were making an irruption into Armenia. [The Mamagonian or Mamiconian race sprang from a certain Mamgo, son of a celebrated king of Djenasdan, or of the Djens, whose country, Moses of Chorene says (Geogr. 96), was near China. See the same writer for particulars respecting the Mamiconian race, lib. ii. c. 78.]

[1] The ancient organization of the Armenian kingdom under the Haïkan dynasty, admitted of certain inferior and petty sovereigns, subject to the king's authority, who were called princes, with the

Such was, in general, the ancient, illustrious, and powerful family of the Bagratidæ, for whom Armenian tradition claims a Hebrew origin, and who certainly did exist in Armenia in the times of the Haïkan dynasties; while under the Arsacidæ they still constituted a powerful aristocratic family, which alone had the right to crown the kings of Armenia. During the Persian and the Byzantine periods, many of them were governors of Armenia. Under the Caliphs they yielded with bad grace to the authority of the "Osdigans" appointed by them, and often managed to get themselves appointed governors of their country, with the Byzantine title of "Patricians," wrung by force from the Caliphs. At last one of them, Ashod, surnamed the Great, obliged the Caliph Motovakkel to acknowledge him independent governor of Armenia, with the title of "Prince of Princes" (A.D. 859), which was afterwards changed by the Caliph Maatmed into the full title of "King" (A.D. 885). Thus was founded the Third Dynasty of native Armenian kings, some of whom reigned under the pompous title of "Shahanshah," that is, "Prince over Princes[1]."

---

privilege of handing down their rank and power from father to son. Thence issued a number of powerful families in Armenia. After the period of the Arsacidæ they numbered 117 in the fourth century. Some of them equalled in power the reigning kings, with whom they disputed the government of the country, and who, by reason of these princes that were subject to them, took the title of "king of kings."

[1] The founder of the Bagratidian or Bagration race is said to have been a Jew, brought by Nebuchadnezzar to Babylon, who

Yet the sentence against Armenia had gone forth. The dynasty of the Bagratidæ soon began to grow weaker and weaker through internal decay, divided, as it was, in many branches, every one of which claimed the title of "King." The chief of these royal families that retained for itself the title of "Shahanshah" exhausted its resources, not only with internal dissensions, but also in fruitless attempts to resist the growing power of the Seldjucide Turks in the interior of Asia, and was thus obliged to make over to the Byzantine Emperor Constantine Monachus (A.D. 1045) its assumed rights and the pompous but empty titles of a power all but extinct. The branch of the Bagratidæ that reigned in Kars soon followed that example towards the Emperor Constantine Lucas (A.D. 1064), and the third offshoot of that ancient family, that had ruled for centuries in the Armenian Albania, held out a little

---

went and settled in Armenia under Rhatch, of the Haïkan dynasty, some six centuries before Christ. Their name came to them from Pakrat or Bagrat, to whom Vagharshak (Valarsaces), first of the Arsacidæ, gave the hereditary dignity of "Asbed" or knight. Under the Arsacidæ, the Bagratide princes were already very powerful; and afterwards they still increased in importance. Their influence spread all over Armenia, but it concentrated itself especially towards the interior, under the chain of Ararat, and round the sources of the Euphrates, of the Chorok, and of the Araxes. Ashod, the son of Symbat, who suffered martyrdom at the hands of the ferocious Buga, the last of the Osdigans (A.D. 856), lived at first in Kars, then in Eraskavors, the present Shiragvan, then in Ani, all three cities in the province of Ararat. But on his taking the title of "prince," he removed to Tovin. Ashod III., however, removed the seat of his government thence back to Ani, about A.D. 961.

longer, but in the same pitiable plight. The last known descendants of it were, towards the end of the thirteenth century, in bondage among the Mongols, where they finally disappeared for ever [3].

But the ancient and illustrious Empire of Byzantium was not in a condition to maintain its hold on the provinces of Armenia which it had acquired, much less to extend its dominion over that country. It is true, indeed, that soon after the Bagratidæ had ceased to govern, under the Emperor Nicephorus Botaniates (A.D. 1080), Byzantium gained a few detached portions of ancient Armenia, that was raised by the Caliph Moktaderbillah (A.D. 908) to the rank of an independent and separate kingdom, on behalf of the Ardzrunian family, that belonged to some of the principal and most distinguished in Armenia [4]. But this was the last advantage the Eastern Empire

---

[3] The last kings of the first two branches of the Bagratide family, both called Kakiks, died violent deaths at the hands of the Byzantine Greeks. The third branch of the Bagratidæ, called Goridjian, from the name of its founder, Goridj or Kurken (George), son of the Shahanshah Ashod III., had the seat of its government in Lori, in the province of Daïk; but afterwards, having been deprived of all its power by the Georgians, it was reduced to the single fortress of Madznapert, in which it lived. After that, a separate offshoot of the Bagratidian race reigned in Georgia until lately; and besides kings of the houses of Karthalinia, Kakheth, and Imereth, it furnished many illustrious families, some of which were long since adopted in Russia under the name of Bagrations, and with the title of "princes."

[4] The kingdom of the Ardzrunian race embraced the whole of the province of Vasburagan, and the seat of the government was in Van, which, according to Armenian traditions, was founded by Semiramis, wherefore is it also called Shamiramagerd.

gained in that direction. The Seldjucides pushed their frontiers further and further towards the city of Constantine, and soon the whole of Armenia was in their power. They made over the government thereof to their Emirs, chosen either from among themselves, or from among the Kurds, some of whom assumed the title of " Shahs of Armenia [1]."

But the intestine discords and dissensions, which soon arose among the Seldjucides, encouraged eager neighbours; not the Byzantines, but the Georgians, who, under King David II. (A.D. 1124), rose against their oppressors, and not only drove them from their native land, but also carried their conquests into the heart of Armenia. From that time, the greater part of Armenia changed hands alternately from the Turks to the Georgians, until at last the incursion of the Mongols (A.D. 1232—1239) put an end to their disputes, spreading, as it did, far and wide, ruin, desolation, and woe; and sealing for ever the servitude of Armenians themselves in their own land.

Yet there remained one last fragment of the

[1] Of the Mohamedan princes or emirs who ruled in Armenia, the most remarkable were the Meruanides, of Kurdish origin, called by Armenians Abakhunian princes (A.D. 984—1085), and the Ortokides, of Turcoman origin, who ruled over the neighbourhood of Agdsnik, partly at Khizn-Keifa (A.D. 1101—1231), and partly in Merdin (A.D. 1104—1328). The masters of Khelat, in the province of Duruperan, and of Miapherekin (in Greek, Martyropolis), in the province of Agdznik (A.D. 1185—1259), took for a long time the title of " Shahs of the Armenians " (A.D. 1100—1243).

historical existence of the Haïkan nation within the borders of the original Haïstan, among the defiles of Mount Taurus, in the ancient and classic land of Cilicia. Thither had fled Ruben, a relative of the last of the Bagratidæ, Kakik II., when that royal race was all but destroyed by the Byzantine Emperor; and there Ruben, aided by others of his fellow-citizens who had previously taken refuge in those parts, got up an independent Armenian kingdom, which handed down an hereditary dynasty that lasted nearly three centuries (A.D. 1080—1342). This dynasty, in the person of Leon II., obtained the title of "Royal" from the Crusaders (A.D. 1198), with whom it always maintained most friendly relations[6].

These Rubenians or Rubenides, who reckoned themselves the fourth Armenian dynasty, knew how to hold out against the Byzantines and the Seldjucides. But they found enemies too powerful for them in the Egyptian Mameluks, against whom they vainly tried to protect themselves by alliance with the Mongols. Their race having died out with Leon V. (A.D. 1342), it was revived, on the female side, from the Lusinian dynasty of Cyprus; but not for long. For Leon VI. was carried away captive by the Mameluks, and brought to Egypt (A.D. 1375),

---

[6] Leon II. was crowned king of the Armenian kingdom of Cilicia, with the blessing of Pope Celestin III., and with the ratification of King Henry VI., by the hands of Conrad, Archbishop of Maintz, in the town of Sis, the capital of the kingdom of the Rubenians.

whence, having been redeemed by the king of Castile, John I., he wandered about in exile over Europe, until at last he died at Paris (A.D. 1391). And then, with him, was the name of Armenia for ever blotted out of the page of history.

With the downfall of the Arsacidæ, Armenians began to emigrate from their country, then made over to the yoke of servitude, and ground down under a heavy load of misery. Already in the fifth and sixth centuries numbers of Armenians were found in Asia Minor; and about the middle of the eleventh century they made up a very considerable community in Egypt. As the misfortunes of their native land increased, so also did they leave it in greater numbers, and spread themselves abroad in various countries: willingly or against their will, in single families or in whole colonies, did they wander over the world.

The wandering life, without a home, to which they doomed themselves by quitting their own land, turned their native disposition, enterprise, and aptitude almost entirely towards traffic and merchandise; so that they became the principal merchants and traffickers between Europe and Asia. Whence it happened that they settled with preference in places situate on the borders of those two continents. After the time of the Mongols, they spread themselves all over the wide limits those hordes had occupied in Eastern Europe; in the khanates of Astrakhan and of Kazan; in the Crimea and the Russian Ukraine, especially in Volhynia and in Galicia. Afterwards they settled under the Osmanlis, in Constantinople, and thence overran the whole eastern shore of the Mediterranean. When the interior of Asia became settled under the rule of the Persian Sophis, they found their way into Iran, whence they passed into India, as far as Madras and Calcutta, and thence returned to Europe. At last, in this same Europe, they in the course of time divided themselves, and went to dwell partly within the borders of Austria, in Vienna and Venice, and partly in the wide empire of Russia, in Moscow and St. Petersburg.

Thus does the Armenian nation exist at present, scattered over boundless dominions, from the Indian Ocean to the Baltic, from the steppes of Tartary to the banks of the Nile, and to the slopes of the Alps and of the Carpathian mountains. Meanwhile their own land, the Haïstan of old, is at present subject to three powers—Russia, Turkey, and Persia.

II. *Of the Armenian Church.*

THE strongest bond of union between the scattered members of the Armenian people is undoubtedly, as we have already remarked, the unity of the Armenian Church. The faith of the Fathers, which outlived all the troubles and disasters that have befallen the nation, being devoutly cherished by their descendants, united them in one body, however scattered they be, under one visible head.

Of the Armenian Church.

According to traditions preserved, not only among Armenians, but in the whole Christian world, the honour of having first received and embraced the Gospel, from the land of Judæa, even in the days of our Saviour on earth, belongs to ancient Armenia. The intercourse by letters between the Saviour and Abgarus, one of the Armenian Arsacidæ, who reigned in Edessa from B.C. 5 to A.D. 32, is a known fact; as well as the image[1], not wrought with hand, of the Son of God, which Abgarus obtained afterwards, and which is honoured by the whole Christian Church, relying on traditions, under the name of the Holy Image. Meanwhile, and at the

[1] [Respecting this tradition of our Saviour's likeness sent to Abgarus, Abulpharaj (Hist. Dynast. Arabicè, p. 112) says, that it was done by Hanan, who was a painter, and who carried the letter of "Abgarus the Black," as he styled himself, to Christ. But in his Syriac History of Dynasties, p. 51, Abulpharaj calls that painter Johannes. Asseman (Bib. Or. vol. i. p. 261) thinks that *Abgar*, the name given to toparchs of Edessa, is Syriac, and means "lame;" but Moses of Chorene (lib. ii. c. 25), who states that he was an Armenian, derives his name from the Armenian *Avak-aïr*, "chief or noble-man," given him first for his gentleness (as if "gentle-man"), and afterwards for his age. Michael Tchamitch, who also says he was an Armenian king, gives full particulars of his life, quarrel with Herod, journey to Rome, illness, &c. (Hist. of Armenia, vol. i. p. 276 sq.); and Euseb. Pamphil. (Hist. Eccl. lib. i. c. 13.) begins the letter with Ἀβγαρος τοπάρχης, which Abulpharaj (Arab.) renders "Abgar the Black;" while the Syriac translation of Eusebius (see Dr. Cureton's Ancient Syriac Doc., p. 2), has "Abgar Uchomo," that means both "Abgar the Black" and "Abgar the Leper." The Armenian version of that letter, as given by Moses of Chorene, begins thus: "Abgar, the son of Arsham, prince of the country," &c., and alludes to his incurable disease, but without mentioning the leprosy. The opinion that Abgar is the same as Akbar is a mistake.]

same time, the living word of the Gospel was brought into Armenia by Thaddeus, one of the Apostles, who was afterwards joined by the Apostles Bartholomew and Judas. All three watered with their blood the seeds of the Gospel which they preached in Armenia. But the superstition that prevailed at the time, which was a mixture of Persian fire-worship with Greek idolatry, was so gross and so ingrained in the people, that a long time elapsed ere the good seed then sown could take root, grow, and yield abundant fruit[1].

But the finishing of the work begun by the Apostles was reserved for S. Gregory, who has immortalized himself in the history of the Christian Church under the name of "the Illuminator," in Armenian "Lusavoritch[2]." He was of the reigning

[1] Armenian historians affirm that the Apostles Thaddeus, Bartholomew, and Judas, whose bones are still preserved and reverenced in sundry places of ancient Armenia, founded, either themselves or through their disciples, several cathedral seats in Armenia, which have preserved an unbroken succession of bishops ever since. Thus the disciples of Thaddeus founded the following episcopal churches: Addæus founded one at Edessa in Southern Armenia; Elisæus founded the episcopal church of Albania in Northern Armenia, or Karabagh; Theophilus founded the church of Cæsarea of Cappadocia, in Lesser or Western Armenia. Besides all these, Armenians attribute the foundation of the church of Siun in Eastern Armenia, in Sisaghan, to one of the Apostles, Eustathius, who was a companion of Thaddeus, and whose bones are now preserved in the monastery of Datev, which is at present within the borders of the Russian dominions. [There is a tradition that S. Thomas also preached the Gospel in Armenia.]

[2] [During the first period of the Armenian Church, from the first preaching by Thaddeus (A.D. 34) to S. Gregory the Illuminator, that Church continued in union with the Church of

family of the Arsacidæ, and lived and wrought towards the end of the third and the beginning of the fourth centuries; a time of trouble for Armenia. That country was then under Ardashir, the father of the Sassanidæ; who, after putting down the Arsacidæ of Parthia, caused the death of Chosroes I., the Arsacide then reigning in Armenia, by the hand of Anak, another man of the same family (A.D. 232). The sons of both the one who was slain and of his murderer then found refuge with the Romans: Dertad or Tiridates, the son of Chosroes, found it in Rome; and Gregory, the son of Anak, was taken to Cæsarea of Cappadocia, where he was brought up from his infancy in the principles of the Christian faith. Providence, however, brought them both back to their native land: the one for the prosperous establishment, and the other for the enlightenment, of Armenia.

But they did not soon come together into agreement, separated as they had been from their infancy. For Tiridates, who was raised to the throne of his ancestors by the help of the Romans (A.D. 259), received from them also his hatred of Christians; so that he rewarded the first efforts of Gregory in preaching the Gospel, by casting him into a deep

Jerusalem. In spite of fearful persecutions, the Christian faith was, to a certain extent, kept alive by bishops who were consecrated either at Jerusalem or by the Greek Church, with which the Armenian Church had liturgies and the New Testament in common, there being as yet no Armenian translation of these books. During this time, the only orders known in that Church were bishops, priests, and deacons. Dulaurier, Précis, p. 14.]

pit, in which the brave martyr spent thirteen whole years of his life. He came out thence at last with glory; and, having baptized Tiridates, he firmly established the faith of Christ in Armenia (A.D. 289). At the request of the king, Gregory went to Cæsarea to be consecrated Hierarch over his new flock of Christians (about A.D. 302); and founded his seat, the cathedral of all Armenia, in the city of Valarshabad, on the spot where he had been accounted worthy to behold Jesus Christ in a vision; and he gave to that place the name of "Etchmiadzin," which in Armenian means "the descent of the Only Begotten." From thence he continued his great work of enlightening Armenia, by sending every where teachers and pastors, and by building churches and monasteries; until, after he had laid the firm foundations of an outward and inward Christian Church in Armenia, he ended his life in solitude, and retired from the world (A.D. 331). Out of gratitude for so great a man does the Armenian Church call herself, after his own sainted name, Gregorian[1].

---

[1] The Orthodox Church also reveres S. Gregory, and keeps his feast on the 30th of September. The sanctuary of Etchmiadzin was reared by him on the ruins of a temple to the goddess Anahid, who was worshipped by Armenians of old. Besides a church in honour of the descent of the Only Begotten Son of God, the sanctuary embraces two more churches: the one sacred to Rhipsime, the other to Gaïane, two holy martyr-women who suffered under Tiridates, and whose memory is also honoured by the Orthodox Church on the same day as S. Gregory's. These three churches, which constitute the whole of Etchmiadzin, are

The successors of S. Gregory on his cathedral chair, who took to themselves the title of " Patriarch²," followed straight in the steps of him, the Illuminator. The conflict they had to bear, however, was hard. For the infant Church had at once to struggle with the heathenism of the country, favoured and kept up, as it was then, by many princes of the land. The neighbouring Shahs of Persia, moreover, did not fail to turn this opportunity to their own advantage, by taking under their protection the enemies of Christianity—partly from fanaticism, and partly from political motives; as at that time Christianity was raised by Constantine on the throne of the Roman Emperors, their natural enemies and jealous rivals. But, of course, the Patriarchs of Armenia were driven to solicit assistance from the Christian Emperors, thus increasing the bitter hatred of the Persian Shahs, not only for themselves, but also for the descendants of Tiridates that took up arms against them. Nevertheless, the Armenian Patriarchs had both sense and strength left to appease strifes, to quell seditions, to thwart perfidious designs, and thus to strengthen the tottering throne of the Arsacidæ without ceasing to look to the welfare of the Church committed to their charge.

the only remains of the ancient city of Vagharshabad or Valarshabad, and have given to that spot the Turkish name of Ütch-Kilise, or " Three Churches."

² [S. Nerses I. was the first to take the title of Patriarch and Catholicos of Armenia. He was present at the Council of Constantinople in A.D. 381.]

Thus, among the near successors of S. Gregory, did the Patriarchs Nerses I. and Isaak (Sa'ak) I. distinguish themselves; both of whom are mentioned in Armenian annals with the additional name of "Great." The latter made famous his long patriarchate (A.D. 390—440) by the translation of the whole of the Holy Scriptures, and of many other works, into Armenian; for hitherto there not only existed no Armenian literature, but not even Armenian characters. This, however, was accomplished by him with the help of Mesrob[3], who founded a whole school of remarkable thinkers and writers, that created what is called "the golden period" for the enlightenment of ancient Armenia. Then, also, did the country live out her last days of an independent existence. For Isaac was obliged at one time to take in hand the rule of government (A.D. 419—422), and at another to abandon his cathedral seat, and wander about in exile (A.D. 428—439). In his days the throne of the Arsacidæ fell for ever; and Armenia was brought under the galling yoke of the Sassanidæ, of those unrelenting enemies of the Christian Faith[4].

[3] [Then, besides the Armenian version of the Bible, "regius versionum," especially that of the New Testament, the Old being translated from the Septuagint, S. Isaac and Mesrob revised the Armenian liturgy, first translated from the Greek by S. Gregory, and added several prayers from the Fathers. That Liturgy has continued unaltered ever since in the Armeno-Gregorian Church, during a period of 1400 years.]

[4] We may notice that among the successors of S. Gregory on the patriarchal chair of Armenia were at first his own sons Aristages

Hardly had they established their rule in that unhappy country, when they raised a persecution against the Christians, many of whom shed their blood for their faith, and with it won the crown of martyrdom. Among those brave defenders of the faith, the Patriarch Joseph I., Isaac's successor (A.D. 454), distinguished himself. Then also did the patriarchal seat of Etchmiadzin itself suffer, being laid waste by the persecutors; so that the successors of Joseph I. were obliged to remove the patriarchal chair thence to Tovin[5].

These calamities prevented the Armenian Church from taking part in the Fourth Œcumenic Council, then terminating at Chalcedon (A.D. 451), whence originated the unfortunate rupture between the Armenian and the Eastern Churches. That Council condemned the heresy of Eutyches, which arose from extreme opposition to that of Nestorius, who had been condemned by the Third Council, held not long before at Ephesus (A.D. 431). Meanwhile a

---

(A.D. 306—314) and Vertanes (A.D. 314—330) [Of these more anon, in the life of S. Gregory]; and after these his grandson Khusik, son of Vertanes (A.D. 330—336). Isaac I., the Great, was also own son to Nerses I., the Great (A.D. 340—374). The two last named are revered as saints also by the Orthodox Church, that keeps their feast on the 20th of November. And to the school of Mesrob belongs Moses of Chorene, who is reckoned by Armenians as one of their first classic authors.

[5] After Etchmiadzin had been forsaken by the Armenian patriarchs, the Patriarch Nerses II. built there a monastery (A.D. 524—533). Nevertheless the place still continued a long time in ruins, whence it was afterwards raised and restored by the Patriarch Gomidas (A.D. 618).

report was propagated by followers of Eutyches in Armenia, which had remained faithfully attached to the decisions of the first Three Councils [*], that the Council of Chalcedon had received and approved the doctrine of Nestorius in direct opposition to the Council of Ephesus [']. This false report was confirmed by the efforts of the Byzantine Emperors Zeno and Anastasius, to quell the conflict of heresies, by arbitrary or fanciful explanations of the disputed dogmas, to the prejudice of the Council of Chalcedon. The Patriarch Papguen [*], then taking advan-

---

[*] According to the testimony of Armenian writers, the Armenian Church took an active part in the first three Œcumenic Councils, by means of her chief pastors. At the First Council were present the Patriarch Aristages and S. James, Bishop of Nisibis. To the Second Council, held at Constantinople, went in person the Patriarch S. Nerses the Great; and S. Isaac the Great, Patriarch, took part, by letter, in the Third Council, held at Ephesus [being then in prison, where he had been cast by order of the Persian Shah Yezdejerd II., during the persecution that was raging at the time].

['] [One of the chief causes of that alienation was this. The letter of Pope Leon I. to Flavian, concerning the Council of Chalcedon, had been incorrectly translated into Armenian, so that, when speaking of our Saviour's two natures, of which the one was divine, the other was subject to human sufferings, the words "the one and the other" were rendered by an Armenian expression applicable only to persons and not to things. Thus, whereas Pope Leon spoke of *two natures*, the Armenians understood *two persons*. So that while, on the one hand, the Pope's letter was approved of as orthodox by the Greek and Latin Fathers at Chalcedon, the Armenian bishops, owing to the wrong translation of that letter, thought that Council had embraced the errors of Nestorius, while condemning those of Eutyches.]

[*] [With him ended the second period of the Armenian Church,

tage of a short respite from the persecution carried on by Persia during the rule of the Marzban Vakhan the Great, called together a National Council in Valarshabad (A.D. 491), for the purpose of bringing to light the different sentiments about which disputes had arisen; and relying on the heterodox decisions of the Byzantine Emperors, there and then annulled the Council of Chalcedon[*]. All this was discovered, only too late, to have been the result of a misunderstanding, and it is now evident that the Armenian Church of S. Gregory wholly rejects the heresy of Eutyches, condemned by the Council

that of union with the Greek Church; with him also began the third period, that of estrangement between those two Churches, from A.D. 491—1175.]

[*] [There were no Armenian bishops present at the Fifth Council (Second of Constantinople, A.D. 553). But in proof of good will towards the Armenian Church, the letter of S. Saak (or Saag, Isaac), written to Proclus, Patriarch of Constantinople, in 435, was read publicly, thus showing that the Armenians were not Nestorians, and that therefore their presence at the Council, in order to clear themselves, was not needed.

At the Sixth Council (Third of Constantinople, A.D. 680), four Armenian bishops were present, according to certain Armenian historians, though others dispute the fact. Any how, the decrees of that Council agree with the Armenian faith.

At the Seventh Council (Second of Nicæa, A.D. 788), there were present three Armenian bishops; so that the Fourth Council of Chalcedon is the only one the Armenian Church did not *de facto* acknowledge, though it does so in reality. As regards the presence of Armenian bishops at the last three, there is some difference of opinion among Armenian writers. The Catholicos Johannes, however, in his letter to the Russian Emperor in 1847, solemnly acknowledges the first three and the last three General Councils, in the name of his Church. See Dulaurier, p. 34, sq.]

of Chalcedon; and that she does so as much as the Eastern Church[1]. But the bond of union, once broken, never could be restored; the less so, as such religious misunderstandings were always kept alive and embittered by the national antipathy and political differences that never ceased between Armenians and Byzantine Greeks[2].

---

[1] [Eutyches and his followers rank among the heretics who are regularly excommunicated by the Armenian Church, which holds the same doctrine as the Greek and Romish Churches concerning the twofold nature and will of Christ. See "Practice of the Christian Faith," by the Vartabed Mser, printed at Moscow in 1850, and published with the consent and authority of the late Catholicos Nerses V. The false reports respecting the Eutychianism of the Armenian Church were of late propagated both by Jesuits (P. Monier, *Lettres Edifiantes*, &c.) and by Protestants, as by the learned Lacrose in *Histoire du Christianisme d'Éthiopie et d'Arménie*, &c., but from want of sufficient information.]

[2] The separation of the Armenian Church from the Church Catholic grew so quietly that the real originator of it is not known. According to Abulpharaj, it began with the Syrian Samuel Barsuma; according to Photius, with a certain Syrian Peter; and according to Euthymius Zygabenus, with Ecuanius Mantacunes. Many accusations were and are now brought against the Armenian Church: but whoever wishes to have a true knowledge of her doctrine, let him read with attention "The Exposition of the Christian Faith of the Armenian Church," published by Joseph, Armenian Archbishop of Russia and Prince Dolgorucki of Argutinski, afterwards Patriarch of Etchmiadzin and Catholicos: St. Petersburg, 1799. Therein may one see with his own eyes that the reproaches made to the Armenian Church with regard to her Confession of Faith are the result of prejudices that have no foundation whatever.

[Our author is at great pains to clear the Armenian Church of Eutychianism, and it is very desirable he should. The charge, however, is of old standing. Greg. Barhebræus tells us that, if Mar Barsumas did not himself introduce the Monophysite heresy

Meanwhile the Armenian Church, finding herself thus severed from the rest, and confined within the limits of the Haïkan nation, became more and more one with it, and constituted its firmest stay, not only in her inward spirit, but also as an outward bond of union among the Armenians, who were already beginning to spread themselves over the world. The Patriarchs, who in consequence of the rupture from the Universal Church now enjoyed in its literal sense their title of Catholicos, that is, "Supreme or General Pastor[1]," saw the whole of Christendom

into Armenia, his disciple Samuel did; and that a great many Armenians were in his time (A.D. 1240—50) addicted to the Eutychianism of Julian of Halicarnassus, but that they had acknowledged their error, and had signed a treaty of agreement with the Syrian Church, from which, however, they soon after relapsed into their former heresy (Fundam. Eccles. in Assem. Bib. Or. vol. ii. p. 296). Johannes, Bishop of Asia (ibid. p. 87), writes, that in A.D. 545 disciples of Julian penetrated into Arabia, Egypt, Sophene, Armenia, and the land of the Arzunians. The Armenians were probably confirmed in that heresy by those Julianists, and of it they are widely and generally accused; as by Greg. Barhebræus, Petrus Meligensis, Petavius, and others. Of them Asseman (Dissert. de Monophys. iii.) says, "Verùm licet Syri, Armeni, Ægyptii, Æthiopesque, eandem hæresim circa Incarnationem Verbi tenuerint olim hodieque teneant; differunt tamen ad invicem ut regione, ita linguâ, ritibus et quibusdam aliis." But as we shall have occasion to see more in detail when treating of the Armenian Confession of Faith, a great deal of misconception, and therefore of difference, originated from the terms used to define ideas, being either insufficient or imperfectly understood. We must also bear in mind, as regards Syrian testimony respecting Armenians, that the two nations were jealous of each other; and also, that all Asseman's writings are from the Maronite point of view, with strong Romish prejudices.]

[1] The term and title "Catholicos" is of Greek origin. In the Eastern Church it was given to bishops sent outside the boun-

in every one of their several flocks. And identifying, as they did in their ideas, the interests of the Church of Armenia with those of the nation, they strove all the more to maintain the unity of faith in it, as they saw its political existence dying out. With this object in view, they did all they could to promote development of instruction and progress among the people. They introduced into the constitution of their hierarchy, besides their usual orders and degrees, a new order of "Vartabeds," occupying an intermediate position between the priests and the bishops; an order whose special object is learning and instruction. These Vartabeds combined their efforts under the Patriarch Moses II. (A.D. 551—594) in establishing in Armenia a new system of chronology and the calendar which is still in use[1]; a step that helped not a little to confirm

---

daries of the Roman empire, with full hierarchical powers over the flocks of their co-religionists, yet subject to the authority of the ecclesiastics by whom they had been ordained and sent forth on their errand. Thus, until the twelfth century, there were subject to the Orthodox Patriarch of Antioch two Catholicos in the interior of Asia, whom William of Tyre compares with the primates of the Western Church. It is therefore probable that S. Gregory received the title of Catholicos from Leontius, Bishop of Cæsarea of Cappadocia, who consecrated him. There are proofs to show that ever since and for a long time the Armenian Church kept up relations with that of Cæsarea; for the successors of S. Gregory until S. Isaac inclusive were always consecrated at Cæsarea.

[1] The Armenian almanack has for some time past been published at Odessa, together with the new Russian Calendar, and is very useful. The Armenian reckoning begins from A.D. 551, under the patriarchate of Moses II.; consequently now is their

the Armenian Church in her national separation from the rest of Christendom. In consequence of this, Georgia, which had hitherto been in communion with Armenia, joined the Universal Church; whence the Patriarch Abraham I. (A.D. 594—617) took occasion to summon a council at Tovin, in order, if possible, to make Armenia take deeper root and interest in the isolation of her own Church [s].

1291st year, begun on the 23rd of August of the current year 1842. But they also date from the birth of Christ, reckoned from His return from Egypt; so that they, in this respect, are four years behind us.

[s] Soon after the patriarchate of Abraham I., when, owing to the downfall of the Sassanidian dynasty by the Arabs, the Church of Armenia passed into the hands of the Byzantine emperors, and the hope of her reconciliation with the universal Church began to revive, at the instigation of the Emperor Heraclius, the Patriarch Ezra gathered a National Council at Erzerum, in A.D. 629, where misunderstandings were explained, and mutual communion was restored. But in spite of the anathemas hurled by the Council at all those who should refuse to come, many of the Armenians not only did not comply, but were, on the contrary, confirmed in their obstinacy. Foremost among them was the Vartabed Johannes Mairagometsi, whose sphere of labour lay in the Armenian Albania. But there is a tradition among Armenians that this reunion of the Armenian Church with the Church Catholic continued after Ezra, and under six patriarchs for the space of eighty-four years. See "Géographie du Vartabed Vartan" in "Mémoires sur l'Arménie," par M. J. St.-Martin, t. ii. p. 425. Others affirm that it ended at Ezra's death.

Fresh overtures, however, were made afterwards towards reunion with the Orthodox Eastern Church: on the side of Photius, Patriarch of Constantinople, in 862, and on the part of the Armenian Catholicos Bakhan, in 965. The Emperor Emmanuel Commenus showed himself most eager towards the Catholicos S. Nerses IV. Shnorhali in 1168; but his efforts had no other results than to lead the Catholicos and the other Nerses, Archbishop of Lampron, both men of high powers and remarkable

After the Persian dominion ceased, Christianity stood a better chance in Armenia. But when the Arabs came, bringing with them their fanaticism of Islam, they raised a fresh persecution against the Church of Armenia. At their first approach on the frontiers (A.D. 649), the Patriarch Nerses III. was obliged to flee from Tovin* into the mountains of

eloquence, to write sundry treatises, both theological and controversial, that are considered some of the gems of the Armenian literature. Generally speaking, as long as the Byzantine empire lasted, the emperors had in view, for political purposes, to put an end to the differences of opinion that severed them from Armenia. But, unfortunately, the Emperors Heraclius and Emmanuel Commenus were the only ones who opened the way to deliberation and conciliation; the others acted either by violence or by intrigues, that only tended to confirm mutual hatred and prejudices.

* [In 647 Nerses III. held a council at Tovin, as it were in confirmation of the one held by the Patriarch Ezra at Garin or Erzerum in 629, the object of which was to seek reconciliation with the Greek Church. There were mutual good wishes on both sides; some even say that Nerses II. administered the Holy Eucharist to the Greek Emperor Constantine II., successor of Heraclius, with whom Ezra had before had relations on the subject of re-union; and others say that Nerses III. himself received the Holy Sacrament in the Greek Church, in token of good will. Nevertheless, the majority of Armenian bishops would not hear of union with the Greek Church, and it then came to nothing. Indeed, the Vartabed Vartan, in his "Geography of Armenia," tells us that, during eighty-four years, six patriarchs, including Ezra himself and his successors, held the doctrine of Entyches, which he calls "the doctrine of Chalcedon," until the Catholicos Johannes IV., surnamed Odsnetsi, from the town of Odsun in Daschir, who purified the Armenian Church of the doctrine of the *ergapnagats*, "holders of two natures," and is therefore called *ergrort lusavoritch*, "the Second Illuminator." Geogr. p. 424, ed. St.-Martin. This shows how far difference between the Armenian and Greek Churches was the result of mutual misunderstanding, caused by terms ill defined.]

Daïk. He succeeded, however, in giving courage to his fellow-countrymen, and with their aid he once more raised the ruined seat of his patriarchate in Tovin (A.D. 654).

The reign of the Bagratidæ restored outward peace to the Church of Armenia. But, at the same time, intestine dissensions, raised by family quarrels among members of the reigning dynasty, ceased not to tear her asunder. The Patriarch Johannes I. saw himself obliged to leave Tovin (A.D. 897—925), the capital of the Bagratidæ, and to transfer his cathedral to the separate kingdom of Armenia, which was then beginning to rise under the dynasty of the Ardzrunians; and there he settled in the monastery of Dzoroï-Vank, in the province of Vasburagan (A.D. 924). His successors, Stephen II., Theodore I., and Eliseus I., took up their residence also in that same province, in a small island of Lake Van, still called Akhtamar. But the Patriarch Ananias (A.D. 943—965), after having also resided a while in that same island, went to the monastery of Varak, in that neighbourhood, not far from the town of Van (A.D. 948); and at last, he again removed thence to a small place called Arkinas, not far from Ani, the residence of the Bagratidæ, and consequently outside the dominions of the Ardzrunian princes. In that same place did three successors of Ananias also dwell. The first of whom, Vakhan[1], or Vakhanik (A.D. 965—970), was obliged

[1] [This Vakhan was an enlightened man, and with the help of Theodorus, Bishop of Melitene, drew up a summary of the Ar-

to flee from thence and again to seek refuge with the Ardzrunians; but the second, Stephen III., was taken captive by them, having been found in arms on the field of battle. This going from one place to another was, on the part of both these patriarchs, intimately connected with the political interests of Armenia at that time.

The Patriarch Sergius I. also left Arkina for Ani (A.D. 993); while his successor Peter I. was during his patriarchate of nearly fifty years (A.D. 1019—1058) a real wanderer, not knowing where to lay his head. He first went to Sebaste, the chief city of the Second Armenia, that had been made over to the Byzantine emperors by the Ardzrunians (A.D. 1021); he thence went back to Ani (A.D. 1025), then a second time to Sebaste (A.D. 1026), and again returned to Ani (A.D. 1029); he thence departed into Dzoroï-Vank, and back again among the Ardzrunians (A.D. 1030), and once more to Ani (A.D. 1034), where, this time, he was deposed by a Synod, at the instigation of the Bagratide who was then in power, and was condemned to go into exile; but having been re-instated in his office (A.D. 1036), he left Ani and came to Ardzen, the present Erzerum (A.D. 1047), whence he passed on to Constantinople (A.D. 1048), then at last he returned to Sebaste, where the Ardzrunians were yet in power (A.D. 1051); and after being definitively settled in the monastery of

menian Faith, intended for the Greek Emperor Polyeuctes, in the hope of forwarding a re-union of the two Churches. Dul. Précis, p. 38.]

Surp-Nishan (A.D. 1053), he ended there his eventful and wandering career (A.D. 1058). This Peter witnessed the extinction of the power of the chief family of the Bagratidæ in Ani.

The Byzantine emperors having got possession with Peter I. of the cathedral chair of Armenia, were naturally not inclined to part with it. Peter's successor, Khatchik II., fain would have fixed his residence in Ani, but he was not allowed so to do, albeit that city then belonged to the empire; but he was called to Constantinople, where he spent three years (A.D. 1060—1063), after which they sent him to live in the small town of Tavplur, in the Third Armenia. His successor, Gregory II., first took up his residence in a small town of that same province, called Dzamentad, and remarkable at that time for being the dwelling-place of a Bagratide of the family of Kars, who had been deposed (A.D. 1065).

The patriarchate of Gregory was a troublous one. He was at first rejected by his own flock (A.D. 1071); then afterwards, having deposed his chosen successor, he managed again to draw to himself the office of Patriarch (A.D. 1072). Then was a distinct Patriarch appointed for the part of Armenia that belonged to the Byzantine Empire, and his residence was fixed at Honi, a town of the Third Armenia. But Gregory returned to Ani (A.D. 1074). Hence, having made over the flock to his successor Basil I., without giving up either the title or the power of Patriarch, he departed into Tchernoï-Ghor [or Black Mountain], on the frontiers of Cilicia and Cappadocia (A.D. 1082). But he there soon met with another rival, who founded his cathedral seat in the small town of Marash (A.D. 1085); so that at one and the same time there were four Patriarchs, every one claiming for himself the name and power of Catholicos over the Armenians. It fell, however, to the lot of Basil (A.D. 1105) to bring the divided Church of Armenia under one pastoral staff. Being now left without competitor, he fixed his residence in Shgur-Anabad, not far from the town of Khesun, among the mountains of Euphratesia. But after the death of Basil, when Gregory III. was chosen there for his successor, the whole province of Vasburagan seceded and chose for itself a distinct Patriarch, who fixed his residence in the island of Akhtamar. This separate patriarchate has existed from that time until now.

Gregory III., the rightful successor to the dignity of Catholicos, dwelt at first in Tchernoï-Ghor, in the monastery called Garmir-Vank (A.D. 1113—1133); he thence went to reside in the castle of Dzovk, situated in the middle of the lake Arni, among the mountains of the Fourth Armenia, nigh unto the sources of the Tigris (A.D. 1133); and thence removed to the citadel of Hrhomgla, now called Orom-Kla, in Euphratesia, not far from where the river Marzban flows into the Euphrates (A.D. 1148). There did the seat of the Catholicos continue for nearly a century and a half (A.D. 1148—1294)[s]. During

[From 1169 to 1179 the Greek and Armenian Churches

Of the Armenian Church. 41

that time rival claims were set up by various individuals; but not for long; as, for instance, in Ani (A.D. 1180—1204) and in Sebaste (A.D. 1203—1207). Hrhomgla was taken by the Mameluks of Egypt, who led away the Catholicos Stephen IV. captive to

were on more friendly terms, and seemed more anxious to come to an understanding. Then Alexius, son-in-law to the Emperor Manuel Commenus, while travelling in Armenia, became acquainted with Nerses, then bishop, afterwards Patriarch, and surnamed Glajetsi or Shnorhali, because of his residence at Hrhomgla, and of the sweetness of his disposition and writings, and asked him to explain to that emperor the reason of difference between the Greek and the Armenian Churches. S. Nerses did so in his celebrated Confession, sending a letter to the Emperor, who, in turn, required, on the part of the Greek Church, sundry alterations in the Armenian ritual, to which Nerses and his bishops would not consent, saying, that "oneness of faith, not of ritual, was the main point." Several letters passed between the Armenian Patriarch and the Greek Emperor, carried to and fro by Theorian, an able man and deep theologian. These overtures, however, were not successful.

Six years after the death of Nerses, a celebrated Council was called together at Hrhomgla, in 1179, at which thirty-three Armenian bishops and neighbouring patriarchs from Syria and Albania were present. At this Council all the conditions that had been proposed by Nerses were discussed, and, by the influence of Nerses, Archbishop of Lampron (N. Lampronatsi), they were all accepted, and ratified by the signature of all the bishops there present; and thus a prospect of union with the Greek Church seemed at last to be realized. But the messengers, entrusted with the letter to the Patriarch and Emperor at Constantinople, were prevented from going further on their way than Cæsarea of Cappadocia, owing to the disturbed state of the country at that time, by the wars with the Crusaders. The letter was then brought back to Hrhomgla, to Gregory; and when, in 1181, the Greek Emperor died, all further overtures of union and peace were at an end. From that time dates the fourth period of the Armenian Church. Dulaur. Précis, p..48, sq.]

Cairo, where he died (A.D. 1298). Then Gregory VII., chosen to succeed Stephen, fixed his abode in Sis, the capital of the Rubenians of Cilicia. Here continued the Catholicos again to reside for nearly a hundred and fifty years (A.D. 1294—1441); when, at last, all these changes of residence were brought to an end, by the seat of the Catholicos of Armenia being once more restored to Etchmiadzin, where it was at first founded by S. Gregory the Illuminator. On the other hand, distinct Patriarchs continued to reside in Sis, where their successors exist at the present time.

When, after an absence of nearly a thousand years (A.D. 454—1441), the chief pastors of Armenia went back to the ancient cradle of their Church—that Church, once so pure, and so brilliant—it presented a wretched spectacle. Ruinous monuments of the ancient life of the nation, memories of former national independent greatness, and of the once flourishing arts of ecclesiastical building and decoration, lay in ruins, waste and desolate. But as regards the people, wandering like mourning shadows among scattered monuments of past ages, amid the ruinous heaps of sanctuaries—ceaseless changes from one form of bondage to another at last extinguished in the nation a feeling of self-respect, crushed its spirit, and nourished miserable passions and mean habits. And when, severed from union with the rest of the world, the patriarchate of S. Gregory was torn asunder and weakened by intestine divisions and dissensions, instead of being for the nation a rock of refuge and a defence, it became a stone of stumbling and a rock of offence for the greed of the meanest ambition, and for the intrigues of the grossest personal interest, carried on by rival parties struggling one with another, to purchase the chair at the hand of Mohammedan rulers.

So was it in Sis, under the government of the Egyptian Mameluks. So also did it happen many a time in Etchmiadzin itself under the reign of the Persian Shahs. The Catholicos Kiriak (Giragos), who was first to return to Etchmiadzin, had to feel the whole force of the baneful love of simony, deeply rooted in the Armenian character, brought to bear against himself; and after two years the chair of Etchmiadzin, which had been offered him, was then taken from him (A.D. 1441—1443). The further matters went, the worse they were. For when the greater part of Armenia became subject to the rule of the Osmanlis, then had one to bargain with them in Kazbina as well as with the Greeks in Stambul; and the chair of Etchmiadzin being now fallen into the lowest depth of degradation and ruin, not only exhausted its own revenues, but borrowed at an insolvent rate: in one word, it became not an ornament, but a burden on the Church. Then, as if to make the cup of such miseries overflow, new dissensions and divisions began to show themselves in the heart of the Armenian people, being sown there by the untiring intrigues of the Propaganda of the Roman Catholics of the West. The Catholic Armenians then separated themselves from the

Armenians who were faithful to their Church, and began to oppress and persecute their brethren; and while spreading dissensions among them, made them over to their enemies, the Musulmans. In short, they undermined and, like worms, fretted the last remaining strength of the National Church of Armenia [9].

[9] The first attempts at union with Rome date as far back as the eleventh century, in the days of the Catholicos Gregory II., who, they say, had a personal interview at Rome with Pope Gregory VII., of whom he came to request help against the Byzantines, who were ever trying in every respect to smother the independence of the Armenian people. With this object in view, did both Gregory himself and his successors fix their residence as near as they could to the governments established in Asia by the Crusaders from the West; and to this unfortunate circumstance it is that we owe the creation of the separate patriarchate of Akhtamar in an island of lake Van, independent alike of the Catholicos resident at Hrhomgla, or of him of Sis. In fact, the Catholicos Gregory, who, when Hrhomgla was taken by the Mameluks, removed his seat to Sis, where the Rubenians, clients of the Pope, were then in power, laboured earnestly in the interests of Rome, preparing the way for a union, which his successor, Constantine II., advocated warmly at the Council of 1307. The people, however, resolutely resisted the decisions of the Council.

In spite of this, the Catholicos Mekhitar shortly after renewed an offer of submission to the Pope, in 1342; but his efforts were also in vain. Meanwhile, during the schism that took place between the Patriarchs of Akhtamar and of Sis, the heart of Armenia was left unprotected; and then it was that the Propaganda pounced upon it like a bird of prey, led on by Padre Bartolomeo, of the order of Preachers (A.D. 1317). At once was an order of missionaries, called "Unitorians," established there for the purpose of furthering the union with Rome, who pushed their advances even to Etchmiadzin itself. Then was it found absolutely necessary to remove the seat of S. Gregory the Illuminator back to Etchmiadzin, in order to stop the internal schism of the Armenian Church, and to protect her from these dangerous

This wretched state of things for the Armenian Church, and for the seat of Etchmiadzin in particular, continued almost uninterruptedly from the latter end of the sixteenth century, to the beginning of the eighteenth. Towards the close of the sixteenth century, the Catholicos David V., having bought the chair of Etchmiadzin rather dear (A.D. 1586), and being unable to pay for it, took in, as partner in the bargain, Melchizedek, Bishop of Karhni, and shared with him the title of Catholicos (A.D. 1593). But as their joint funds did not suffice to defray the necessary expenses, they called in a third party to the purchase, who should also bear the title of Catholicos, namely, Serapion, Bishop of Amid (Diarbekr), who then took the name of Gregory XIII. (A.D. 1602). These three Catholicos very soon fell out. At first David and Melchizedek intrigued together against Gregory; but after having deposed him (A.D. 1606), they took to quarrelling together.

This happened during the reign of the famous Shah Abbas I., who wrested from the Turks a con-

enemies from without, who were preaching re-union. But the Armenians, faithful to their Church, fought strenuously against these Unitorians; among them the Vartabed Gregory Datevetsi especially distinguished himself about A.D. 1400. Unfortunately, however, these disturbances were not settled only with the bloodless weapons of mere words; but, as might be expected, Rome's interference gave occasion to disgusting and dreadful scenes, which took place chiefly at Constantinople, in the seventeenth and eighteenth centuries. At last things came to such a pass, that even quite recently (1828 and 1829) the Turkish government was obliged to send all the Armenian Catholics out of Constantinople to Ancyra.

siderable portion of ancient Armenia, together with Etchmiadzin, and restored it to Persia. He, therefore, took advantage of the confusion prevalent in the Armenian Church, and offered his protection to the two rivals. Melchizedek, who at first lost in his game with the Shah, and who was exposed by him to the most humiliating insults, afterwards got the better of it, and came into favour, but at a very high price; having pledged himself to pay to the Shah a yearly tribute, for the payment of which, not only the nation, but even the clergy, were subjected to intolerable straits and privations. At last, having exhausted all common patience, he fled into the Russian Ukraine (A.D. 1624), which was then under the government of Poland, and already inhabited by a great many Armenians; he first went to Lemberg, and afterwards to Kamenets-Podolsk, where he finished his life, ended in apostacy from his own Church to that of Rome (A.D. 1626)[1].

Isaac V., whom he had left to succeed him at Etchmiadzin, was obliged to go to law with David, and at last fled into exile among the Turks (A.D. 1624—1629). Under his successors, Moses III. and Philip[2] (A.D. 1629—1655), the Church of Armenia had a little breathing-time. But under the Catholicos Jacob IV., who succeeded Philip, a

[1] Unfortunately, Melchizedek had the example of this apostacy set him by his predecessors, Stephen V. (A.D. 1541—1547) and Michael (A.D. 1547—1556).

[2] In his time Etchmiadzin was raised from the ruinous state into which it had fallen during the troubles of the preceding times.

certain restless Vartabed, called Eleazar, proclaimed himself Supreme Patriarch of all the part of Armenia which was under Turkish dominion, choosing Jerusalem for his residence (A.D. 1664); whence he ceased not to annoy Jacob, until he was made to succeed him at Etchmiadzin (A.D. 1680). Then followed troubles and disturbances without end, raised after the death of Catholicos Abraham III. (A.D. 1737). Lazarus, Archbishop of Smyrna, arrogated to himself the chair of Etchmiadzin by means of various intrigues; but he disgraced it during fourteen years (A.D. 1737—1751), by acts of unheard of tyranny and of unparalleled wickedness; to which the venerable Peter II., who had been consecrated in opposition to him by the choice of the people and of the clergy, fell a victim (A.D. 1748). In those days the chair of Etchmiadzin fell to the lowest state of degradation.

But at that same time, when the measure of the calamities, that pressed heavily on the cathedral chair of the whole Armenian Church, was full, Providence already prepared in the future a new era of deliverance for the suffering children of Haïk. Early in the eighteenth century the thunder of the victorious armies of Russia was heard across the Caucasus. And then did the Armenian people turn their hopes towards the powerful Sovereign whose dominion made itself known always and every where by kindness, by Christian charity and universal philanthropy. These hopes were not disappointed: already in 1724 Peter the Great kindly welcomed an ambassage, sent him from the Albanians of Armenia, and, by an Imperial edict, promised his protection to their clergy. A like promise of support, with another charter of the same kind, was again given to that clergy by Katharine I., in 1726. And at last, Simeon, Patriarch of Etchmiadzin, in the days of Katharine II., had the credit and good fortune of obtaining from her the promise of protection for the whole Church of Armenia, confirmed by a formal edict and charter addressed and given immediately and expressly to the chair of S. Gregory, in 1766. From that time peace and quiet began to reign in the Armenian Church. And now that Etchmiadzin forms part of the Russian Empire since 1828, a solid prosperity is for ever secured to that first cathedral seat of Armenia; to this one bond of union and spiritual life for the children of Haïk[1].

Such is the Armenian Church, as it has continued to our own times, a remarkable monument of original and purely oriental development of Christianity. In the midst of all the troubles and disasters that befell her, she subsisted and maintained herself unmoved in her faithful attachment to her high origin. Her isolation from other Churches had the

[1] Besides Etchmiadzin, the Russian Empire now contains the very heart of Ancient Armenia, remarkable for the most precious monuments. Thus, within the boundaries of Russia we find, not to mention Ararat, the ruins of Artaxata, of Erovantashad, and Tovin, ancient capitals and seats of Armenian kings and patriarchs; as, for instance, the so-called "Throne of Tiridates" in Karhni, and the "Holy Well," or ditch, into which S. Gregory was cast, called in Armenian, Khorvirab.

effect of, as it were, "petrifying" in her the forms she had received in the first centuries of Christianity. And in this respect she presents a comforting spectacle to the zealous advocates of Christian orthodoxy, even by the side of all the misfortunes that resulted from her separation from the Universal Church. She protested and protests aloud against all the novelties, in time introduced to divide the Western Church from that of the East: for the faith and doctrine of the Armeno-Gregorian Church, as well as her ecclesiastical constitution, are the same in their fundamental and original features as those from which the Orthodox Church of the East never departed, but to which she has clung with unshaken loyalty. This was the real cause of the schism wrought in the Armenian Church by Rome [1].

[1] As, for instance, the introduction of "*filioque*" into the Nicene Creed by the Roman Catholic Church of the West, and borrowed from her by all the so-called Evangelical Churches, that never was nor ever is heard of in the Creed as professed by the Armeno-Gregorian Church, wherein, on the contrary, the Holy Ghost is definitively and decidedly stated to "proceed from the Father only." See the "Confession of Faith of the Armenian Church," edited by the Catholicos Joseph, St. Petersburg, 1799, pp. 34, 59. [This is the treatise already mentioned above, p. 32, note.] Likewise the Armenian Church, in spite of the few cases of apostasy from her to the Roman Church, which she must admit, has never received nor acknowledged the supremacy of the Roman Chief Priest over the whole of Christendom. [The Romish Armenian schismatics make in the Nicene Creed other alterations than the one here mentioned.]

III. Of the Armenian Hierarchy.

As regards the hierarchical arrangement of the Armeno-Gregorian Church, late political events have introduced sundry changes, besides a few others that do not affect the nature of hierarchical order. Formerly there were subject to the Catholicos of Etchmiadzin a number of Bishops, Archbishops, Metropolitans, and also Patriarchs, who, for the most part, only took the titles of defunct eparchies[5]. At present, however, the hierarchical subdivision of the Armenian Church of S. Gregory is brought as much as possible into agreement with its actual wants.

We have already remarked that two distinct patriarchates were erected in the Church of S. Gregory—Akhtamar and Sis. Besides these, there existed in olden times a separate patriarchate of the Albanians or Aghwans of Armenia, the origin of which, however, is ascribed by Armenian historians to S. Gregory[6]. Over and above all these the title

[5] In former times, there were reckoned, under the Supreme Patriarch Catholicos of Etchmiadzin, forty-two Archbishops and about three hundred Bishops. The title of *Metropolitan*, but without all the usual rights, belonged to four of these Archbishops, namely, to the Archbishops of Sebaste, Melitin, Martyropol, and Siun.

[6] The Armenians affirm that S. Gregory the Illuminator, after preaching in Albania [a province of Armenia, between the Kur and the Caspian sea], gave her for pastor his own successor Gregoris, with the title of Patriarch. This Gregoris is a Saint of

of Patriarch was afterwards assumed by the Armenian Bishop of Jerusalem (A.D. 1310) and of Constantinople (about A.D. 1461). Lately, however, the Albanian patriarchate was done away with, in subsequent arrangements of the Russian Government, and made immediately dependent on the Catholicos. On the other hand, the Turkish Government has gathered, under the title of "Patriarch of Constantinople," the chief authority over the several eparchies found in the Ottoman dominions; this Patriarch, however, to continue, in general, subject to the chair of Etchmiadzin. But to the Patriarch of Jerusalem was granted an exemption, in favour of his own eparchy, from reference to the Patriarch of Constantinople; and the Patriarchs of Akhtamar and of Sis still preserve their titles, but nothing more[1].

According to the division finally settled at the local Synod of Constantinople, held the 20th of November, 1830, the rule of the Armeno-Gregorian

the Armenian calendar, and his bones are preserved and worshipped by the Armenian Church in the monastery of Amaras or Amaren in Karabagh, not far from the Araxes. In that monastery is also found the chair of the patriarchs of Albania, who resided sometimes in Berda, sometimes in Gandja (the present Elizabethpol); but afterwards settled definitively in the monastery of Kantsasar, in the neighbourhood of Gandja. Of these the Patriarch Isaiah was the first to seek relations with Russia, by heading an embassage to Peter the Great, from whom he obtained protection, secured by official documents.

[1] The Island of Cyprus, together with Palestine, forms the eparchy of the Patriarch of Jerusalem. The patriarchate of Akhtamar extends over two cities and thirty villages only; and that of Sis, over three cities and forty villages.

Patriarch of Constantinople extends over the folowing eighteen eparchies, subdivided into twenty-six vicariates.

I. The Eparchy of Taron, the seat of the Eparch of which is at Mush, in the convent of S. John the Baptist. The vicariates are: (1) Arakelots, in the monastery of the Holy Apostles; (2) Surp-Johannes, in the monastery of S. John the Theologian; (3) Amrtola, in the monastery of S. John the Baptist; (4) Keghi, in the monastery of Keghi.

II. The Eparchy of Cæsarea; the seat of the Eparch thereof is in Cæsarea of Cappadocia (in Armenian, Gaïseri and Majak), in the monastery of S. John the Baptist. The vicariates are: (1) Surp-Daniel, in the monastery of the Holy Prophet Daniel; (2) Tomarzaa, in the monastery of the Blessed Virgin; (3) Tara-Vank, in the monastery of S. Sergius.

III. The Eparchy of Nicomedia, the seat of which is in the monastery of the Blessed Virgin, Tchark-hapan. There are two vicariates attached to the small towns of (1) Ada-Bazar and (2) Nor-Kiugh or Bazar-Keghi.

IV. The Eparchy of Brussa, the seat of which is in the cathedral-church of the Blessed Virgin. There are two vicariates attached to churches in the small towns (1) of Cotina and (2) of Pantrma.

V. The Eparchy of Smyrna, the seat of which is in the cathedral-church of S. Stephen, protomartyr. It has no vicariate.

VI. The Eparchy of Galatia, the seat of which is

in the monastery of the Blessed Virgin. There are vicariates attached to churches of the small towns of (1) Aphion Kara-Hissar and (2) Polu.

VII. The Eparchy of Eudokia, in Armenian Tokat, the seat of which is in the monastery of S. Anna. The vicariates are: (1) Shabin-Kara Hissar, in the monastery of the Holy Apostles; (2) Tamzara, in the monastery of S. Sergius; (3) Atsbiter, in the monastery of Surp-Nishan.

VIII. The Eparchy of Amasia, the seat of the Eparch being in the monastery of the Blessed Virgin. It has one vicariate only, in Sepukha, in the monastery of S. Gregory the Illuminator.

IX. The Eparchy of Sebaste, the seat of which is in the monastery of the Holy Cross. No vicariate.

X. The Eparchy of Kars or of Erzrum, the seat of which is in the monastery called Mutruk. Its vicariates are: (1) Garmir-Vank, in the monastery of Garmir-Vank; (2) Gasaï-Kale, in the monastery of the Blessed Virgin; (3) Khatchka-Vank, in the monastery of the Holy Cross; (4) Sper, in the monastery of S. John the Baptist; (5) Erzinka, in the monastery of S. Nerses; (6) Derjan, in the monastery of S. David; (7) Kars, in the monastery of Kosha-Vank; (8) Utch-Kilise, in the monastery of S. Gregory the Illuminator.

XI. The Eparchy of Van, the seat of which is in the monastery of Surp-Nishan, called Varaksk. The vicariates are: (1) Nareg, in the monastery of S. Gregory of Nareg; (2) Ter-Uskaï-Vordi, in the monastery of Ter-Uskaï-Vordi; (3) Lim, in the monastery of S. George the Victorious; (4) Ktuts, in the monastery of S. John the Baptist.

XII. The Eparchy of Aghin, the seat of which is in the monastery of Amenaprgitch (that is, of the Saviour). It has two vicariates attached to the churches of (1) Arapker and (2) Kuruchaï.

XIII. The Eparchy of Trebizonde, the seat of which is in the cathedral-church of the Blessed Virgin. The vicariates are: (1) Gümüshkhan, in the monastery of the Blessed Virgin; and (2) Babert, in the church of that place.

XIV. The Eparchy of Tigranocerta, or of Diarbekr, the seat of which is in the monastery of the Blessed Virgin Pardzragayats. There are two vicariates in the monasteries of (1) Balu and (2) Kharberd.

XV. The Eparchy of Oorfa, or Edessa, the seat of which is in the cathedral-church of the Blessed Virgin. It has no vicariate.

XVI. The Eparchy of Adrianople, the seat of which is in the cathedral-church of S. Theodore. It has one vicariate only, in Shumla, attached to the church of the place.

XVII. The Eparchy of Tekirdag or of Thrace, the seat of which is in Redestona, at the cathedral-church of S. John the Baptist. It has no vicariate.

XVIII. The Eparchy of Egypt, the seat of which is in Alexandria, attached to the cathedral. No vicariate.

Under the immediate superintendence of the Catholicos of Etchmiadzin, at the present time, are certain eparchies that belong to Persia, besides those that are included in the Russian Empire.

The Persian eparchies of the Armenian Church are only two, which are subdivided into three vicariates, as follows:—

I. The Eparchy of Ispahan, the seat of which is in the neighbourhood of Ispahan, at a place called Novaya-Djulpha, in the monastery of Amenaprgitch. It has one vicariate only, in the East Indies, at Calcutta.

II. The Eparchy of Tebriz, the seat of which is in the monastery of the Holy Apostle Thaddeus. It has two vicariates: (1) Achbak, in the monastery of the Holy Apostle Bartholomew; and (2) Darashamb, in the monastery of S. Stephen, protomartyr.

In Russia, the Government of the Armeno-Gregorian Church, as settled by the Emperor's will, on the 11th of March, 1836, is divided into six eparchies, five of which are managed by Archbishops, and one constitutes the province governed by the Supreme Patriarch or Catholicos of Etchmiadzin himself. The five other eparchies, governed by Archbishops, are as follows:—

I. The Eparchy of Nakhitchevan or of Bessarabia. To it belong the Armenian churches of St. Petersburg and Moscow, and those found in the governments of New Russia and in the province of Bessarabia. The Archbishop resides at Kishineff.

II. The Eparchy of Astrakhan. To this eparchy belong all other Armenian churches in the empire, except those about the Caucasus. The Archbishop resides in Astrakhan.

III. The Eparchy of Erivan. It consists of the former province of Armenia, with the addition of what was the province of Ordubat, and a portion of the province of Karabagh. It is under the immediate rule of the Supreme Patriarch Catholicos of Etchmiadzin, who has under him four vicars: (1) in Erivan; (2) in Nakhitshevan of Armenia; (3) in Shuraghel; and (4) in Tatev or Datev.

IV. The Eparchy of Georgia. It extends over churches in Georgia and around Elizabethpol, with the addition of the distant places Bortshalin, Kazakh, Shamshadil, and a part of Bambak; also the neighbourhoods of Akhaltsik, Imereth, and Guria. The Archbishop resides in Tiflis, and has three vicars: (1) in Elizabethpol; (2) in Akhaltsik; and (3) in Imereth.

V. The Eparchy of Karabagh, which consists of the neighbouring provinces of Karabagh (with the exception of a province governed by the Metropolitan of Siun, in Datev), of Shekinsk, and of Talshinsk. The Archbishop resides in Shusi, and has a vicar in Sheka.

In 1842 the number of churches in the above six Eparchies within the Russian Empire was 955, 15 of which are cathedrals; the Gregorian Armenians in Russia number about 500,000, while those who have joined the Romish schism muster only 15,000.

The Catholicos of Etchmiadzin is supreme over the whole Armenian Church of S. Gregory the

Illuminator. Even the Armenians of Constantinople, of Jerusalem, and of Sis, like those of India, acknowledge him over them, albeit they have in those cities archbishops with the nominal title of Patriarch, without, however, the power of consecrating bishops. The Catholicos of Etchmiadzin alone has the right of episcopal consecration, as well as of blessing the holy oil², which the priests of Armenian churches, from all parts, come to fetch at Etchmiadzin, every seven years, when that ceremony takes place.

The Catholicos of Etchmiadzin is chosen by the votes of the Armenian bishops of all lands, who, for that purpose, come to Etchmiadzin, where the election takes place; after which he is appointed by the Emperor of Russia, under whose rule the Armenian Church enjoys great peace and many privileges.

[² There is an interesting account of this ceremony in Muravieff's "Travels," vol. ii. p. 184 sq.]

INTRODUCTION OF CHRISTIANITY INTO ARMENIA.

I. THE ACTS AND MARTYRDOM OF THE HOLY APOSTLE THADDEUS.

II. THE ACTS AND MARTYRDOM OF THE HOLY APOSTLE BARTHOLOMEW.

[INDJIDJEAN, in his "Antiquities of the Armenian Nation" (vol. iii. p. 182), says, that "As Haïasdan (Armenia) was the first in the days of Noah to receive the knowledge of the true God, so also was it the first to receive the preaching of Christ's Gospel. And that, as in after time the light of Truth in it disappeared, driven as it was by the darkness of the grossest idolatry, so also did the country again receive fresh light at two different periods: first by the preaching of Thaddeus and of Bartholomew [1], in the days of Abgarus; and again, after the land had fallen back into idolatry, by the efforts of S. Gregory the Illuminator, more than two centuries later."

As might be expected, so confused is the tradition respecting S. Thaddeus, that even S. Jerome was of opinion that he is the same as Lebbæus (S. Matt. x.),

[1] [Who each brought with him, according to tradition, a wonder-working relic: S. Thaddeus, the spear with which our Saviour's side was pierced; and S. Bartholomew, a picture of the Blessed Virgin, painted by S. Luke. The spear is preserved in the convent of Aïri-Vank in Kashni, but the image is lost. Both these relics are figured on most altars and churches in Armenia, where they have not been effaced by Popish influence, in order to substitute for them the images of S. Peter and S. Paul. Vartan, Geogr., p. 420, and Muravieff's Travels in Armenia, vol. ii. p. 190. The spear was brought from Aïri-Vank to Etchmiadzin, and laid in the cathedral, when this was restored.]

also called Judas the brother of James (S. Luke vi.), and the probable author of the Epistle of Jude (S. Jude 1): the cause of this mistake may be owing to the fact that the title of "Apostle" is by Eastern writers frequently given to the seventy disciples mentioned by S. Luke (chap. x.), as well as to Timothy, Titus, and others who have no claim to it. Thus Agathangelos, in his History (p. 512, ed. Arm.), ranks "Barsabas, Mark, Luke, Barnabas, and others like them, among the Apostles, like unto whom they were endued with supernatural gifts and power." Likewise does Solomon, Bishop of Botsrah (Deburitho, chap. 48), extend the list of Apostles to many besides those who are so called in Scripture, while (in chap. 49) he gives in detail the names of the twelve Apostles, as well as those of the Seventy from among whom twelve drew back, as Judas Iscariot did from among the Twelve. These "twelve apostates were Simeon, Leech, Barkurba, Kleon, Hymenæus, Kandrus, Klethon, Demas, Narcissus, Silicispus, Thaddeus, and Maruthas; in whose place the following fifteen were admitted into the number of the Seventy: Luke the physician, Apollo the elect, Amplius, Urbanus, Stachys, Publius, Aristobulus, Stephanas (not he of Corinth), Herodion the son of Narcissus, Olympas, Narcissus, Mark the Evangelist, Adæus [Addeus], Aghæus, and Mar-Maris;" wherein we notice that Addeus came in instead of Thaddeus.

This opinion of the Bishop of Botsrah is at variance with the tradition generally received in most of the Syrian and Armenian Churches. For Moses of Chorène (lib. ii. c. 28 sqq.), who gives in detail the letter of Abgarus to our Saviour, our Saviour's reply to him, as well as Abgarus's letters to Pilate about our Lord and the Christians of Syria, tells us that Thaddeus, who was one of the seventy, was sent by S. Thomas to Edessa, where he cured Abgarus, and ordained bishop a certain silk-mercer, named Khoharar, to whom he gave the name of Addeus, and whom he left behind him when he went from Edessa into Armenia to King Sanadrug, who was sister's son to Abgarus. Jesujabi, Bishop of Nisibis, however (Assem. B. O. vol. iii. p. 298), affirms that this Thaddeus was one of the twelve Apostles, as does also the Sahidic work mentioned by Zoega (Codd. Sahid. p. 229), as well as the Ethiopic account of the same Apostle in the *Gadla Hawaryāt*, that seems to be a translation of the above Sahidic treatise; and in both of which Thaddeus,—who preached the Gospel in Syria and Mesopotamia, according to the Sahidic, but in Syria and Dacia (i. e. Daïk, a province of Armenia), according to the Ethiopic tradition,—is called "Judas, who is Thaddeus, the brother of our Lord." Although Thaddeus, also called Judas and Lebbæus, was a brother, or a next of kin, to James, and not to our Lord, yet the tradition preserved in these African accounts evidently makes him one of the Twelve.

Further confusion arose also from mistaking the names Thaddeus and Addeus, each for the other, as by Jesujabi of Nisibis and Jacob of Serug (Bib. Or.

vol. i. p. 319 cet.), Elias of Damascus and Amrus (Ass. Bib. Or. vol. iv. p. 13). Abulpharaj (Hist. Dyn. Arab. p. 113) only mentions Addeus as sent to Abgarus; as he does in his Origines Eccles. Syr. (ed. Overbeck, p. 417 sq.), where Ade, or Addeus, alone is mentioned as first Patriarch of Edessa (as also in Doctr. of the Apostles, Anc. Syr. Doc. p. 34). The accounts of Eusebius, however (Hist. Eccles. lib. i. chap. 13), and of Moses of Chorene seem to be the most trustworthy. They both make Thaddeus one of the Seventy, who was "sent by Judas, who is Thomas[1]," to Edessa after our Saviour's ascension; but Eusebius, who, like Moses of Chorene, drew his information from the public records of Edessa, says nothing of the consecration of Addeus, first Patriarch of Edessa, whose teaching of Abgarus, after the departure of Thaddeus for Armenia, is given at

[1] [Eusebius l. c. says that Thaddeus was sent to Edessa by Ἰούδας ὁ καὶ Θωμᾶς, "Judas who is also called Thomas;" a particular which Moses of Chorene omits, though he professes to have drawn his information, as Eusebius did, from the public records of Edessa. Eusebius, however, is right; for "Judas Thomas" occurs in Dr. Cureton's "Ancient Syriac Documents," pp. 3, 32, 33 of the text, as well as in S. Ephraem's VIIth "Discourse on Faith," as it is given in Assem. Bib. Or. vol. i. p. 101, but not in the same passage as printed in S. Ephr. Opp. vol. iii. p. 16. Grabe also mentions a MS. (Spicileg. SS. Patr. vol. i. p. 324), where we read: κατὰ κλῆρον ἔλαχεν ἡ Ἰνδία Διδύμῳ Ἰούδᾳ τῷ καὶ Θωμᾷ; a passage which occurs almost word for word in Itiner. S. Thomæ (in Fabric. C. Ap. N. T. vol. i. p. 820): κατὰ κλῆρον οὖν ἔλαχεν ἡ Ἰνδία Ἰούδᾳ Θωμᾷ καὶ Διδύμῳ; concerning which book S. Athanasius (Synops. SS. vol. ii. p. 154) says: ἐξ ὧν μετεφράσθησαν ἐκλεγέντα τὰ ἀληθέστερα καὶ θεόπνευστα. ταῦτα τὰ ἀναγινωσκόμενα: so that Valesius in his notes on this passage of Eusebius' Hist. Eccl. is not to be followed.]

length in the ancient Syriac documents published by the late Dr. Cureton (p. 5 sq. of the text), and in which he is throughout called "Adé the Apostle[1]."

Although S. Thomas, who is said to have preached the gospel in India, went also into Parthia and the eastern parts of Armenia, yet the two Apostles who are looked up to by the Armenian Church as the messengers of truth to her country, are S. Bartholomew and S. Thaddeus, who, whether he be of the Twelve or of the Seventy, was the first to preach Christ to the sons of Haïk, and is therefore said to be "the Apostle of Armenia." His acts and martyrdom, according to the Armenian Church, are as follows.]

[1] [See also Assem. B. O. vol. iv. p. 3—15, for much information respecting the two Thaddæi or Addæi, who are often distinguished, but as often confused by the Syrian Church.]

INTRODUCTION OF CHRISTIANITY INTO ARMENIA.

I. The Acts and Martyrdom of the Holy Apostle —Thaddeus[1].

Writers who have searched into the subject agree with the general tradition, that the man with long hair, the bright star, the holy Apostle Thaddeus, came among us from the northern parts[2]. He had

[1] [Translated from the Armenian, Venice, 1853.]

[2] [This does not apparently agree with the statement that Thaddeus was first sent from Jerusalem to Urha or Edessa, and thence to king Sanadrug in Shavarshan, a town of Ardaz, a small province of Vasburagan, between Lake Van and the Araxes. This however may, perhaps, refer to his return into what M. Tchamitch (in his Hist. of Armen. vol. i. p. 191) calls "the interior of Armenia, from his preaching in Upper Armenia, even to the Albanians," who inhabited the country situated between the Kur and the Caspian Sea, considerably to the north of Armenia proper.

We may also notice the fact that, whereas the Armenian Church knows Thaddeus by his Greek name, "Thaddœos," and also by his Syriac one, "Thaddé," and uses both alike, she yet only mentions Addé, for Addeus, as the name given him by Thaddeus himself; "which name," says M. Tchamitch, l. c., "is called Adé in Syriac." He is right as regards the number of letters in the Syriac names Thadé and Adé, but doubling the consonant may be a local idiom. The fact is, however, that whereas Abgarus is said in the Syriac writers to have been a Syrian

received by lot the whole of Armenia, to preach in it the Word of life, and to be the first in it to be honoured with the crown of martyrdom. He came to call all men to the heavenly feast, sent as he was for this purpose by Jesus Christ the Saviour of us all, soon after His ascension into Heaven, after He had laid His right hand on His Apostles and breathed on them the Holy Spirit, the Comforter and the Light of Truth; having blessed and strengthened them with bright words, and then sent every one of them, to the parts allotted to him, there to preach the Word of life. For this holy Apostle was filled

king, he is claimed by Moses of Chorene, the Catholicos Joseph, M. Tchamitch, and other Armenian authors, " as their own blessed king Abgarus," whose name they derive from the Armenian, while the Syrians do so from the Syriac. (See Introduction, note, p. 23.) But, as we know from Herodotus, Strabo, Pliny, and other Greek and Latin authors, the term "Syria" was of a very wide meaning, embracing, at one time, nearly the whole of Armenia, whose name is by many derived from Aram; so that, for a large portion of the country to the north of the present Syria, the names Syria and Armenia often were interchangeable.

Some confusion in the traditions respecting S. Thaddeus, may also be owing to the great jealousy which existed for a long time between the Armenians and the Syrians. Until the invention of the alphabet by Mesrob, and the revival of letters that followed, the Church Service was chiefly performed in Syriac, by Syrian priests. The whole of the south-west of Armenia, between the Tigris and the Euphrates, the Sophene, and the neighbouring provinces, were dependent on Syria as regards religion and letters; and in the fifth century, Syrian bishops were there so powerful, that they several times attempted to seize on the patriarchate. Hence arose both jealousy and enmity between Armenians and Syrians, each of whom claim the same Apostle, but each in their own way. See Moses Chor. lib. iii. c. 64, 65, in St.-Martin's Mém. Arm. vol. i. p. 10 sq.]

with bright thoughts, when, having received for his lot the Armenian nation, he arrived in Mesopotamia, preached the Word of life, and wrought great signs and wonders; then returning thence, he came to Urha [Oorfa]; and going into the house of Tobias, he healed all manner of sickness and of diseases, and enlightened the people with the light from heaven.

Meanwhile, king Abgarus having heard of the holy Apostle Thaddeus and of the wonders he wrought, began to think that he was the man sent to him by Christ. Then Thaddeus came to the king's house; and when Abgarus beheld him, and the sign of heavenly light on his countenance, he was awed, and falling on his face to the earth, he worshipped him. But the holy Apostle, drawing near, laid his hands on him in the name of our Saviour Jesus Christ, and enlightened him and all his house with heavenly light. He also cured of an evil disease Abdias, son of Abdias, who was a great man at the court of Abgarus; and having enlightened the whole city, he left there some of his disciples. Yea, even king Abgarus himself, who had been healed by the holy Apostle, became a preacher of the Word of life, and wrought signs and all manner of good works; and he with all other believers in the place received the blessing of the holy Apostle.

Then the holy Apostle himself took his disciples and hastened to come into Armenia, to king Sanadrug, in the province of Ardaz[3], to the small town

---

[3] [A province of Vasburagan, between the Araxes and Lake Van.]

of Shavarshan, the royal palace and summer residence of the kings of Armenia. There he preached the Word of life, and wrought signs at the court and among the whole army, and cured all manner of illness and of evil diseases. And many from the court[1] came out to the holy Apostle, and heard from him the loving language of the Gospel, and saw the signs he wrought: how he cleansed the lepers, made the lame walk, cast out devils, and healed all manner of the worst diseases. And at the sight of these wonders many believed in Christ.

Then came [to Thaddeus] the king's daughter, whose name was Sandukht, of tender age, beautiful in form and of a lovely countenance, the like of whom was not to be met with in the whole country. She came to the holy Apostle by night, and heard the word of the Gospel, and the voice of the heavenly hosts; she hearkened to it, she threw herself at his holy feet, embracing them with tears; she was taught by him for several days, and left him neither day nor night; and thus joined to him, she was confirmed in the love of Christ our God. Then the holy Apostle, seeing her ardent feeling of love for Christ, took her and baptized her in the name of the Father, of the Son, and of the Holy Ghost. And there came a sign of heavenly light

---

[1] [According to M. Tchamitch, king Sanadrug himself believed and was baptized with his court, but afterwards fell back into idolatry, and put to death his own daughter, who continued in the faith, as we read in this history.]

upon that holy virgin, and from the midst of the light a voice of angels from heaven; so that many others at that hour believed in Christ. But the priests of the idols went and told it all to their lawless and wicked king Sanadrug.

Then that abandoned king gave orders that all the believers should be put to death. But a sign from heaven appeared over them, and many believed in Christ, and fear came upon the heathens, many of whom were terrified by the brilliant light, and could not even raise their heads to speak to the holy Apostle. Then the Saviour appearing said, "Stand firm, Thaddeus, for I am with thee to deliver thee." And Thaddeus seeing the Saviour Christ, threw himself before Him with tears, and said, "My Lord and my God, leave me not alone; for behold I am come to a barbarous race of men at this king's gate, by Thine order and in Thy strength. For Thou, O Lord, didst say: Go ye into the whole earth, and preach the Word of life; he that believeth and is baptized shall live; and he that believeth not shall be damned. Now, since I came hither I began to preach the word of Thy holy Gospel which Thou hast put in my mouth, but they will not hear; for of them that believe some are put to death, and others are driven to prison with cudgels; and they wish also to lay hands on me. For the light of Thy holy Godhead has soon plunged them into the depths of painful sufferings, and has brought them to the cruel death of being beaten with rods; but some they have not been able to find."

Then the Lord said, "Arise, and show thyself to them, and bear up, for many afflictions and much distress shall befall thee; for there are not here of them that will receive the preachings of My Gospel; only a small number out of many. But I will keep them, and will take them to Myself; and to them that are made perfect [in death] for My name's sake, will I give an abode in My Father's house."

Then Thaddeus said unto the Lord, "I also will make haste to reach unto the light of Thy Godhead, and be filled with heavenly love from the brightness of Thy glory." And the Lord answered, "Be glad and rejoice, for I will fulfil thy request." And the holy Apostle went back with great joy in the Saviour.

He went to the prison by night, where they kept S. Sandukht and other believers; when the gates opened of their own accord, and the holy Apostle went in, and said, "Peace be with you, beloved of Christ." Then they took courage when they saw the holy Apostle. And coming to Sandukht, he kissed her chains, and said unto her, "Blessed art thou, sister of the heavenly king." And having strengthened them with words of the holy Gospel in the love of Christ, he made sign that they should keep silence and pray; and spreading his hands towards heaven, he said, "I give Thee thanks, O my God and Lord Jesus Christ, only begotten Son of God, who didst come upon earth to save mankind; look down now from heaven, Thy chosen abode, on Thy maid-servant Sandukht, who has given up her youth to thee; keep her now, O Lord, and strengthen her and her companions for the struggle; cause now the light of Thy Godhead to shine over them, and put to shame the darkness of the enemy; for Thou alone art the God of gods and the Lord of lords. Show forth the token of Thy power on those who are in danger of their life, for they are Thine, and in Thine awful Name will they be strengthened unto eternity."

No sooner had the holy Apostle ended his prayer, than an awful noise was heard, the ceiling of the prison was raised up, and a light shone from heaven, brighter than the rays of the sun; and in the midst of the light the Lord Jesus was seen bringing these glad tidings to the champions for the faith: "Be strong and stand firm, for I will come and take you to Myself; and thou, Sandukht, who hast come after Me, and hast despised the honours of this world, and hast called Me thy Father, I will give thee the supreme light and greater grace than to all the rest."

At the sound of this voice their bonds were loosened, and rising up they gave glory to Christ God, and said all together: "O Lord Jesus Christ, our God, we give Thee thanks for Thy love of us, seeing that Thou didst come to visit us, in search of us when lost, and that Thou didst save us from the worship of idols, and gavest us power to overcome our unseen enemies. And that Thou hast strengthened us by a voice from heaven, bringing us the glad tidings from the brightness of Thy Godhead; that Thou hast broken our bonds, and hast healed the bruises on our bodies. But now, what can we offer unto Thee, O God! except we present ourselves as a sweet-smelling offering unto Thy Father?"

When they had ended this prayer, they saw, at the time the brightness of the light disappeared, the holy Apostle praying; who, rising from his knees, blessed them, and embraced them with a loving and heavenly embrace.

But the keepers of the prison having seen these signs and wonders, looked and saw the gates of the prison standing open, and the holy Apostle Thaddeus in the midst; and being struck with fear by the light, they bowed down, and tottering, fell at the feet of the Apostle, and said: "We also believe in thy God; receive us and put us in the number of the believers." They then embraced the feet of the man of God, and with tears entreated him, and said: "Forgive us, thou holy man of God, that not willingly, but unwillingly, we kept the company of believers in great distress, from fear of a wicked king. But after seeing the light shine over thee in the prison, we saw the bonds of the prisoners loosened, we knew thee among them all as their teacher and the leader of heavenly light. We acknowledge firmly and know that He whom thou preachest is the Maker of heaven and earth. And we believe with all our heart, and confess, that He is God, and that no one can separate us from thy God, neither bonds nor distress. Now arise and hasten, O holy man of God, and put us in the company of Christ, as, may be, we shall die for fear of the glory of thy God."

Then the holy Apostle knew that this call was from God, and that they had seen the light shine from heaven, and had heard the awful sound of a voice, and he said unto them: "Brethren, fear not; in return for your devoting yourselves to God, and for your believing in His only Son Jesus Christ and in the Holy Ghost, I will entreat Christ on your behalf that He will vouchsafe unto you His forgiveness for what ye did ignorantly; for our Lord loves us men, and is pitiful, and seeks to find all those that are lost in their sins, as ye were. But now, having loved you according to His infinite mercies, and having kindled His divine light in your hearts, He has taught you to know Him, that He alone is God, and that there is none else. Now, therefore, stand firm, and be strong in the faith of Christ God, and forget for yourselves the vain and deceitful lusts of the flesh that lead you astray." And when the holy Apostle had done speaking, he said unto them: "Arise and pray!" And he looking up to heaven with groans, said: "Father of our Lord Jesus Christ, through Whom Thou hast been pleased to make Thyself known unto these men, and hast called them unto Thyself; keep them now with Thy holy right hand, and leave them not to wander either to the right or to the left, but make them fast in their ardent love for Thee, their God; purify them with heavenly freedom from above, that being made one with Thee, they may continue in the love of Thine only begotten and beloved Son."

And having ended prayer, he took them that same night, and baptized them in the name of the Father, of the Son, and of the Holy Ghost, to the number of thirty-three, both men and women, who had believed at that hour, and who belonged to the class of gaolers.

But Satan the accursed, taking the form of a man, went to the prison, and from afar said with a loud voice to the warders, "What profit is it to you to have forsaken the great goddess Anahid[5], and Bisithon, the mother of the gods[6], to go wandering after a man that is a Jew, who teaches you a

[Anahid or Anaïtis was a Persian goddess, chiefly worshipped in Armenia, as Strabo tells us: ἅπαντα μὲν οὖν τὰ τῶν Περσῶν ἱερὰ καὶ Μῆδοι καὶ Ἀρμένιοι τετιμήκασι, τὰ δὲ τῆς Ἀναίτιδος διαφερόντως Ἀρμένιοι. She is often alluded to in the Avesta as Anāhita, pure, spotless, e. g. in the Aban Yasht v. 4, ardivī çūra Anahita, "the welling mighty Taintless" goddess. She was the personification of the pure waters in nature, that were supposed to flow from Mount Hakairya, and that fertilized the earth, as being derived from Ahura-Mazda. She is often identified with Diana, and also with the so-called Syrian Venus, whose worship was celebrated with most licentious rites all over the East and West, as far as the Canaanitish worship reached, in Malta, at Carthage, and in Spain. For a full account of her, see Windischman, "Die Parthische Anahita," 4to, and the works of Justi and Spiegel, but especially the original authorities themselves. She was the patron-goddess of Armenia, as we shall have occasion to see in the Life of S. Gregory the Illuminator.]

[The Armenian editor, in a note, says: "By Bisithon we must here understand Neptunus, who was not "the mother of the gods," but the brother of Aramazda, the father of the gods. It seems, however, that this Aramazda is here meant, and that Sanadrug meant him, by mentioning him together with Anahid."]

new doctrine, and ruins you by deceiving your hearts? Come, return, and guard the land of Anahid, and I will pray all the gods to forgive you."

But Thaddeus, who understood that the man was only speaking with the artifice of the Evil one, said, "O thou teller of lies, stand back, wretched man that thou art."

Then Satan, hearing the voice of the holy Apostle, said, "I hear thy voice, but I know not who thou art."

And the holy Apostle said to Satan, "Then see me, another servant of Christ God; thou foul and impure spirit, evil and shameless, how long wilt thou not stand in awe of God? By the power of God come out thence, and get thee behind me, thou wicked serpent."

After this rebuke from the Apostle, the evil spirit disappeared into darkness, and was tormented by the holy angels. And the faithful in the prison, seeing the awful torments of the evil spirit, were confirmed in the faith of Christ; when the devil, lifting up his voice, wept bitterly, saying, "Woe is me, I am overcome by the Crucified, and I perish; but I know what I shall do; I will enter into the hearts of the rulers, and I will provoke them against the king, and he will put you to death."

To him the holy Apostle answered, "Get thee behind me, Satan; the Lord rebuke thee." On hearing this the devil disappeared, went and entered the palace, and raised the barbarians against the saints.

And when it was morning, the king took counsel

about his daughter Sandukht, what to do with her; he could not give orders that she should be put to death, by his fatherly feelings of pity for her whom he loved so much, and that made him weep bitterly. He then sent one of his ministers to the prison, to bring his daughter Sandukht, and to search the highways for Thaddeus, who had led her astray, and bring him also with her. But when that prince came with great pomp to the prison, he found the door of it ajar, and wondered, and looking within he saw a great light around those that were inside, with a great multitude, and the holy Apostle standing upright, and teaching them the Word of life. And when he saw all this and the light that shone so brightly, he was seized with fear, and fell to the earth, tormented with invisible torture, and frightened at the terrible voice of the multitude within. But the holy Apostle having knowledge of it, came out, and seeing him fallen and writhing on the ground, took him, laid his hands on him, and healed him; and that minister, as well as the twenty men that were with him, believed. He was a great man placed over the worship of all the gods, the comptroller of the king's household, and the third in rank and office among the Armenians. When rescued from the grasp of Satan, he wept bitterly, and said, " I have lost the helmet on my head."

And as he could not go into the prison for fear of the heavenly powers, he hastened back to the palace, and by provoking the wicked and lawless king, turned him to command that they should put all those believers to the sword. And in that day two hundred were slain. Then a loud voice and a sound coming from the heavenly hosts were heard greeting the martyrs; and many of the heathens perished for fear thereof. And when it was night, a heavenly light spread all over them; when the holy maiden Sandukht sent to her own home, unknown to her father, to fetch from thence fine linen cloth; and taking her sainted companions in the faith, she wound their bodies and kissed them, saying: "Blessed are ye, brethren and sisters, who have been made worthy of the heavenly joy. Remember me, your handmaid." Then she buried them near to her own palace, taking care that no one in the royal hall should be made aware of it; and then hastened back to prison.

But Sandukht, seeing the holy Apostle in prayer and a bright light spread over him, was seized with fear, fell on her face, and with tears kissing the Apostle's feet, said: "My Lord and my Father, who didst find me when I was gone astray, and didst make me to know my heavenly Lord Jesus Christ, God's only begotten Son, now pray for me and bless me, that I may soon join my companions, and be made worthy with thee to see the Lord Christ."

Then the man of God seeing the tears Sandukht did shed, and her ardent feeling of love for Christ, said to her: "Blessed art thou, daughter of the heavenly King, have patience yet a while; and then shalt thou see the light of all creatures."

He also comforted other believers in the holy

words of the Gospel, and said: "Stand firm, for ye shall now receive the crown of light." And when his discourse was ended, they brought in Bread, which he took and blessed, and gave to Sandukht and to her fellow prisoners, after he had himself tasted a little of it, and then of the Blood; they blessed and gave thanks and praised the holy Trinity; and then signing themselves with the sign of the holy Cross, they fell asleep.

Meanwhile the holy Apostle stood praying and said: "O Lord my God, Father of our Lord Jesus Christ, I cannot sufficiently thank Thee for Thine abundant mercy, in that Thou didst call me, unworthy though I be, to the lot of the Apostleship, and didst purify and cleanse me, and make me a temple of the Holy Ghost, and didst give me this land by lot, where I preach the word of Thy holy Gospel. For them that have believed in fear of Thy holy name, wilt Thou make me perfect, and then receive them as a sweet-smelling savour in the light of Thine own Godhead; mingle them with the bands of angels in the heavenly hosts, and receive us also as a sweet-smelling offering to Thy Godhead; keep this Sandukht, who is yet a spotless maid; give her patience to fight through her martyrdom; and then place on her head the crown of light."

And when he had ended his prayer, the Saviour appeared to him, and said: "Peace be to you, My beloved." Then Thaddeus seeing the Saviour, fell on his face and worshipped Him. And the Saviour said: "I have heard thy prayers, and I have given thee what thou requirest of Me; and I will make perfect the band of martyrs, with Sandukht and the other disciples. I will also kindle the light of My Divine nature over your bones, and where offerings shall be made by vows over you for My name's sake, the prayers and supplications of those who make them shall rise up to Me unhindered, and the more so on thine account. Thou shalt appear strengthened this day, and thou shalt neither fear nor be dismayed, for I am with thee, to save you all."

Then Thaddeus answered: "My Lord and my God, have mercy on me, and leave not those who have believed in Thy holy name, but after my death keep them with Thy right hand; and, O Lord, forsake not this Thine inheritance which Thou hast given me. But, O Lord, after driving away the idolatry and all error from among these barbarians by Thine awful Divine power, do not treat them according to their own wickedness, for their evil adversary will deceive them, put them to shame, and scatter them abroad. So crush and destroy him, frustrate the evil intentions of his wickedness, grant to these Thy servants to have their lot above in the light of Thy Divine Presence, and make them an eternal assembly, and children of the heavenly mansions, that they may with one heart and with one voice glorify the Holy Trinity in the sweet-smelling savour of their life."

Then the Lord answered: "I have heard thy supplications; I will not leave them that have believed out of My hands until the end of the world, nor yet the lot of My inheritance, but I will soon accomplish thy desire, for I will enlist them in the company of those who are with Me in heaven, and I will make them partakers of My Divine light; I will make them unto Myself a noble assembly, and I will put My Gospel in their minds; I will drive away from among them the Evil Beast, and I will surround them with the hope of My Divine nature. I will look on them, and I will have mercy on them; and thou, rejoice and be glad." The Lord then blessed Thaddeus and rose up to heaven.

The holy Apostle then drew near and awoke the believers his disciples, and Christ's holy handmaid Sandukht, and said to them: "Let us pray." And he then began to pray and to sing this Psalm: "I will praise the Lord at all times." And after singing this and many other Psalms, they glorified God with tears, and were in great joy. Then said the holy Apostle to the believers, "Stand firm and endure, for now shall ye receive upon your heads the crown of light." And looking upon the holy maid Sandukht, he saw her face bathed in tears, and he said, "Be not fainthearted and be not afraid;" for he thought she was beginning to fear.

Then said Sandukht, "My lord and my spiritual father, I am not fainthearted; but I rejoice and am glad, for I am hastening to see Christ my hope, and to be in His presence for ever; I earnestly long to behold the heavenly light."

The holy Apostle then said to her, "Blessed art

thou, my sister and my daughter, for thou art about to obtain that which thou longest for, and to take upon thy head a crown of light; thou shalt stand before God, the King of Heaven, and thou shalt be found honoured above many, because of the devotedness of thy walk on earth."

And when it was morning, many officers of state and other grandees came to the gate of the prison. Having brought out the holy Apostle and Sandukht, and the other Christians that were in the prison, they led them away bound to the king's palace, but Sandukht came free. Then raising her voice, she said rejoicing, to her companions in the faith, "Stand fast, brethren, and be strong in Christ, for the threats of an earthly king are nothing. To Him alone look ye now, to the King of Heaven in Whom ye have believed. Give Him your mind and your devotion, and He will give you strength; for He alone is God, and besides Him there is none else; He will keep you from vain and deceitful snares."

But while she was thus exhorting her fellow Christians, the king called her from within; she went in to him and he said, "Come near, my daughter;" but she did not look at him nor did she go near him.

Then the king said, "Deniest thou me, and lovest thou that deceiver? If thou turn not from thy present mind, I swear by all the gods, that I will put both thee and him to a painful death."

The holy maiden then said, "Call him not a deceiver, who turned me from darkness to light, and gave me to know my Lord the Maker of heaven and earth, and the only Son of God, with the Holy Ghost Who comes from them. I hasten to my Lord Christ, He is the Lord of lords and the King of kings; He is the light and the life of all creatures."

The king then said, "Who is He Whom thou callest God and Father?"

Sandukht answered, "God. God is He Who made all things out of nothing, and established all things made by the Word of His mouth; but your deceived mind and your darkened imagination have forsaken God your Maker, Who made and established you out of nothing. And ye worship the ghosts of dead men that neither see nor hear, that are akin to devils, that doom to perdition your darkened minds, and make you the children of hell. And now ye have to go into outer darkness with your leader Satan, where there is weeping of eyes and gnashing of teeth."

At these words the king was very wroth, and commanded to bind and to flay her alive, and then to burn her. And the executioner drawing near, bound the holy maiden, when one of the believers ran and told the holy Apostle that they had bound Sandukht, and that they were going to torment her. Then Thaddeus said with tears, "My Lord Jesus Christ, look down upon Thine handmaid, strengthen her, and put to shame the wicked enemy of the Truth." Meanwhile the holy maiden, while being bound, as they laid hands on her and were about to flay her, cried unto heaven, and with a loud voice said courageously, "My Lord Jesus Christ, hasten to my help, for Thou art my Father and Creator, my refuge and my life, forsake not the lost sheep of Thy flock."

And as the maid cried there was an earthquake, and a light shone from heaven, when a voice was heard saying, "Be of good courage, my daughter, for I am with thee to deliver thee." Then were her bonds loosened, and the executioner, and many with him, perished in the brightness of the light; and fear having fallen upon the king and all that were with him, they all thought themselves about to perish. But the holy maiden hastened to the Apostle, and embracing his feet said, "My lord and my spiritual father, lo, Christ soon loosened me from my bonds, and put to shame Satan and his servants." And they arose and praised the Lord.

Then came a minister from the king, who fell at the Apostle's feet and said, "The king has sent me to thee, saying, 'I have sinned against thee and against thy God. Forgive me and pray that His anger at our fearful wickedness may be turned away, lest we perish altogether; and we will do all thou listest'. The king commands to set you free from your bonds."

Then Thaddeus, seeing him and hearing the king's command, melted into tears and prayed, saying, "O Father of our Lord Jesus Christ, look upon Thy congregation, and do not unto these men according to their sins. Forgive them, for they know not what they do." This short prayer being ended, they loosened the bonds of all the believers. And then there was an awful sound of an earthquake, and the minister seeing it feared greatly. But the Apostle said, "Fear not, but go, and tell thy king what things thou hast seen."

He went, and told the king, "I have seen the Apostle, who is not like a man, but more than a man. There was a light around him, and while he prayed all anger and vexation passed away from my heart."

Then the king, being set on by the wicked one, said, "May be he will forgive my wrath against him; yet the great gods Aramazd and Anahid are the support of the world and the glory of our kings."

Then the minister believed with all his house, and he was baptized and received the name of Samuel; they could not find the like of him in the whole land of Armenia; and he shaved his hair and became a disciple of the holy Apostle. And the king hearing of it, commanded that a burning nail should be thrust through his shoulders, and thus was he perfected in death, and with him also many other disciples of the holy Apostle, who had come with him. Then three or four arrived from the land of Armenia at that hour, whom they tormented, some by nailing them with red-hot nails to wheels which were thus set on fire, while others were put to the sword; so that in that day were eight martyrs thus perfected, over whom a sign of light appeared that caused a great fright to the heathen. And when it was night the holy Apostle came with other faithful men, and taking up their bodies, wound them up in their own robes of state with spices, and laid them in small clay coffins in their own homes, taking care that no one should know it.

And that same night the holy maid Sandukht came, and throwing herself before the holy Apostle, said, "Blessed art thou, my lord and father, for having made so many people worthy of the crown of Christ."

To which the Apostle replied, "Blessed art thou also, for being worthy of accompanying them; rejoice and be glad, for soon shalt thou also arrive in the kingdom of Christ." She then comforted all the believers, feeding them with bread, and covering them with raiment, allowing them to be in want of nothing; and she preached the Word of Life, and converted many through the signs and miracles which she wrought.

Then a woman of rank, by name Zarmantukht, who was related to the king, believed with all her house, which the holy Apostle took and baptized: in number, two hundred. But the king having heard of it, gave order that Zarmantukht alone should be put to the sword; over whom, after she was thus perfected, there shone a sign of light, whereby many believed on the day of this saint's martyrdom. The king hearing of this, roared like a lion against the holy maid Sandukht and said, "She it is that deceives most of them;" and he commanded her to be slain with the sword. But the holy Apostle hearing the order given by the wicked king, prayed to Christ the whole night in behalf of Sandukht.

When it was morning, Sandukht coming to him, threw herself at his feet, and embracing them said, "My lord, I have been thinking in my heart what Christ, Who is my Light, will do to me; for while asleep during the night a light shone over me, and in the midst of the light a man surrounded with light, whose likeness I could not see for the exceeding brightness of the rays of His light, then called to me and said, 'Sandukht, arise and hasten to put on My light.' And I, bathed in tears, replied, 'My Lord, I am not worthy.' But He, rebuking me, clothed me with light as with a garment; He placed a crown of light upon my head, He adorned me with bright ornaments of light, and I stood amazed. But He said, 'Rejoice, O Sandukht, for I will not leave thee.' Then suddenly there was an awful sound, and I awoke, and getting up I glorified Christ God, Who had thought me worthy of such a marvellous vision."

When the holy Apostle heard this, he understood that this day she should pass from this world, and be clothed upon with the glory of the heavenly hosts, and wear on her own head the crown of light; he then said to her with tears, "Blessed art thou, O Sandukht, for He that appeared to thee this night is Christ Himself; because He saw thine ardent, earnest love for Him, therefore did He appear to thee, and therefore will He the more establish thee in the light of His Divine nature. He will now clothe thee with His light as with a cloak, and He will place upon thy head a crown of light; for thou shalt abandon thy gross earthly body, and thou shalt put on the heavenly light, since thou art made worthy to wear on thy head the crown of victory in martyrdom. Thou shalt be adorned with the light of heaven above, and shalt dwell in the brightness of the Godhead; and thou shalt at all times be in the joys of that supreme light. And as to His saying to thee, 'Rejoice and be glad, for I will never leave thee,' it means that Christ is inseparable from His beloved ones; and that He gladdens them evermore who abide in their love for Him, their God."

When the holy maid Sandukht heard from Thaddeus the explanation of the marvellous vision she had seen, she was bathed in tears, and falling at the feet of the Apostle, she said to him, "Blessed be thou, my father, who hast begotten me anew, and hast taught me to know Christ, the living Light; for thou hast been to me the path of life and the draught of immortality. Ask, then, Christ that He may soon gather me unto Himself."

Then the holy Apostle said, "Behold, thou shalt soon come into the Light of life with Him for Whom thou longest now."

And to this Sandukht replied, "My Lord, I beseech thee, that until my passage hence thou wilt stand by me; for I cannot exist away from thy love in the Spirit."

Then they arose and prayed, and lifting up his

hands unto heaven, Thaddeus said, "Remember Thine handmaid, O Lord; give her patience in her struggle this day, and put to shame the enemy; that all those who believe in Thee may know that Thou alone art God in heaven above and in the earth beneath." Then turning towards the holy maid kneeling by him, he blessed her and said: "Stand firm, Sandukht, and Christ will give thee strength."

Hardly were these words uttered, when suddenly there came to the door of the prison cruel officers and soldiers, towards whom the holy Apostle came forth to meet them, and stood in the midst of them.

Then they led the blessed maid to the place where she was going to be put to death, when she said to those who led her, "Bear with me yet a little while, that I may pray unto my Lord and my God." Then looking up to heaven with tears, she said, "Heavenly Father of Thy beloved Son Jesus Christ our Lord and Saviour, look down from heaven Thy holy dwelling, and vouchsafe unto me Thy loving mercy and pity. Receive me, Thine handmaid, in the name of Thy beloved Son, as a sweet-smelling savour, and make me meet partaker of the heavenly light of Thy Divine nature, that I may delight myself in the infinite, abundant, and eternal blessings Thou hast promised unto all those that love Thee." Then taking leave of the holy Apostle, she received his blessing; and drawing near to the place where preparations were made for her martyrdom, she said, "Arise, fulfil the will of your father Satan;"

and then, of her own accord, she willingly gave herself up to be bound.

Then the executioner drawing his sword, went as about to slay the holy maid Sandukht, but instead of that, he smote his chief officer and killed him. When the heathens saw this they became all the more enraged, and seizing the holy maid, they rushed upon her, and there they all beat her to death. Meanwhile the handmaid of Christ continued to pray, saying, "Lord Jesus Christ, receive me into the everlasting habitations, for I rejoice and am glad of the suffering and of death for the sake of Thy holy Name; Thou hast strengthened me and enabled me to overcome those who fight against me, for Thine is the victory, and unto Thee belongs eternal glory, Amen."

At that same moment a young man smote the breast of the holy maiden and drew blood, whence came forth a sweet smell; and she gave up her spirit to Christ in a good confession of the Father, of the Son, and of the Holy Ghost.

Then from heaven shone forth light like a pillar of fire, and there was an earthquake with an awful sound of the voices of heavenly hosts, praising God; and the pillar of light stood over that holy corpse three days and three nights. And that day as many as two thousand souls believed, both men and women, who did not move from the place where the body of holy Sandukht lay.

Afterwards the holy Apostle came by night and baptized them in the Name of the Father, of the

Son, and of the Holy Ghost. And taking the body of Sandukht, he laid it in that same spot, covered it with earth, and thus made invisible the resting place of the sainted princess.

Then, three days after the death of Sandukht, towards morning, as the holy Apostle was praying, the Saviour appeared to him and said, "Peace be unto thee, my beloved; make haste, to-day shalt thou come to the fighting ground; yet endure, for many sufferings shall come upon thee, but I will not leave thee;" and blessing him, He disappeared.

Then the holy Apostle prayed, saying, "I give thanks unto Thee, Father of our Lord Jesus Christ, that Thou hast not left me out of Thy hand in these barbarous lands, but that Thou hast had pity on me. Now receive me as a sweet-smelling savour to Thy Divine essence, and strengthen me for the conflict; receive and remember, O Lord, Thine handmaid, Sandukht, who has passed hence unto Thee, and put her among the companies of Thy saints, who for Thy Holy Name's sake have fought and overcome; and satisfy her with the light of Thy Divine nature; and keep those who have believed and who have put their trust in Thee. Hear now their supplications and their prayers, O Thou Friend of sinners; and set not aside the requests of those who cry unto Thee day and night, but ward off the wicked adversary from them and put him to shame, that he may not venture near the company of those who believe in Thee. Strengthen Thy servants in the love of Thy commandments, by persevering in them unto the end."

Having thus ended his prayer, he blessed the believers, and said, " Children, since ye have given yourselves to God, and have been enlisted in the company of Christ, stand firm in the faith, and Christ God will give you strength; He will increase your number, and will put to shame your wicked adversary the Devil, who leads astray the heathen; and will make you tread him under foot for ever. But lo! I am passing hence unto my Lord Christ, and I will pray Him to send you His mighty angel to defend you against the yoke of heathen errors, wherever He may lead you, and purify you in the furnace of His divine light, to be unto Him a noble company. For He now is unto you a Father, Lord, and King; He will keep you, and not leave you."

When the believers heard that Thaddeus was soon to pass hence to Christ, they were all in tears, and falling at his feet, they embraced them, saying, " O, sir, who hast quickened our spirits, pray for us, and entreat Christ that He may not let us go from His hand."

To whom the holy Apostle himself, bathed in tears, answered, " O Lord Jesus Christ, let not go out of Thine hand Thy small company now around me, but keep them with Thy holy right hand." And dismissing them, he sent them every one to his own home.

But after the believers had gone with the heavenly blessing, two officers of state came by order of the wicked king, and a great multitude with them, searching everywhere, thinking that they should not find more Christians than they did a day or two before. But the holy Apostle being made aware of their approach, went out to them, and said, "I am he whom ye seek." Then they took him and brought him to the king. The king seeing him, said, "Art thou Thaddeus?" And he said, "I am." And the king, looking at him, saw his face very brilliant and awful; he feared greatly, and said, "Why didst thou unsettle the mind of my fair daughter and win her over to thyself, removing her from her father's throne, hung with purple and gold embroidery; and why didst thou make her hate our gods and make her like unto one of the poor, until I made her perish with the sword in the bitter indignation of my grief?"

Then answered the holy Apostle, and said, "With regard to the holy maiden of whom thou speakest, it is true that I rescued her from the chilling and Satanic delusions of the dark works of your worship, as you offer it to Anahid, worshippers as ye are of devils. And I won over her heart to Christ, making Him known to her through the heavenly birth of Baptism; and I removed her from thine own abominations, her father though thou be. Christ has clothed her in the glory of heavenly rays of light. For when thou thoughtest to make her perish, He made her pass from death unto life, and winged her flight to the realms of light, where, being in full enjoyment of divine love, she moves among the bands of Seraphim, at all times praising and glorifying the Most Holy Trinity; for there is ineffable light, and life eternal. But ye have a deceived mind, and a darkened imagination, and forsaking the Creator of heaven and earth, Who made you out of nothing, and placed you upon earth, wherein He gives you both breath and life; ye have gone astray after the worship of idols that work death, deceived and led astray as ye are by the wicked and abominable Satan, who has cast you into the bonds and snares of death; and ye have, as your portion, to be cast with him into outer darkness, where there is weeping and gnashing of teeth."

Then the king was very wroth, and said, " Such a man ought not to live." And having led away the holy Apostle, they cast him bound into the walled den wherein were kept wild beasts that fed on human flesh. Then they let into it two lions; but these went, and crouching at the feet of the holy Apostle, licked his shoes, and howled, fawning. The Saint then prayed, and his bonds were loosened; and making a sign to the lions, they each retired to his own place.

But the king grew more and more enraged at this, and commanded that the furnace of fire be kindled and made very hot, and they cast Thaddeus, bound, into the midst of it. But he prayed and said, " Lord Jesu Christ, send me Thy help."

Then there arose at once a strong wind with a refreshing dew, that scattered the fire of the furnace among the wicked heathens, and the terror of heavenly voices destroyed them all; so that the king fled to his palace, where, seized with an evil disease, he lay in doubt what to do.

The holy Apostle, however, being full of the hope of heaven, was happy and as bright as light. And in that day, four hundred and thirty-three people believed, who cried and said: "Great is the God of the Christians!" Thaddeus then arose and baptized them at that same hour; whereat the wicked king being enraged, gave orders to put them to death. But the holy Apostle strengthened them in the faith of the Gospel that gives us life, and rising he prayed, saying, "O Lord Jesu Christ, my God, forsake not this Thy holy company, but strengthen them in their love for Thee their God; and receive me, O Lord, as a sweet-smelling offering unto Thee."

Having ended his prayer, he blessed them all, and committing them to Christ, he said, "Arise, go to yonder high place, which is above us, and ye shall look upon the scene of my martyrdom; I have given you for leader Zacharias, a beloved of Christ, my fellow-worker and servant in the Lord. He will teach you the word of the holy Gospel, which the Holy Ghost has put in his mouth; and after having established you in our holy faith, he will soon come to me, and accomplish his martyrdom." Then he blessed them and they went.

And a troop of soldiers coming with officers, took the holy Apostle, and brought him to a small, narrow valley on the top of a hill, and to a quarry there. But he praying, said, "O Lord God, Father of our Lord Jesus Christ, receive me now; and show forth a token of Thine awful divine power, that they may know and acknowledge that Thou alone art the God of all creatures. O Lord, I beseech Thee, do not let go out of Thy hand the portion of Thine inheritance which is in this land; and reckon not to the inhabitants of it this sin, for they know not what they do. Convert the mind of these heathens, and make them to acknowledge Thee as their God, O Thou lover of mankind and merciful Lord."

Having ended his prayer and signing himself with the sign of the Cross, he said to the executioner, "Do what thou wilt." Then the executioner arose upon the Apostle, and smote with the sword Zemendos, his own brother, and killed him, who was a chief set over all the roads of the kingdom, and a trusty councillor of the palace. But the holy Apostle, seeing that he was dead, was grieved, for he was the friend and protector of the believers, and entertained strangers hospitably. And going towards the dead body, he looked up to heaven and said, "Father of our Lord Jesus Christ, look down from Thy Throne in heaven, and bring this dead body to life, that they may know that Thou art God." Then he took hold of the hand of the corpse and said, "I say unto thee, in the name of Jesus Christ the Son of God, arise and stand up." Then the dead arose and stood, and falling at the feet of the Apostle, said, "I believe in thy God, that He alone is God, and that beside Him there is none else." And Thaddeus laid his hand on his wounds and healed him. And in that hour eight hundred and twenty souls believed, at the head of which was Zemendos, whom Christ raised from the dead through the holy Apostle Thaddeus. To whom the Apostle said, "Behold, Christ, the Son of God, has brought thee to life; He has saved thee from the errors of thy fathers, and has made thee worthy of the heavenly light. Now be strong, and stand firm in the faith of Christ, and He will keep thee and all the believers with thee."

Then he arose and baptized them, embraced them with heavenly love and blessed them, and committed them to the Holy Ghost, saying, "Go ye in peace, the Lord is with you." Then he prayed himself over the believers, and said, "O my Lord Jesus Christ, keep them; put to shame the wicked one, and receive me, O Lord!"

No sooner had he ended his prayer, than the king, being wroth, commanded him to be put to death at once; and at that moment he was made perfect in death with the sword. But as he was dying, a sweet smell came from his body, with an awful and terrible sound of a voice, while the light of heaven shone over the Saint. Then there was a great earthquake, and the earth being rent asunder by the power of God, received the body of the holy Apostle, and the impious bystanders fled[1].

---

[1] [A Syrian account (Ancient Syr. Doc. p. 110) says that Adé, who preached at Urha (Edessa) and in Mesopotamia, in the days of Abgar, was from Paneus (Pancas?), and that when among the Zophenians (in Sophene, a province of Armenia), Severus (Sanadrug), son (sister's son) of Abgarus, sent to slay him at Agel Hasna, together with a youth, his disciple. (Agel is a town of the fourth Armenia, a province of which was called Sophene. —St.-Martin, Mém. Armén. vol. i. p. 97.)]

But the believers being strengthened by the light that shone over them, the holy Thaddeus being among them in a body of light, they cried with one voice and said, "O holy Apostle of God, our father, remember us and forget us not!" because they fancied him risen and present with them in the body.

Then they rose, and going down into the place where he had been slain, they understood that he had been put to death with the sword, and that the rock rent asunder had received his body [8]; and they wept. And that day three thousand and four hundred and thirty-three, men and women, believed, and gave glory to the Holy Trinity on high.

I Samuel, bishop, unworthy servant of Christ, have told the martyrdom of the holy Apostle Thaddeus and of the holy maid Sandukht, and I have given it to the whole land of Armenia. May those who read it and who commemorate these two chosen of the Lord, think me their humble servant, worthy of remembrance in their prayers!

Saint Thaddeus was perfected in death on the 13th of December, at the ninth hour; and Saint Sandukht, on the 8th of the same month: to the glory of the most Holy Trinity. Amen [9].

[According to Armenian tradition, S. Thaddeus, whose tomb is in Ardaz, consecrated his son Theophilus Bishop of the First Armenia, which included Cappadocia. Wherefore did S. Gregory go thither, as it were to be consecrated by S. Thaddeus himself. His son Theophilus, says the same tradition, is the Theophilus for whom S. Luke wrote his Gospel. Vartan, Geogr. p. 434.]

[It is needless to say that not a word of these Armenian legends occurs in Abdias, which only gives Romish stories. The Ethiopic account of S. Thaddeus or Judas is also very different.]

II. THE ACTS AND MARTYRDOM OF THE HOLY APOSTLE BARTHOLOMEW[1].

S. BARTHOLOMEW having for some time companied with S. Thomas on his way to India, afterwards parted from him, and went into Media and Elymais, and in the country round about, visiting Parthia, where he made many converts.

He thence came into Koghth[2], a province of Armenia, and hastened to enter into the work fallen by lot to Thaddeus, according to the order he had received from the Holy Ghost. He preached there the Word of life, which the people of those parts received with joy and great gladness, believing and yielding themselves obedient to it; and were of him enlightened by baptism. He left among them elders, who had been magi, but were made disciples by him, and through whose hands God wrought many wonders in divers places, wherever they went; for they turned many from their vain worship to that of the true God, and the graces of the apostolate rested on them. It was in the twenty-ninth year of king Sanadrug's reign that S. Bartholomew came into Armenia, according to the command of the Holy Ghost, who had chosen the Apostles to call the heathen to the faith. And S. Thomas, by

---

[1] [Translated from the Armenian. Ven. 1854, p. 22 sq.]
[2] [A district of the Armenian Albania.]

virtue of his being chief guide of the Apostles engaged in the evangelization of the East, wrote to S. Bartholomew not to omit to preach the Gospel about Armenia, as well as in every place where Thaddeus had been, who was one of the Seventy.

But when S. Bartholomew came to the plains of Ardash[3], he fell in with one of the Twelve, Judas, the brother of James. They planted a cross on the spot where they met, and afterwards parted with great joy at having seen each other: Judas went to his own district[4]; but Bartholomew went into Her and Zarevant[5], districts of Armenia, where he wrought signs and wonders among the sick; cast out many devils, enlightened many, comforted others with words of teaching from the Holy Gospel, and called upon them to abide firm in the faith they had received, and to continue faithful. And having laid hands on them one by one, he committed them to the grace of God; he then left them and came to Urpianos[6], a city of Armenia. And there came to

[3] [Or Ardaz, a district of Vasburagan, in which S. Thaddeus laboured, and where he lies buried. See above, p. 66, note 2.]

[4] [Judas, the brother of James, is said to have preached the Gospel in Armenia; hence, possibly, some of the prevailing confusion with regard to Thaddeus and Addeus, and to the two Thaddæi. The Vartabed Vartan, in his Geography (p. 422, ed. St.-Martin), says that " Thaddeus is buried in Ardaz (though Syrians claim him for Edessa), S. Bartholomew in Salamazd, and Judas, the brother of James, in Ormi "—all in Armenia. See for Syrian accounts of S. Bartholomew, Assem. Bib. Or. vol. iv. p. 3 sq.]

[5] [Two districts of Armenia, to the east of the Gordjaïk.]

[6] [This town is not known among Armenian writers. It is a corruption of some other name, as "Germanica," a country in

him all those who were tormented with divers diseases, whom he healed and enlightened with holy baptism.

Okohi, sister of king Sanadrug, who was sister's son to Abgarus, heard of S. Bartholomew; she then came to him in secret, and having heard from him the Word of life, she believed in our Lord Jesus Christ, she and all who belonged to her; and having put on the habit of a nun, she renounced the glories of the world, and went about with the Apostle, ministering to him.

The king hearing of this, became furious, like a wild beast thirsting for blood; and sent Terentius, a captain, with his men, who, when he came to the Apostle by order of the king, had pity on him. The Apostle then began to preach to him the Gospel of the kingdom; and the Lord opened his understanding to receive his words; but he was a leper. The Apostle then took him by night, and baptized him; and lo, a cloud of light hovered over the place, and a light of fire shone all round the water in which he was baptized. And as he came out of the water, there fell from him, as it were, a hard skin like the bark of a tree, and like a leaf of the vine, and light enveloped him like a garment; at the sight of which marvels many believed in the Lord. But when the king heard of all these wonderful things, he became more enraged than ever, and sent at once another of his chief ministers, who should forthwith exter-

which S. Bartholomew is said to have preached, is a corruption of Caramania.]

minate the Apostle and the rest of the believers, and hearken to nothing else.

They came, and laying hold on the holy Apostle, on Okohi and Terentius, they brought them to the palace. There the Apostle was scourged for one hour by six men; and as he was left for dead, they dragged him and cast him outside the city; but he continued alive by the power and the help of the Lord, in whom he had trusted. And after having thus lain for three hours, while a great crowd from the city and the neighbourhood was standing around him, he began to move his hands, to stretch them and lay hold with them; he then rose and stood upright, and spreading his hands towards heaven, he said, "O Lord God, Father of our Lord Jesus Christ, let not go from Thy hand this Thine inheritance, for the supplications which Thomas, Thaddeus, Judas, and myself, have offered Thee in behalf of this land, that it may not be trodden down by the enemy; but vouchsafe to the inhabitants of it Thy mercy and pity, that they may be converted from the worship of their vain idols, and recover themselves from the error of their ways of ignorance and unbelief. Then give them a Pastor and Guide, that they may know Thee, the only true God, and Him whom Thou hast sent, Jesus Christ. And now receive me, O Lord, and help those who believe in Thee."

When he had said this, the place where he was trembled, and behold, an arch of light rose over the Saint, who, looking up to heaven, gave up the ghost; when a sweet smell was scattered abroad, and the holy Apostle Thaddeus stood before them in the same form as that which he had while in the body; and they disappeared to the place whence Thaddeus had come. Great fear then fell on them all, and that day more than two thousand people believed, while they all glorified God for what had taken place; and a light in the form of an arch continued over the body of the Apostle twelve days.

But they slew with the sword the blessed Okohi and Terentius, and many others with them. And seeing the body of the holy Apostle, they removed it to some other place of rest, together with other martyrs, to the glory of the most Holy Trinity. Then it thundered, and the deaf heard, the blind saw, the dumb spake, and they all were healed of whatever disease they were taken, as many as believed in our Lord Jesus Christ, through the preaching of S. Bartholomew. Then they all together lifted up their hands to heaven, and with one mouth glorified our Lord Jesus Christ, unto Whom, with the Father and the Holy Ghost, belong glory, honour, and power, now and ever, world without end. Amen[y].

---

[y] [S. Bartholomew is, by the Syrian Church, identified with Nathanael (Assem. Bib. Or. vol. iv. p. 3—5); but by the Egyptian Church, Nathanael is said to be the same as Simon, the son of Alphæus, as it appears from Zoega, Codd. Sahid. p. 229, and other documents. It need hardly be said that the Latin and Ethiopic accounts of the martyrdom of S. Bartholomew differ from this.]

THE LIFE AND TIMES

OF

S. GREGORY THE ILLUMINATOR.

HISTORY

OF THE LIFE AND TIMES OF OUR HOLY FATHER

GREGORY THE ILLUMINATOR
(*GREGOR LUSAVORITCH*)[1].

CHAPTER I.

Of the time and place of his Birth.

[2] IN the days when kingdoms and nations had been set one against another, and changed at the bid of one stern ruler of them all, the valiant Arsaces arose, about sixty years after the death of Alexander the Great, and reigned over the Persians and the Parthians; thus checking the further inroads of the Macedonian empire, already on the wane, by founding the family of the Arsacidæ. War followed upon war, until he had brought the whole East under his rule, during a reign of thirty-one years. After him came his son, Ardases, who reigned twenty-six years, and was succeeded by Arsaces the Great, who, in order to bestow rank and dignity on his

---

[1] [Translated from the Armenian. Ven. 1749.]
[2] Moses of Chorene, lib. ii. c. i. n. 2, and Lives of the Saints, Nov. 13.

brother, Valarsaces, set him king over Armenia, giving him the North and West as limits of his dominions. From that time the two kingdoms of Armenia and of Parthia were subject to the same family, Parthia taking the first rank and Armenia the second.

'This went on until the reign of Ardases the Great, King of Armenia, who, being of a hasty and overbearing disposition, and very powerful withal, assumed supreme authority, bringing the Parthians under his own hand, and thus raising the throne of Armenia above that of Parthia. After him, however, Tigranes, his son, when sick unto death, restored the highest rank and power to the throne of Persia; and from that date the kingdom of Persia was accounted first, and that of Armenia second, until the time that Philip became emperor under the Roman rule.

'In those days, Ardashir, a Persian prince of the city of Sdahr, headed a rebellion, and drew to himself the rulers and satraps of Persia and Assyria, all of whom set at naught and thrust from them the Parthian yoke, to which they had yielded until the reign of Arsaces the Great; and with one consent chose and set king over themselves this Ardashir, son of Sasan. He at once gathered his troops together against the king of Persia, Ardavan, son of Valarsaces, and slew him; and then ruled over the kingdom of Persia in his stead.

' Moses of Chor. lib. ii.
' Agathangelos, and Moses of Chor. lib. ii. 69.

⁵ The reason of the success of Ardashir was this. Ardavan, king of Persia, was a fire-worshipper and addicted to magic; and it came to pass one day, as he was with his wife in his chamber, that he began to talk to her, and said, "Know that if at this time any one attempted to raise a rebellion, I do not doubt he would succeed." Meanwhile, one of the maids in waiting, Ardatukht by name, who happened to be in the room behind the curtain, listened and took notice of the words spoken by the king, and brought them at once to Ardashir, who had before been on familiar terms with her. This gave Ardashir the idea of rising against Ardavan; but he feared the attempt. The words of the maid, however, gave him both pleasure and courage; and as a reward, he swore to her that, if he succeeded, he would make her his wife, and raise her to the dignity of queen. Being thus confirmed in his thoughts of rebellion by this foreboding, he ventured to make known his intentions to his most intimate friends.

He then excited to rebellion, and also encouraged the Persian and Assyrian princes, who longed to become rulers in their own houses, and to be set free from the galling bondage of their Parthian king; and he gathered them all together against Ardavan. And when, during the fight, Ardashir was brought face to face with Ardavan, Ardashir addressed him thus: "Trouble thyself no further; neither do thou foolishly doom to destruction the Persian and the Parthian nations, whose heart is

⁵ Sim. Metaphrastes.

not to thy rule, but rather to that of Ardashir, even to mine. If thou hearken unto me, thou shalt live, and I will give thee a place wherein thou shalt find every thing thou canst require. Remember the words thou didst speak in the ears of the queen in thy chamber; then take counsel with thyself: be wise, and live."

Having heard this, Ardavan turned to his attendants, and said, "How bitter is woman!" He then commanded that his wife be put to death; not knowing how else his words could have reached Ardashir. Then replying to him, he said, "Better it is for me to die, than to give my kingdom into the hands of the slave Ardashir." And thus saying, he rushed forward to fight him, and raised his spear to thrust him through, when Ardashir feigned flight; but, turning round upon Ardavan, who was pursuing him, he sent an arrow through him, and killed him. Then he forthwith gathered together all the princes and governors, who at once set him up king instead of Ardavan. Such is the account of the success of Ardashir, left us by Metaphrastes, who not only wished to confirm the voice of the stars, but also to state the occasion on which Ardashir had raised his hand in open rebellion against the king of Persia.

*When the news of the revolt reached Chosroes, king of Armenia, he at once hastened to send help to Ardavan, ere he were put to death; but he could not do so in time to prevent his untimely end; for he heard of his death even before he set foot in

* Agathangelos, and Moses of Chor. lib. ii. 68.

Assyria, and he went back sorrowing. Afterwards, however, his mind became bent on avenging upon Ardashir the blood of his relative Ardavan, who was next to him in royal rank. He sent messengers to gather together to battle the armies of the Georgians and of the Albanians. At the same time he opened the gates of the fortresses of the Alans and of his own, while he brought the hordes of the Huns into Assyria, to spread desolation therein. He laid it waste as far as the province of Dispont, destroying populous cities and most romantic villages, until he left the whole country desolate and without inhabitants.

Then, as a preparation for the coming struggle, they sent messengers right and left to the provinces and to the strongholds which had yielded themselves subject to the rule of Chosroes, to whose aid Albanians, Caspians, and others readily came at once with abundant supplies of men and horses, together with other reinforcements from various quarters, all bent on avenging the blood of Ardavan. Ambassadors had also been sent into Parthia for the same purpose; but the satraps, heads of families, and other princes who had already given their allegiance to Ardashir, turned a deaf ear to the call of Chosroes.

Meanwhile, Chosroes having brought together his own forces, and those of his allies who had come to his aid, marched against Ardashir. Ardashir, on his side, came to meet Chosroes with a great army; but instead of beating him, he was himself beaten and put to flight by the Armenian host, which pursued and utterly routed and discomfited him, scattering in all directions, and sweeping away from the face of the earth and from the roads and passes of the land, all the remnants of his army. Thus did the king of Armenia conquer the country, hold and rule by repeated blows, during the space of ten years, all the provinces which afore had been subject to the yoke of Persia; and after laying them waste, he drove back Ardashir, and constrained him to take refuge on the borders of India.

Ardashir, then, seeing that he could not resist Chosroes, nor subsist before him, became perplexed, anxious, and undecided in his counsels, from which he could find no outlet. He therefore called to himself the great men of his kingdom, the satraps, governors, princes, and magistrates, to aid him in devising means of escape or of rescue. He made them various and great promises, even unto giving the second rank in the kingdom, next to the throne, to whomsoever would, by craft or otherwise, compass the death of Chosroes, either by poison or the sword: if by one of the nobility, so much the better; but if not, by whomsoever it might be.

Then one of the chief men among the rulers of Parthia, Anak by name, stood up in the midst of the rest assembled, and promised to do it.—Strange, heedless folly of a man, thus taking in hand so awful a deed, without care or concern of what may follow, and rashly risking both his own life and that of his kindred! Thus pledging himself with an oath to deal treacherously by a king of his own kin, as if he were a stranger of another tribe; we shall, however, see how this fiendish act on the part of Anak was overruled by God's great power and mercy, and made to lead to the enlightenment and conversion of the Armenian nation. For the present, however, let us continue our narrative. The king answered to Anak, "If thou do this deed honestly and sincerely towards me, I will restore to you Parthians, your ancestral and noble territory of Balkh; I will put a crown upon thy head, I will honour thee, and thou shalt be called second after me."

Anak then gave orders to his household to prepare for a journey. He took measures, prepared and got himself ready with his brothers, and with his whole house he removed from Persia to the borders of Armenia, under pretence of emigrating, on account of his having rebelled against the king of Persia, towards whom he must now deal with caution, if not with subtilty. Wherefore, when some time after the armies of the Persians found their way into Assyria, they, as if driving him thence, made him come to the borders of Aderbigan.

Chosroes having heard this, sent some troops to his assistance; and, by order of the king, they brought him to the province of Ardaz, in a plain country, where it happened that he took up his abode close to the monument raised to the memory of the holy Apostle Thaddeus. There, as generally reported, did Okohe, the mother of S. Gregory the Illuminator, conceive him, whereby he became endowed with the grace of the Apostle. And thus he, who came into being near the Apostle's tomb, accomplished what was lacking in his conversion of the country, as Moses of Chorene tells us, who borrowed his information from trustworthy sources. Nerses Shnorhali also makes mention of it in his History of the Armenian nation; and we find it alluded to in the section of the hymnal dedicated to S. Gregory the Illuminator, in these terms: "The child is given, a living remnant of the Apostle's remains." Then, in due course of time, Okohe his mother brought forth the little innocent. How he was called to holy orders in the true service of God, and in due form, the following narrative will show.

'After these things it came to pass that Anak went to meet Chosroes in the province of Udi, in the city of Khaghkhagh, his winter quarters, where he was frankly welcomed by the king, and treated with every mark of respect and pleasure at his presence. For Chosroes could have no reason to fear aught from him, seeing he came to him with his brothers and his whole household. While Anak, who thus found grace with him, showed him confidence, and said to him in false, feigned words, "Hither have I come to thee, that we may together seek to wreak our vengeance on our common enemy." Thus deceived, Chosroes received him with great honours, even unto seating him next to himself on the throne. And Anak continued there two years

' Agathangelos.

watching his opportunity to bring about his treacherous design.

But in the second year after Anak's arrival at the Armenian Court, and while Chosroes was making preparations for an inroad on the Persian territory, the traitor Anak began to dwell on the oath he had nefariously made and on the promises of Ardashir; and the longing he felt for the throne of his ancestral land of Balkh led him at once to plot against Chosroes. One day in the spring, when he and Chosroes were gone hunting, Anak and his brother, under pretence of saying something in private to the king, took him aside from the rest, and drawing a dagger he kept hidden in his side, raised his hand, smote Chosroes to the earth, and slew him. Then he and his brother, jumping on their horses, fled for their lives.

When the king's attendants became aware of what happened, they raised a loud and tumultuous cry, while the princes rushed to the king's assistance; and others, with the Armenian troops, pursued Anak and his brother. Of these, some occupied the passes by land, while others, placing themselves between the bridges cast over the Araxes, made sure of their prey among the defiles of the country; thus driving into the river Anak and his followers, who, finding themselves hedged in on all sides, must at last come to the river, which at that time, being swollen with the melted snows, rolled tumultuously in a deep and rapid stream; so that if they attempted to escape from the Armenian soldiers by crossing the river, they would assuredly perish in it.

But ere the breath of life had departed from Chosroes, and whilst his blood was yet warm, he commanded the whole family of Anak, man and woman, young and old, to be put to the sword. Then was it that, by God's will and counsel, two children from among His sons were saved by their nurses, who escaped with them. The one took refuge in Persia, and the other, who, in the foreknowledge of God, was to become the Light of Armenia, was taken to countries under the dominion of Greece, as we are going to show more in detail.

*A certain man named Burdar, of a family both rich and distinguished, who had come from Persia with Anak, travelled as far as Ardaz; and starting thence, went and sojourned in Cæsarea of Cappadocia. There he took to wife a woman whose name was Sophia, the sister of a believing nobleman called Euthalius, with whom he continued for the space of one year, and then set off with his wife to return to Persia. But Euthalius having gone after them, overtook them in the province of Ararat, and persuaded them to go back with him to Cæsarea. Then, as Burdar tarried in the city of Valarshabad, where the house of Anak was, and where the child Gregory was also just born, the nurse of that new-born babe, that was destined to become the Light of Armenia, happened for some reason or other to come in to Sophia. And when the orders of Chosroes were being executed,

* Moses of Chorene, ii. 77. Legends of Saints, Nov. 18.

and that calamity befell the house of Anak, Euthalius went in to Okohe, the wife of Anak, and, taking the babe in his arms, he hid him in some safe place together with his nurse. And they continued thus concealed a certain time, until the excitement was over.

Euthalius then took his sister Sophia and her husband, with the child, who was then about two years old, and brought them all to Cappadocia, to his own city Cæsarea. Wonderful, unsearchable providence of God, in thus preparing for Armenia the Light of her holy Father Gregory! whose true history remains unto this day, written for our use. Thus writes, for instance, Moses of Chorene, who, wondering at it all, says, "All this, I willingly admit, was wrought by God's Providence, who then made a way for our salvation. If not, with what hope or object in view would they have thus brought a Bactrian child to be reared on Roman soil and under the Roman dominion, teaching him at the same time the faith of Christ?"

* The following wonderful occurrence is also told of him by credible historians. As on the journey they once had to spend the night under a tree, an angel came down from heaven in the form of a dove, alighted at the child's feet, and greeting him by name, called him Gregorios, which is interpreted "watchful," in token of his future watchfulness in all things. The form of a dove also, in which the angel appeared, showed, as it were, beforehand the

* Legends of Saints. Life of S. Gregory, by Anton.

nature of his angelic life, which he spent from his cradle to his grave, without spot and innocent, nurtured as he was in the graces of the Spirit. And in consequence of this apparition, when in after time he was consecrated at the second birth of holy Baptism, was he then named Gregorius; as we are told, not only in the Lives of Armenian Saints, but also in the Life of S. Gregory, carefully written in Italian.

This birth, therefore, took place, according to the most careful calculations, in the year of our salvation two hundred and fifty-eight. We will now proceed to give an account of his early years.

CHAPTER II.

How S. Gregory was brought up by his nurse, and taught in the paths of wisdom, and of a godly life.

[1] No one can describe the care and solicitude with which Sophia devoted herself to the Bactrian child, Gregory, whom she had been directed by a vision from God to bring up. So that, when he grew out of childhood, his whole life and conduct was marked by the progress he had made, both in the wisdom of the wise and in the service of God. For, while he was yet of tender age, she had him taught letters, and after that, when he was a little older, he applied

[1] Agathang., Metaphrastes, and the Lives of Saints.

himself to philosophical studies. But, above all, he ceased not continually to cultivate his mind with the letter and inspired wisdom of the Holy Scriptures; so that we may say that, like Christ when an infant, S. Gregory sucked the pure divine milk of the Word, and grew thereby till he reached manhood.

From his remarkable countenance every one who beheld him might understand the nobleness of his intelligent soul. For the brilliant gifts with which he was endowed shone brightly from within, like a lamp from within a lantern, into a beautiful form and into all the graces of his urbanity of conversation and manner, and already marked him out as destined one day to be one of the great men of the earth. But especially Sophia, guided and, as it were, instructed by God, did her utmost to educate, in all the teaching of useful and good knowledge, as far as in her lay, the young Gregory, who was being prepared, by the eternal decree and wisdom of God, to become not only the Light of Armenia, but also to scatter the thick gloom of heathenism, that brooded over eastern nations, by the bright sunbeam of his faith; to be their overseer and pastor, to strengthen and confirm them in the light of that faith, and thus, by the grace of our Saviour, to guide and order them in the keeping of God's commandments, and in the protection of His Church.

But at this time something very remarkable about him showed plainly that he did not, like other children, yield obedience by constraint to examples or rules set him to follow; but that he gave himself to it of his own accord, readily and willingly; as taking interest in good things, in a modest bearing, in a daily walk ordered in the fear of God, in works of humility, of obedience, of brotherly love, of abstinence and prayer. To other works of God's service also did he give himself up with a willing mind; making such progress in them as to astonish the happy lady Sophia and her friends and acquaintances. For he was pure and immaculate in his life, which he directed Godwards; he was humble, modest, quiet, obedient to his instructors, and adorned with discretion and urbanity of manner. So that, even in his natural bodily constitution, that bespoke the dignity of his high Parthian ancestry, he was brisk, of a fine, tall figure, erect and of a beautiful form, with handsome features, well made in body, and in all respects faultless.

² But prepared, as he was, to become the Illuminator of the Armenian nation, he received from the Giver of all good gifts excellence of sentiment, largeness of heart, and penetration of mind, and at the same time a great readiness in doing what circumstances required; and thus, by the constant practice both of his perception and of his activity in doing, he became eminent in every way. Of this his hidden man in the heart, the lady Sophia knew nothing; neither did she understand why he was thus, as it were, making diligence to fulfil what God had decreed from everlasting, by giving himself up wholly to the pursuit of good works.

² Anton, c. ii.

Oh the infinite goodness of God towards men, incomprehensible in its counsels, whereby He, the kind and careful God, appointed and fitted S. Gregory to be Illuminator of Armenia, how and when He pleased! Was it not, then, possible for Him to choose some saintly man out of a race already enlightened, and, enlightening him with wisdom and a perfect conversation, to take him by the hand, and send him to preach the Gospel in Armenia, and thus become the Illuminator of that country? He might, indeed, have done so if He would. But He who kindly takes care of all, did not so order it; because, had He so done it, we, Armenians, should not have appeared the special objects of His care, neither would His great power have been so clearly displayed towards us, as in the ways and means He used in calling our Illuminator, who was of a nation in which no trace of the worship of God existed any where.

But He who provides for all, who brings light out of the darkest shadows of death, detached him from the roots of heathen parents of whom he was born, and brought him, in the way we have just described, into a country enlightened with the Christian faith. And in this way did He commit him into the hands of pious instructors, that should train him in the fear of God and in innocency of life, until he reached the age of man's estate. So that, while his bodily form was growing to perfection, was he trained in the knowledge of the wise among men; and while his conversation was disciplined in the fear of God, was he perfected in knowledge and in holiness of life. And over and above this, abounding in all spiritual graces and mental gifts, he was thus fitted to become the Sun of Armenia, and through untold deeds of endurance and of long-suffering was he thus to enlighten the East, as we are about to relate.

CHAPTER III.

Of the marriage of S. Gregory while a layman, and of his giving up the married state after the birth of his two sons.

[1] As S. Gregory was of the royal stem of the Parthian Arsacidæ, the lady Sophia, his foster-mother, who was well aware of it, took care that he should marry as soon as he was of age, in order that the succession to his house should not fail. He, however, had no such intentions, neither would he of himself have sought the married state; choosing much rather to lead an ascetic life, as he had planned in his own mind to do. For he set at nought all the glories of this life, and counted as nothing the pomp and vanity thereof, desiring that which is incorruptible, and longing to devote himself to

---

[1] Moses of Chorene, ii. 88. Lives of the Saints, Nov. 18.

works that bring eternal glory to the real and true man. But he who was always so obedient and so considerate of his parents' wishes would not in this case appear deaf to their entreaties, but resolved to hearken to them.

In a vision from God, therefore, a maid, rich, modest, and pious, was allotted to him for his bride, whose name was Mary, the daughter of a prince of high rank, called David. She bare him two sons, the elder of whom was called Vrthanes, and the younger Arisdaghes. These two children, owing to the circumstances of their birth, sucked holiness and innocency of life with their mother's milk; for ere they could articulate distinctly, and while as yet their tongue only stammered in children's talk, they already made mention of the mystery of the Most Holy Trinity, and of the unity of the Godhead..

For while these noble babes were yet in their cradle, their parents bestowed as much care in rearing them in the fear of God, as when they became children. The perfect holiness of their life shows this to have been the case, as we shall tell it in detail in its proper place. For S. Gregory and his wife Mary determined to entrust them to a wise teacher who loved God, who at the appointed time should impart to them all the liberal arts and sciences; and, above all, the knowledge of the Holy Scriptures. Thus did they come to manhood with all the advantages of a rich and easy position in life.

S. Gregory, however, three years after having

received these two virtuous, sensible, and obedient children, made known to his wife his intention regarding holiness of life, asking her consent to their mutual abstinence from all intercourse with each other, in order to cultivate a closer union with God. Mary, who, for the love of God, was herself much disposed to lead a retired life, gave her consent, not by constraint, but readily and willingly. They then, for several days, asked of the Lord in prayer, to show them how they should carry out their intention. Then, by the efficacy of spiritual graces, they were confirmed within themselves in their purpose, and enabled to carry it out, by leaving all their property for the support of their children, and by no longer living together; so as to devote themselves unhindered to the contemplation of heavenly things, and to good works in the service of God.

'Then Mary, taking her younger son Arisdaghes, who was yet a mere child, entered with him a convent of women, and there spent her whole life as a nun. But he, when he came to manhood, went and joined himself to an anchorite, called Nicomachus[5], and took orders; while Vrthanes, his elder brother, being advised by his guardians, chose the married state, as Moses of Chorene tells us. These facts, however, are not told alike by all historians. And if we read any where that Vrthanes went with his mother into the convent, it would

---

[4] Moses of Chor. ii. 77.

[5] [Who lived near Cæsarea of Cappadocia, as we shall see hereafter.]

only be to remain there a very few years with her.

On the other hand, the blessed Gregory was after all this led by the Holy Ghost to go to Tiridates, king of Armenia, intending to make amends for his father Anak's deeds, by attaching himself as a slave to Tiridates, after having made known to him the fraud by means of which his father Anak had slain Tiridates' own father Chosroes, as we told above; S. Gregory's purpose being to win over to eternal life, through the Gospel of Christ, the son of him who had been slain by his father, and thus to make amends for his father's crime. Mark, then, at this time the supreme righteousness of this man and the wonderful love of him who, with the prospect of royal rank, as heir to all the pomp and wealth promised by the king of Persia to Anak, takes no thought for it all, but rather sets it at nought, and seeks to bind himself as a slave for the sake of saving the soul of his brethren—after the example of the infinite, ineffable, unsearchable Word of God, Who made Himself of no reputation, but took the form of a servant; and Who, instead of the rest and consolation that was set before Him, rather chose the Cross. Thus longing to become a follower of our Saviour, did S. Gregory attach himself to Tiridates, being strengthened by the grace of the Holy Spirit, so as to become the light of the whole Armenian nation.

Tiridates himself was the son of Chosroes, king of Armenia. S. Gregory, having borne witness before him of the faith of Jesus Christ, was by him grievously tormented; but at last, not only did the saint turn him, but also the whole of Armenia, to the true worship of God. And albeit our chief object is to relate the testimony borne to the faith of Christ by the holy Father Gregory, and the light of the Gospel which he spread all over Armenia, must we nevertheless begin with saying something about Tiridates himself, and his cruel treatment of S. Gregory; and first, about his birth and education.

CHAPTER IV.

How Tiridates, the son of Chosroes, king of Armenia, escaped with his sister out of the hands of Ardashir, king of Persia; of his birth, and deeds of valour, and how he received his crown from the Roman emperor, in token of his triumphs over Armenia.

⁶ WHEN Ardashir, king of Persia, heard how treacherously Chosroes had been put to death by Anak, he was much pleased; and that day made a feast to his court in honour of the event. Then gathering together his forces, he hastened unhindered against Armenia, putting to flight at the same time the

⁶ Agathangelus, ch. i. 15. Moses of Chor. ii. 73, 74.

Greek army sent at great risk to aid the Armenians. He laid waste a large tract of country, and assumed the whole authority in his own hands for about six and twenty years. His son Shabuh [Shapur] succeeded him, and reigned one year. During these troublous times, the princes of Armenia were put in great straits, and were at a loss what to do; when the house of the Arsacidæ, escaping from their own country, took refuge among the Greeks. One of them, by name Ardavazd, a nobleman of the Mantagunian race[1], having taken charge of Tiridates, the son of Chosroes, laid him at the emperor's gate; whence Tiridates was taken to dwell with the prætor Licinianus. Meanwhile another prince, called Oda, of the family of the Amadunians, having taken charge of the daughter of Chosroes, sister of Tiridates, fled with her to the stronghold of Ani[2], and hid her there, where she was brought up. But as to Ardavazd, who had rescued Tiridates and brought him to Greece, when Ardashir heard that he was of the Mantagunian race, he gave orders that his family should be entirely destroyed.

[1] [The Mantagunians were descended from Miandaco, to whom Valarsaces granted certain privileges. The whole race was exterminated by Ardashir, when he heard that the sons of Chosroes had been saved from death by the Mantagunian Ardavaz. Moses of Chor. ii. 7. 75. See note, Introd. p. 15.]

[2] [This fortress of Ani in Sophene, in Higher Armenia, must be distinguished from Ani, the capital of the whole country, in the province of Ararat. For full particulars of both, see St.-Martin, Mém. Arm. i. p. 72 sq., p. 111 sq., &c.; Indjidjean, Ancient Geogr. of Armenia, p. 7, 417; Moses of Chorene, and Geogr. of Vartab. Vartan. p. 418, ed. St.-M.]

*Both Moses of Chorene and other trustworthy historians [1] tell us much of the courage and valour of Tiridates. From his childhood he was accustomed to ride, to break-in fiery horses, and to throw the dart with skill; and with a natural turn for such warlike pursuits, in which he indulged, he became skilled in them, the more so as being by nature gifted with extraordinary strength and courage, he was greater than most of the men of valour who had preceded him. Greater, for instance, than Cleostratus, who in a wrestling-match could throw down his adversary by merely taking him by the neck; or greater than Cronus of Argos, who, taking hold of the hoof of an ox, would overturn and bravely overcome him; inasmuch as he, Tiridates, having seized two wild bulls, each with one hand and by one horn, bruised and crushed them together. Then, on another occasion, when contending in a chariot-race, his own chariot was upset while his charioteer was driving, and he lay on the ground, overturned by the skill of his adversary; he jumped up, and rushing forward, laid hold of the chariot, and thus at once stopped the four horses tied to it.

Then, again, when Probus was carrying on war with the Goths, a dreadful famine took place; and as his soldiers could find no corn in the granaries, they rose up against him, and slew him. They also proceeded to do the same to Licinianus, but they could not hurt him in any way, because Tiridates alone

* Moses of Chor. ii. 76.
[1] [Tacit. Ann. vi. xii. xiii. xiv. xv. xvi.]

standing up against them, would not allow one of them to come near the store-house. It also happened in a fight between the Romans and the Persians, that his horse was wounded, so that, when the Roman troops were routed, he had no horse whereon to ride and flee with them. But he, taking his armour and the trappings of his horse, plunged into the great river Euphrates that was flowing before him; he swam across the wide and deep stream, and reached in safety the opposite bank, his own troops, and Licinianus, who all wondered at his courage. Thus writes the intelligent Moses of Chorene. Nerses Shnorhali also makes mention of the same thing in his ancient history of Armenia.

Tiridates, however, was not only endowed with strength and power of body, which are but little in comparison with strength of mind and the moral powers of man; but in mind was he also sensible, prudent in his discernment, brave in council and just in his judgment, wise in his government, and in his whole conduct he was civil and correct, according to the light of nature. For while yet a youth, he excelled not only in soldiery, but also in liberal arts; and above all he was well-trained in philosophical acuteness, in civil economy, and in the affairs of the kingdom, as the manner is for noble sons to be. Being thus taught by innate justice and by public example, he became well-informed, and made proof of it in the rule of his kingdom, even before he received Christ's holy faith. And when he reached manhood, he was of a good figure, tall and well-made, of a commanding appearance, with a loud voice, of a beautiful countenance; so that to a flexible make of body he added lightness of heart, beauty of features, and was in all respects faultless and perfect.

Not many years after Diocletian became emperor of Rome, Hrtche the pugilist, king of the Goths, levied troops in order to make war against the Roman emperor. When, therefore, he came into the kingdom of Greece, he sent some one to parley with him in these words: "Why then, should we fight together with our whole forces, to ruin our armies, and place the country in imminent danger? Therefore do I, alone on our side, come forward to fight with thee alone on the side of the Greeks: let us come forth and go to some place and fight. If I overcome thee, the Greeks shall be subject unto me, and serve me; but if thou overcome me, our people shall become obedient to thy rule; and thus shall we settle our limits on either side without a wanton shedding of blood."

When the emperor heard these words, he was afraid, shuddered and was troubled, inasmuch as he had no chance of settling the business according to the terms of the parley, for he was of a diminutive size and weakly; and being in a great strait, he knew not what answer to return. But he gave orders to call together all his forces from all sides; and his captains and princes came to him in haste,

* Agathangelos, Nerses Shnorhali, Metaphrastes, &c.
* [The Roman empire is often thus mentioned in Eastern writers.]

every man with his troop. Licinianus also came with his legions, and with him Tiridates, who was to be brought before the emperor.

'And so it was that, as they came to a certain city, too late to enter in at the gates, they had to pass the night by the wall outside, for it was the usual time at even when the gates are shut. But as no provender could be found there for the horses, they looked about for some; when they descried a quantity of hay stored up and ready on the other side by the wall. Thence Tiridates crossed over to the other side, and threw over to this side to the troops bundles upon bundles of hay until they had enough; and after the hay he also flung over into the middle of the troops a number of asses; then himself crossed over and came down, to the astonishment of Licinianus.

'Then, on the morrow, when the princes came to the emperor, he began to tell them of the challenge sent to him by the king of the Goths. But Licinianus answered, "Let not the heart of my lord the king be troubled. There is here, at thy gates, a man, Tiridates by name, of the royal house of Armenia, who will easily settle the matter for thee." He then began to tell him of some of Tiridates' deeds of valour, and what he had done the evening before, in order to prove the truth of his words respecting him; and after that he brought

---

' Agathang.
' S. Metaphrastes, ix. Agathang.

Tiridates before the emperor, who conversed with him. The emperor then commanded to set the battle in array. Then when Hrtche came to the field of battle, where he was encamped, the emperor sent him word, by way of answer, that on the morrow they would meet each other face to face, equipped for the fight, according to his words.

The next day, therefore, in the morning, the emperor commanded that Tiridates should be arrayed in the imperial robes. Nobody knew any thing about it, as the news had gone through the host, that it was the emperor himself who was going to fight the king of the Goths in single combat. And having brought together the troops at the sound of the trumpet, he hastened to come before the enemy. As soon, therefore, as the would-be emperor and the king of the Goths, Hrtche, came in presence of each other, they spurred on their horses and rushed upon each other. At that moment, Tiridates being strengthened by the will of God, made the king of the Goths prisoner, and brought him before the emperor. Then Diocletian decorated Tiridates and honoured him greatly, making him withal many valuable presents. He placed a crown upon his head, and clothing him in royal purple, proclaimed him king of Armenia. He gathered together into his hands the whole forces to assist him in establishing his kingdom, and then sent him away to come and take possession of his illustrious ancestral land of Haïk. So write both Agathangelos and Nerses Shnorhali in their re-

spective histories⁶. But when king Tiridates came
into Armenia, he had to fight more than one battle
ere he could attain the rule of the country. But
this will we tell in our next chapter.

As regards S. Gregory, it is certain that while
king Tiridates was with Licinianus avenging the
Romans, getting himself a name in the world by his
deeds of courage and valour, the holy Father having
bound himself in service to him as a compensation
for his father Anak's crime, sojourned for the time
among the Parthians, as we mentioned it above⁷.
And for a number of years he continued, in great
humility, Tiridates' faithful and intimate servant,
having endeared himself to him by repeated proofs
of devotedness, not only during the campaign, but
under other circumstances also. Yet how was it
that the king never discovered who was this faithful
servant, and for what cause he had thus devoted
himself to him? He never once asked him about it,
neither did he make inquiries elsewhere, albeit he
ceased not to wonder at Gregory's life and conduct,
full of grace, innocent, pure, and irreproachable, so
that he loved him with especial fondness, consulting
him as an intimate friend on the most important
matters of the kingdom. So much so, that he decorated him and conferred on him the distinction of

---

⁶ [And S. Metaphrastes also—εἰς τὴν πατρῴαν ἀρχὴν ἀποκαθ-
ίστησι τὸν Τηριδάτην. S. Greg. Ill. ix.]

⁷ [According to S. Metaphrastes, however, it would appear that
S. Gregory was with Tiridates before his encounter with the
Goth. S. Greg. III. viii.]

being chief among his commanders, as a reward for numberless proofs of faithfulness and attachment. And when Tiridates received the kingdom and returned to his own land, S. Gregory was attached to him with the rank and position of a rich noble among his captains.

CHAPTER V.

How Tiridates came with a great army to his own land of Armenia, and obtained the kingdom after much fighting.

[a] As soon as Tiridates received his crown at the hand of the Roman emperor, as a reward for his triumph over Hrtche, king of the Goths, he departed with a large army from among the Greeks into Greater Armenia; and finding there a considerable army of Persians, who were trying to take possession of the country, he met them in battle, put to flight, discomfited, and exterminated the greater part of them, and the rest he drove back within the borders of Persia. And, as Moses of Chorene writes, he took into his own hand the whole government of the country, not without much fighting, first, in Ar-

---

[a] Agathangelos. Moses of Chorene, ii. 79.

menia, and then in Persia, being triumphant every where.

This, then, was the extent of the kingdom of Tiridates and of his ancestors: it was bounded to the westward by Cappadocia, to the northward by the Caspian Sea and Marsia; to the southward, by the chain of Mount Taurus, as far as Sarmatia, having also reduced the kingdoms of Georgia, of Albania, and of the Massagetæ into subjection to the Armenian rule; so that the countries over which Tiridates and his ancestors ruled in Greater Armenia were fifteen in all.

The first was the province of Higher Armenia; (2) the province of the Fourth Armenia; (3) Aghdzen; (4) Duruperan; (5) Mush; (6) Gordjans, also called Kurds; (7) Persarmenia; (8) Vasburagan; (9) Siunia; (10) the province called Artshag; (11) Phaidagaran, wherein is the capital, called by a new name; (12) Udi; (13) Kukar; (14) Daik; (15) Ararat, which was the original abode of the Armenian people.

These fifteen countries, or provinces, were divided into one hundred and nine districts, of which all those that still go by the same names as of old are found in Moses of Chorene, and are also mentioned by name in the history of Tiridates[*]. The capitals, however, were these: Valarshabad, Ardashat, and Armavir, in the province of Ararat; Vanar, in the province of Vasburagan; Tebriz, in the province of Phaidagaran, that still goes by the same name; Nisibis and Edessa, in Mesopotamia, all of

[*] [Written by Agathangelos, who was his secretary.]

which may be found mentioned by name in the annals of the country.

Who can adequately describe the valour, courage, and bravery of king Tiridates? Once on a certain occasion, while fighting against the Persians, he surpassed the deed of Elianus[1] of old, and stuck his spear into a heap of wounded. And at another time, some valiant men from among the Persians wishing to try the firmness and valour of Tiridates, shot a number of arrows at his horse, that fell wounded, throwing the king to the ground; but he, standing upon his feet at once, fell upon them, and, instead of being himself hurt, threw down several of the enemies, put them to death, and taking the horse of one of them, mounted it and escaped. Then, again, another day, he, and on foot, destroyed a whole troop of elephants with his sword. Amid such exploits did he continue both in Persia and in Assyria, making inroads into the country, even beyond Dispon (Ctesiphon).

When Tiridates began his return into Armenia, several of the Armenian princes came to meet him at Cæsarea in Cappadocia. And when he was come into his own kingdom, he found Ardasias, also called Oda, who had brought up his sister, Chosrovitukht, and had kept safe both his treasure and his castle with great care and perseverance, as told above; for he was a prudent man, enduring, active, and wise. For although at that time he did not know the wisdom of God, he nevertheless felt the vanity of

[1] i. e. Eleazar. See 2 Sam. xxiii. 9.

idols. So also was his adopted child, Chosrovitukht, a maid modest and chaste, like one of the virgins of old; who never did let loose her tongue like other women. Tiridates, therefore, highly honoured Oda, feeling great gratitude for so much faithfulness, and gave him the office of chiliarch, as a reward for his good services. But, in particular, he raised Artavazd, his nurse's son, to the dignity of commander-in-chief of his forces, in gratitude for the safety which he owed him, and for the ancestral greatness and glory he had reached.

Tiridates' accession to the throne happened in the third year of Diocletian, in the year two hundred and eighty-six of our salvation. He was sixteenth king of the race of the Arsacidæ, who reigned independent over all Armenia, as told by the best historians. He took to wife the lady Ashkhen, daughter of the king of the Alani, of equal stature and size with himself in all respects, touching whom Moses of Chorene thus writes: "Tiridates sent his equerry Sambad to bring Ashkhen, daughter of Ashkhart, to be his wife, who was in no way inferior to him in stature. He then commanded that she should be reckoned to the family of the Arsacidæ, that she should be clad in purple, and have a crown placed upon her head, in order to be married to him, the king. Of her was one son born to him, called Chosroes; but he was not like his parents in appearance and stature. Tiridates' sister, however, Chosrovitukht, never married, but continued single all her life."

After this, Tiridates began to seek vengeance on his enemies all round for all the depredations his ancestors had suffered at their hands. He fell on them in war and in fight; he surprised them, came upon them unawares, drove them hither and thither, destroyed them, and laid waste the kingdom of Persia and the land of Assyria. He put their armies to the sword, and took from them untold spoil and booty. He brought the troops of the Huns, the ravagers of the world, in great numbers, and took possession of the borders of Persia, carrying desolation in their land; wherefore was it said in a proverb: *Like the imperious Tiridates, who, stalking along, demolished the banks of rivers, and dried up the whirlpools of the sea.* For he was superb in his dress, energetic and strong, and of a robust frame, yet of a flexible figure, tall, broad, manly in his bearing, and indomitable in fight. As he had been in wars all his life, he acquired a great name for all his victories, gained several tokens of his individual valour, and left in many places splendid remains of his triumphs.

Having thus described some of king Tiridates' bodily advantages, and given some idea of his strength of mind, we will now proceed to give an account of the remarkable deeds of our holy Father Gregory the Illuminator, of the divine grace, and of the supernatural strength of spirit with which he was endowed, to the glory of Christ our Saviour.

CHAPTER VI.

Testimony of the holy Father Gregory the Illuminator, given before Tiridates, king of Armenia, touching the faith of Jesus Christ, when the king tried, by entreaties as well as by threats, to turn him to the worship of his gods.

[2] THE first year of his reign, Tiridates, after having discomfited and driven back the forces of Persia, by dint of wars and victories, and having thus taken in hand the kingdom of his ancestors, went with all his court, with the satraps, princes, and other great men of the realm, into the province of Egegheats and to the town of Erez or Erzenga[3], in order to bring offerings to the temple of the goddess Anahid[4], as a homage to her, paid in gratitude for all the success she had granted him. He came and took his abode with his court on the banks of the river Kail.

How awful is the darkness of blindness which original sin has left in man! Tiridates, in his ignorance, attributed to the vain goddess Anahid the blessings and the prosperity he had received from

[2] Agathangelos, and Legends of the Saints.
[3] [A city of Higher Armenia, celebrated for its temple of Anahid, afterwards destroyed by S. Gregory. Erez was embellished by Tigranes II., and was always a principal city of Armenia. See St.-Martin, Mém. Arm. i. p. 71. Indjidj. Anct. Geogr. p. 14, 114.]
[4] [The patron-goddess of Armenia. See note, p. 74.]

the Creator of all things, not knowing what he was doing; because no ray of the unapproachable light of grace had yet reached him. But, see now, how great is the meekness, pity, and the long-suffering of our Saviour towards men, Who thus made this occasion the dawn of light, then about to shine over the land of Armenia, when brought to the knowledge of God. For at this time He brings forward His faithful servant, the blessed Gregory, in full strength to stem the foul torrent of all manner of wickedness and idolatry, to fight, check, and expel the Prince of Darkness; and thus to raise the nation out of the gloom of idolatry into the bright light of the knowledge of God.

For while the king was with his attendants, with wreaths and clustered branches of laurel, going to offer a sacrifice to the idols, he perceived that his friend Gregory would have nothing to do with it; whereat he became very angry, inasmuch as, from the many faithful offices of Gregory, he fully expected that he would also be one with him in paying due honour to his goddess.

But the saint said to him, "The Lord of all teaches us, in serving our lords, to pay every attention that does not defile the soul[1]; wherefore I never grudged thee any act of such a service, neither did I ever do aught by constraint. But as to the service that places the soul in danger, and that estranges us from our Creator, with it ought we never to have any thing to do; yea, not even when

[1] 1 Pet. ii. 18.

he who gives the order is our emperor, and has power over our life."

We will now relate how all this happened.

In a short history of the life of the Saint, it is told that when the king had robed himself in order to bring to the goddess the offering of sundry chaplets of the most beautiful and sweet-scented flowers, he began to reason in his own mind what men among his nobles were the best and purest in morals, for them to hand the flowers, so as to make his offering the most acceptable to the idol. But among all his friends he could find no one such, except it were his friend and servant Gregory. He then caused to be brought to him the most beautiful bunches and chaplets of flowers; and choosing the best, he placed them on a tray of silver and gold, to wave them before the goddess. Thus prepared, he handed the tray to Gregory, saying to him, "Take this from my hand, and offer it as a gift to my goddess[a], the glory of our land; for I have found thee alone worthy to do it."

Now may we see the wonderful power of the grace of God, and the firm faith, hope and charity of the witness for the Lord Christ. For the king's command was urgent, and his manner haughty and defiant; moreover, not one of the nobles there present was favourable to Gregory, inasmuch as he alone appeared to the king the best among them,

---

[a] [Τηριδάτης δὲ—μᾶλλον εἴχετο δεισιδαιμονίας, ἄλλοις τε θύειν εἰδώλοις καὶ δὴ καὶ Ἀρτέμιδι, ἣν ἐτίμα τε διαφερόντως καὶ φίλην ἡγεῖτο θεόν. S. Metaphr. S. Greg. Ill. x. p. 953, ed. M.]

and was singled out by him for special honour. See, however, that the blessed man is in no wise troubled, neither does he feel perplexed; but on the contrary, with a brave answer does he thrust from him the impious order of the king, and raising up his hands, he draws back farther and farther, saying, "God forbid I should obey such an order as this. I came to wait on thee, and with devotedness to obey thy commands, but not to worship thy idols; for they are no gods, but the work of men's hands." The king feeling ashamed at these words, was very much grieved.

He then began to address him thus, "Thou, a man from another country, who didst come to join thyself to us, how darest thou resist our orders? And what right hast thou to worship a god we do not worship?"

Thus spake the king, not knowing who, whence, or what manner of man was S. Gregory. But God turned his mind from slaying Gregory outright. For the king thus said within himself, "What would it profit me to put him to death at once? may be I shall bring him to yield by means of threats or even torture." Thus did the king reason with himself, because he was greatly attached to him. He therefore ordered him to be removed from his presence, and to be put in ward in his own house, and there to be kept in confinement that day. Then came the nobles of the realm to him, blaming him for not obeying the king's orders, and advising or enticing him to worship their idols, in accordance with the king's wishes. But the blessed Gregory preached to them the knowledge of their Creator.

On the morrow, however, the king commanded him to be brought before him, when he addressed him thus, "For many years past have I seen that thou hast devoted thyself to my service with all thy power and with singleness of mind; and satisfied as I am with thy past services, I had in my mind to raise thee to great honour, and to maintain thee in it for the rest of thy days. Therefore did I impart to thee my counsels in war and in peace, hearkening to thy advice for thy faithfulness' sake; so that I never could have imagined that thou wouldst have thus dealt by me. What then have I done, or what has happened to make thee refuse to obey my commands?"

S. Gregory answered and said, "Because God orders that those who serve lords according to the flesh should be obedient to them[1], therefore have I served thee with all my strength, as thou thyself bearest witness. But, inasmuch as it is not meet to give another the power and to do him the service due to God alone, therefore does it behove me not to hearken to thee in this matter. For He alone is the Creator of the heavens and of the angels who there celebrate His glory and greatness; He is also the Creator of the earth and of men, whom it becomes to worship Him, and to do His will. Likewise every thing that is in heaven above and in

[1] Eph. vi. 5.

the earth beneath, in the sea and on the land, is also the work of His hands."

Then said the king, "Know then, that thou hast now made of no avail all thy past services, of which I have myself borne thee witness. Instead, therefore, of the easy life I had in store for thee, I will even double thy hardships; instead of the honours I was to have bestowed upon thee, I will degrade thee; and for the rank and glory which awaited thee at my side, shalt thou have the prison, chains, and death that cuts off the hopes of life in men. Such is thy lot, if thou wilt not consent to worship my idols, and especially this great Anahid, who is the glory and supporter of our race, whom even kings honour and worship,—among others, the kings of Greece; for she is the mother of all wisdom, the benefactress of all men, and the mother of the great and valiant Aramazda[8]."

To this Gregory answered, saying, "Hitherto have I served thee honestly with singleness of mind, because it is written that servants should obey their masters in the flesh; for the Lord is the rewarder of them that do well[9]. Thus have I never had an eye to any reward from thee, but only from the Creator of all, by whom all things, both visible and invisible, are upheld and maintained. But as to what thou sayest, that thou wilt even double my hardships instead of my happiness in life, or even

[8] [This, as we said above, at p. 75, was a mistake of Tiridates, who evidently was not well versed in his own mythology.]

[9] Eph. vi. 5, 8.

take me out of this world; in so doing thou wilt only double or hasten my joy in Christ, whose kingdom endures for ever, and whose loving kindnesses and mercy never fail. And when thou sayest, 'I will degrade and revile thee, instead of giving thee proofs of respect and esteem,'—thou wilt only thus bestow upon me the honour of angels, who evermore sing and rejoice in Him who made them. And when thou sayest furthermore, that instead of honour and rank thou wilt give me the prison and chains,—happy am I, for having set before me the example of my Lord; I shall rejoice with Him, and be glad of the gladness He gives.

"Then, if thou drive me away from among them that sit at thy table, lo, then shalt thou make me the guest of Abraham and of the other righteous men who sit at meat in the kingdom of heaven. If thou put me to death—what of that? then wilt thou only rank me among the legions of Christ, made up of all the Fathers, the righteous, the Prophets, Apostles, and Martyrs, and all the rest of His chosen. Then, as to cutting off my hopes of life in death, as thou sayest: the hope of such men as thou and those who worship dumb idols that have no breath in them, and that are the work of men's hands, is indeed cut off from the life everlasting; while the hope of those who love and serve God is thus increased. Thy gods, and she whom thou callest the Great Lady Anahid, once were mortals [1], who at one time existed, but were afterwards worshipped by men; because,

---

[1] [Here also is S. Gregory in error as regards Anahid.]

at first, devils taking various fanciful forms under which they might be worshipped, persuaded and induced men to build to them temples, to raise statues, and to worship them; idols as they are, that can do neither harm nor good, which can neither reward their worshippers, nor yet injure those that set them at naught. Such are the gods ye worship, through your gross intellect and blindness of heart, instead of the true God, to whom you owe all the good things you enjoy; gods of stone, of silver, and of gold, things which God made for the service of man.

"But for my part, I will worship with all obedience, with all intelligence and with awe, God the Father and maker of all things, and His Son the framer of all things, and the Spirit who gives life and shape to all creatures; who made every thing, and who can destroy it, and who, in His mercy, may once more bring it into being. Our life, O king! is not without hope; because we worship the living God, who is able to quicken us whenever He will. For even though we be dead, we yet live; because as the Son of God died and rose again to life, so also shall we; since He came to set before us an example of what life is, in His resurrection from the dead. Thus, we who die for His sake, shall also live in Him, at that day, the day of the Resurrection, when He shall appear to take His saints unto Himself and to avenge Himself of His enemies, the workers of iniquity, and the worshippers of your idols."

Then said the king, "When thou sayest, 'I had not an eye to thy rewards, neither did I want them,' I see that thou seekest thine own death, and that thou lookest to this burial ground, in which many gone before us are buried, as thy reward. So then will I lose no time in sending thee thither. But first, show me who is that Christ of whom thou speakest, that I may know; and who is the rewarder of thy services, whom thou callest thy Creator? Is He, may be, the keeper of the burial ground, whither thou longest to go; or is He, perhaps, the keeper of the prison, who will break thy bonds when once thou art in chains? And what are those endless joys of which thou speakest; and whose coming is that? I know not; neither do I understand what are those angels thou talkest about, and that hope of yours, and our hopeless state. Now then, tell it me all, quietly. But I will not forgive thee for having insulted my gods by saying that they are human, thus lowering them to the rank of mortals; because thou hast set them against us, as well as against our kings, saying, as thou didst, that the kings who worship them are void of sense."

To this the blessed Gregory answered, "Christ is the Son of God, through whom God made the world; He is the Judge of the quick and dead, who rewards good to them that do good, and evil to them that do evil, being, at the same time, as thou hast just said, the Keeper and Warder of burial grounds; for He keeps the bones of all men, and will raise them again to life at the general resurrection, as He showed it to us in His own person. For of His own accord He died and went into the grave; but neither death nor hell could of themselves hold Him captive; for after three days He at once rose from the dead, and by His resurrection He brought to light the resurrection of the dead.

"For He is Himself the Resurrection and the Life, who keeps the spirit of every man in life, and who will renew us at the general resurrection and give us new bodies. Then will He openly reward every man according to his works; Who even in the bonds with which thou threatenest me is wont openly to show His mercy and to deliver those who put their trust in Him. Then will there be endless joy and pleasures for evermore, when His beloved ones, who had kept His commandments, whom He had called and invited, shall by Him be crowned with immortality in His eternal Godhead; when the wicked shall also by Him be made immortal in the torments prepared for them. His coming is the day on which He will come and do all this. And His angels are they that wait continually on His great and glorious Godhead, in His everlasting kingdom. And our hope is—to look for these things.

"On the other hand, your hopeless condition lies in this, that ye do not know your Creator according to His commandments, neither do ye seek to become acquainted with Him. Thus are ye like the horse and mule, that have no understanding; yea, ye know less than the ox or the ass, for ye do not know your Creator, who, therefore, will in His own good time put a bit in your mouths and gag them, so that ye will not be able to come nigh Him¹. But as to what thou saidst, that I set the gods at enmity with you: who can ever be at enmity with things that neither feel the honour paid them, nor resent any amount of contempt? For they rest on nothing but the dreams of men raving mad: they have a mouth and speak not, they have eyes and see not, ears and hear not, a nose have they and smell not, hands have they and handle not, they have feet and walk not, neither is there any breath in their mouths. Like unto them are they that make them, and that put their trust in them²."

Thus did the blessed Gregory boldly speak bright words full of grace of the Spirit; while the king, enraged at this, gave order that he should be tormented by the executioners. But his tortures, the patience with which he bare them, and his testimony to Christ, will fill many a chapter. We will now begin and tell them all in detail.

¹ Ps. xxxii. 10.   ² Ps. cxxxv. 15 sq.

CHAPTER VII.

Concerning the first sufferings S. Gregory willingly endured for the sake of Christ, out of love for Him.

⁴ THE more S. Gregory rose against the abominations of idolatry, as we have just seen, the more Tiridates became enraged against him, when, shouting aloud, he said to the saint, "How many times have I commanded thee, O man, not to repeat these tales, that are not fit to be heard! I have had respect unto thee on account of thy past services, and I gave thee the good advice honestly to go and serve my idols, and live; but thou, on the contrary, taking from them the honour due to them, callest them things of naught. Thou hast insulted the great Anahid who supports and protects life in our land, and with her the valiant Aramazd, the creator of heaven and earth⁵; and the other gods hast thou called things without breath or speech. Thou hast also insulted us by calling us horses and mules: now, therefore, as returns for all these insults, will I give

---

⁴ Agathangelos and Lives of Saints.

⁵ [This is more correct. *Ahurô-mazdaô*, the Lord endowed with wisdom, also called *Çpentô mainyus*, the Holy Spirit, is in the Avesta worshipped as Creator of all things, as for instance in these beautiful lines of the Yaçna, i. 2: *Nivaêdayêmi datushô Ahurahê-Mazdão yó nô dadha, yó tatasha, yó tuthruyè, yó mainyus çpeñtô-temô.* "I proclaim the Creator Ahura-Mazda, who created us, who formed us, who kept us in life, I proclaim and worship Him who is the Spirit most holy."]

thee over to be tormented, and will I put a bit in thy mouth and gag thee; and thou shalt learn that such is the reward the words thou hast dared to speak in my presence have got for thee. Is it then nothing that I should have condescended to speak to thee and to pay thee a certain respect, and that thou shouldest reply to me as if I were thine equal?"

Then the king commanded that his hands should be tied behind his back, that a bit be put in his mouth, and a heavy lump of rock-salt upon his shoulders. They then made him, thus harnessed and with his face to the earth, run for some time like a beast of burden, because of his saying to them, that they were like horses and mules, that have no understanding and have no thought to seek after God. But the saint endured this torture with long-suffering in hunger and privation, and valiantly by the grace of Christ.

After that, they proceeded to put an instrument of torture on his chest, and then to tie cords to it, and thus bound they heaved him up and down against the walls of the palace. And he remained seven days thus tied up, bound and suspended. Oh, the wonderful solicitude of the Saviour for His beloved witness! For we see what wonders He wrought in him through these torments: not only did He vouchsafe unto him endurance, but He also filled him with joy at the hope of his eternal reward in heaven. For during the whole time he was thus tormented, not only did he neither complain nor show signs of pain, but with a joyful heart did he glorify the Lord Jesus Christ, to the astonishment of the bystanders, who went and told it to the king.

After seven days, Tiridates commanded that he should be released from his bonds and cruel torture. So they brought him and placed him before the king, whole, unhurt, and rejoicing in heart. The king wondered greatly at seeing him in no wise weakened in body or altered in his serene countenance; and he asked him how it was he had been able to endure, to suffer, and exist until that day, and what he thought of being tied with a bit in his mouth, carrying a burden exactly like an ass or a mule, and laden like them in their place? "Those very gods, Gregory," said the king, "whom thou didst revile, saying they cannot move, have thus requited thee; and if thou wilt still refuse to pay them all due homage, and if thou still continue to insult them, thou shalt be made to suffer worse things than these."

To this Gregory replied, "As regards the idols which thou callest gods, they are assuredly the work of men, since they are figures of wood, stone, silver, and gold, wrought with more or less skill. Of them not one ever spoke, or took knowledge of any thing; neither of thee nor of me. Nay, thou bearest witness thyself, that none of them told thee one word of all the sufferings thou didst inflict on me for their sakes; for of stone and dumb as they are, they are not touched with the feelings or pains of men.

Then, as to that lump of salt thou didst bind upon me, I trust in my Lord, the possessor of heaven and earth, and in His Son, who is equal with Him in power, and in the Holy Spirit, that He will season my lack of savour with the seasoning of the salt of truth that endures for ever, and that He will give me to bear the easy yoke of humility.

"And I look to the eternal reward He, who loves men, and who exalts the humble, will of His great mercy give me at the great day, when He shall set apart His own servants, and give them eternal rest, together with the reward of His greatness. But those who worship gods of stone, they shall fall into the deep like a stone, as the prophet says[6]. And as to those that bow to graven images of wood, thus does he speak concerning them, 'The fire was kindled among the trees of the field; it will destroy the wicked and shall not be quenched[7].' And to those who worship gods of silver and gold, he says, 'Their silver shall not be able to deliver them, in the day of the Lord's anger[8],' of Him who has power to bind heavy burdens on them; and on all those who resist the truth, who are sinners, and who, like thee, work iniquity."

Notwithstanding the bright light of truth thus proclaimed by the saint, Tiridates grew no wiser, being as yet enveloped in a thick gloom of ignorance and heathenism; but turning with renewed zeal to his idols, he prepared to inflict fresh torments on S. Gregory, as we shall see in the next chapter.

[6] Exod. xv. 5.   [7] Jerem. vii. 20.   [8] Ezek. vii. 19.

CHAPTER VIII.

Of the second torture endured by S. Gregory; of his humility, patience, and of the prayers he then offered.

*No sooner had S. Gregory finished his answer, than the king commanded him to be hung by one foot; then all manner of filth to be burnt under his head, as long as he thus remained hanging with his head downwards, and withal, to beat him with a heavy green stick. Thus did the blessed man continue suspended for seven days, during which ten men beat him in succession by order of the king; while, in addition to the torture of being thus suspended and beaten at the same time, the stench that rose continually from under him choked and stopped his breathing. Oh, the terrible thick darkness of him that wanders from the knowledge of God! Tiridates acted thus against S. Gregory, from deep religious feeling, but without understanding; and, as he said to the saint, that for fear of his idols he would not remember S. Gregory's long and faithful services, as the ~~holy Father~~ Gregory of Nareg writes.

Yet, in the midst of such horrible tortures, the saint did not even utter a groan, neither did he show signs of pain; because, raising his mind to God in the deepest and fullest thoughts of the king-

---

* Agathangelos, Lives of Saints, and Metaphrastes.

dom of heaven, borne thither by his lofty soul, he
was filled with untold consolation and joy of heart.
And thus, the wonderful joy of heaven that gladdened his spirit appeared on his countenance,
lightened up from the fulness of his heart within,
to the admiration of beholders; while himself ceased
not to pray to God all the time.

But those whose office was to stand by him
understood not what he said. Albeit he spake to
them many things about God, and preached to them
the worship of Him. He began with saying to them
that in the beginning God made the heavens and
the earth, and having created man placed him in a
garden of delights. But man having transgressed
the commandment of God, was driven out of that
garden; and then all manner of troubles, enmities,
and of other miseries have come upon us all. Moreover, he also taught them God's infinite love towards
men, whereby, having planned our salvation, He sent
us teachers and prophets, who told beforehand of
His Son being made flesh, of His sufferings, of His
cross, of His death which He suffered of His own
accord, and of His resurrection; men who foretold
fully our being renewed through Him, and restored
to our former state of innocence in God. S. Gregory also told them of the second coming of the
Son of God, to judge the world and to make those
who do well inheritors of the kingdom of heaven,
and the evil-doers, on the contrary, partakers of the
torments prepared for them—the fire that is not
quenched, the outer darkness, the worm that dieth

not, and all the everlasting punishments which the servants of sin treasure up for themselves.

The ~~holy Father~~ Gregory of Nareg makes mention of S. Gregory the Illuminator in his exposition of the Song of Songs, in these words, "Ten men, during seven days, ceased not to beat him while he was thus hanging, but they could not lessen the watchfulness of his heart by such grievous torments. For during those days he incessantly conversed with God in prayer, and poured forth in supplications his earnest longing for our salvation." We will now give some idea of his prayers at that time; not all of them, but a few only for the sake of brevity, yet complete such as they are. These few prayers will prove no great interruption to the narrative, but will rather help us to follow it.

The saint beginning to pray to the Father, said thus, "I thank Thee, Lord, for having made my unworthiness worthy of Thy favour. For from the beginning Thou didst love the creatures of Thy hands, and didst give them the first delights of the rest of Thy glorious Paradise. And if we had continued stedfast in the commandments which Thou gavest us, in order to guard us against the temptations into which we easily fall, Thou wouldst have given us a life both healthy, immortal, innocent, and pure, free from pain and sorrow, as well as from old age. For even after our blessed state in Paradise, and after getting into our present earthly condition, Thou tookest man to Thine immortal state; as, for instance, Enoch into the company of angels, and broughtest him at once into Thy kingdom, which Thou hadst prepared for our glory, even before the world was. Since the eye has not seen, nor the ear heard, neither has it entered into the heart of man to conceive the things which, from the first, Thou didst prepare for them that love Thee, and which Thou wilt give to them who love the day of Thine appearing in glory.

"But when the enemy saw us thus blessed by Thy loving-kindness and good-will towards us, he envied us the crown of glory we then wore; and from his jealousy came into the world all manner of calumny, of disorders and debauchery, that shut out man from life and from rest, and spoiled and defiled all that in Thy goodness Thou hadst vouchsafed unto him.

"But when Thy divine nature took pity on our human infirmity, and would not let us go out of Thy hands, Thou didst send upon earth Thy beloved ones, the Prophets, as lights in the world, who made known the mysteries of Thy light, by preaching Thy holy will, and foretelling the coming of Thy Son into the world, who was to come in order to take away the sins which had shut out men from the glory of God. They preached Thy Word in the world, and for that, they were put to death by torture, after living for Thee in the world, in the midst of various troubles and trials.

"Wherefore, even though they rise up in war against me, shall not my heart be afraid, neither will I cease to put my trust in Thee, even when they stand up to fight against me. I will put my trust in Thee, who didst send into the world Thine only begotten and beloved Son, Light of Light, and Life of Life; who came to put on our human likeness from the womb of the Virgin, that He might bring us back to Thy divine nature through His own likeness. Neither did He suffer any change from His divinity: for He now is what He then was. But because He loved men, therefore did He become like ourselves, that He might bring us under the influences of His divine grace.

"Because men loved to worship images in the similitude of men, made of wood, the work of the carpenter, therefore came He in the similitude of man, that He might bring the makers, the lovers, and the worshippers of idols into obedience to their own image of the Deity. And instead of carved figures of wood, He planted the Cross in the midst of the world, that those who were accustomed to bow to images of wood, might, from habit, also bow to the wood of the Cross, and to Him who is on that Cross in the likeness of man.

"And as men were also wont to delight in temples of idols, and in sacrifices which they offered to dumb images, therefore also didst Thou call the whole world to the sacrifice of Thy Son, saying, 'Behold, I have prepared My dinner, My oxen and My fatlings are killed[1].' And Thou didst increase the joy in the Cross of Thy Son, and didst satisfy the whole world with His life-giving Body, which became the

[1] S. Matt. xxii. 4.

food and sustenance that is sufficient for all Thy worshippers all over the world. But for them that would not come at Thy bidding to Thy spiritual marriage feast at Thy Table, hast Thou prepared an imperishable destruction in eternal torments and endless condemnation.

"Then, because men ate and drank of that which was offered in sacrifice to their gods, therefore did Thy Son shed His Blood on the Cross. For that wood is to men instead of their carved images of wood; and He Himself, instead of the human similitudes of impurity; His Blood also is in place of the cup of their joyful libations of blood. For He came and redeemed us with His Blood from our hard bondage, and set us free from the servitude of the wickedness of sin, by His divine nature. For we are the price of the Blood of Thy Son; being saved and made free by the Blood of His Body.

"For we are not masters of our own selves, that we should walk according to our ideas of ease and comfort, or according to the opinions of any mortal man, even though he be our lord and master after the flesh. We must honour them only as Thou hast commanded; for they can only torment our bodies; but Thy Son Jesus Christ has power to cast into everlasting torments both our souls and bodies, into the fire that is not quenched and the worm that dieth not."

Then, addressing his prayer to the Lord Christ, he said—

"But, O Lord, give me patience to bear the

sufferings of this present fight of affliction, and have on me the same pity which Thou hadst on the thief who was with Thee sharing the tortures of the Cross. And, O Thou Friend of sinners, vouchsafe unto me Thy grace, whereby all the righteous live, as well as sinners also, by reason of Thy forgiveness and long suffering. Thou causest Thy sun to rise on the evil and on the good, and sendest rain over the just and the unjust. For Thou restrainest Thy wrath, but showest mercy and pity to all men in every place."

Then again, praying to the Father, he said—

"Lord, give me grace to endure all these bitter torments that tear me to pieces; that I may be worthy to hold fast the treasure of the light of faith Thou hast committed to me, which is to know Thee and to do Thy will. For Thou wilt not despise them that put their trust in Thee, who have once gloried in Thine only begotten Son Jesus Christ, whom Thou hast sent. For Thou didst send Him to die for sinners, that He should take our sins upon Himself, and bear on His Body the chastisement of our transgressions in His agonies on the Cross; that He should accomplish that for which He was sent, and give the graces of His favours to them that believe in Him. Grant me, O Lord, to receive my crown with those whom Thou hast counted worthy to die for Thy Name's sake, whose deaths are remembered before Thee in glory; that I may be worthy to rise in presence of Thy Son, with all them that long for Him, in the brightness of

His light. Now have pity on Thy creatures, according to Thy great goodness, and look with favour upon the land of Armenia; that her people may also know Thee and Thine only-begotten Son, the Lord Jesus Christ, Who was sent from Thee to us, and Who put on the body of our human nature."

Then again, addressing his prayer to Christ, he said—

" And now, merciful Lord, Who saidst, ' Behold, I am with you even unto the end of the world,' let us not go out of Thy hand, but strengthen us to do Thy will, that we may be able to endure unto the end the struggle and warfare we bear for the sake of Thy great Name; that the merit of our faith may be evident to Thy servants, to the praise and the glory of Thee, my God; for it will then appear unto all that no enemy can prevail against those who put their trust in Thee. And now, Lord, in Thy great mercy and kindness, make us of the number of the righteous, and leave us not in the sins of our fathers, nor in the worship of fire to which our ancestors were given, nor yet in the lawlessness of those that came before us. And give us all to know the power of Thy divine nature in creation, that we perish not in the vanity of heathenism.

" And now, Lord, strengthen Thy servant for Thy Name's sake, that he may overcome the power of the enemy. Raise and scatter the gloom of wickedness, of idolatry, and of heathenism from the earth, out of mercy and loving-kindness towards Thy creatures; for Thou gavest Thyself for Thy flock. Leave not the sheep of Thy pasture, but lead them in righteousness; for Thou alone art able to forgive sins, to blot out transgressions and the unrighteousness of Thy creatures, that they may worship Thee alone and do Thy will only; until they glorify Thee as their God, to stand before Thee in Thy judgment, and at last to enjoy Thine infinite goodness in Thy kingdom above.

"But Thou, who givest abundantly to all, grant us to bear witness to Thy divine nature. For Thou didst come and didst die for Thy creatures, and didst mingle our mortal nature with Thine immortality. Therefore will we bear witness to the life that is within Thee, even unto death; so that we be numbered among Thy witnesses. For what else can we do for all the good we have received at Thy hands, if it be not to give up ourselves to do Thy commandments, and to fulfil Thy holy will? that we may become inheritors of Thy kingdom with those who pleased Thee and found grace with Thee, and offer ourselves in sacrifice unto Thee, our God. Let us lose our lives, that we may find them again on the day of resurrection, and then live evermore at Thy right hand, clothed in spotless robes, and free from sin, with the company of those who live in Thee, at the right hand of the Lamb, in the joy of Thy saints, of those who love Thee, their God.

"And again, O benevolent Lord, Who didst come in great humility, and didst take upon Thee the form of a man; Who didst give Thyself up in all patience, and Who didst not turn away from insults, nor Thy face from the spittle; Who didst give Thy cheek to him who smote Thee, and who for our sakes didst drink the vinegar mingled with bitter gall—strengthen the heart of all men in Thy service, that they yield themselves obedient to Thy yoke, which is light, and escape everlasting torments. Then will the earth be filled with the fear and service of God, and those that dwell in it shall be led by Thee, so as not to go astray from the paths of Thy Truth, but be invited to Thy table in Thy kingdom, and delight themselves therein. For Thou didst come to be slain like a lamb for the sake of all, whom Thou hast caused to rejoice by reason of Thy Body, which Thou didst give for the salvation of all men; and of the river of Thy pleasures Thou gavest them to drink of Thine own precious Blood, shed for the life of the whole world. Have pity on them, that they may remember, and turn and come to Thee from all the ends of the earth, and that all they that go down into the pit may worship before Thee. For Thou art able to raise them again, to quicken them, and to make them worthy of Thy love for them; since they, too, are saved by Thy Blood, and by Thee delivered from the thraldom of darkness.

"Then will they, for whom Thou didst die, know Thee; for they, too, are Thy servants, and they will become worshippers of Thee; for let not Thy wrath be kindled against them. Make them children of the light, and sons of the morning, that Thy name be glorified all over the world; since Thou art glorified in Thine everlasting kingdom, Thou who art one in Thine essence, in Thy truth and in Thy nature[1]; who in Thine own sufferings didst give an example to Thy beloved ones of what it is to suffer in humility, while Thou didst show Thy saints by Thine own doings how they may come to Thee by enduring insults for Thy sake.

"Wherefore we of the earth, earthly, should bear some little trouble on account of our sufferings; for Thou, Lord, didst humble Thyself, and didst take every thing upon Thyself, and didst bear the afflictions and the sufferings of the whole world. Now, therefore, strengthen me readily to endure with firmness the strait in which I am, that I may rather glory in my sufferings, so that I be reckoned with Thy beloved ones, in the day when Thou shalt give them the unspeakable boon of Thy glory, which is in store for those who put their trust in Thee, unto all eternity, world without end, Amen."

These and other prayers and discourses did the blessed saint utter during the seven days he was hanging and being beaten. His words were then written down by the head scribes and shown to the king, who, however much he felt surprised and wondered, yet did not relent from his cruelty, for

---

[1] [See the Introduction, pp. 29—34, on the supposed Monophysite character of the Armenian Church. But the subject is fully discussed in "The Doctrine of the Armenian Church," which was intended to form the second part of this work. It is now ready, and will probably appear at some future time.]

fear of his idols. He commanded to take him down from his hanging position, and to inflict on him another kind of torture, which we are now about to relate.

CHAPTER IX.

Of the third and fourth tortures of S. Gregory, and of the heavenly joy with which he replied to the questions the king put to him.

[1] AFTER S. Gregory had thus been hanging eight days by one foot, being all the while beaten with green sticks all over his body—sufferings which he counted as nothing,—the king commanded him to be taken down and brought to him. He then began to converse with him and said, "What is the matter with thee, Gregory, or what is thy choice: still to share life with me, as thou hast hitherto done from thy childhood, or to die for no reason, for the vain imaginations and fancies of thy mind, which thou wilt still cherish?" To this the blessed Gregory replied, "I hasten to leave the body and to put on life everlasting. And now give what orders thou wilt concerning me, even to put me to death."

"No," said the king, "I will not grant thee thy

[1] Agathangelos and Metaphrastes.

wish, and an early death as thy reward, to give thee rest from thy torments into what thou callest everlasting life; but I will command that these be continued bit by bit, that thou mayest not be buoyed up by the thought of dying soon; thus bringing upon thee the vengeance of my gods for thine insults and self-will, in not consenting to worship them."

So saying, the king commanded that two wooden clubs, the size of a shin-bone, be brought, and then fitted like the bars of a wine-press; then placing both his legs in between them, they tied them tight with knotted cords, which they twisted until the blood gushed on the fingers of the men who did it. But the saint continued joyful with wonderful endurance, magnifying Christ God, so firm and so rooted in the faith of Christ, as to prefer having his heart of flesh taken out of his body, and giving himself over to the executioners, rather than denying and forsaking Jesus Christ.

While he was so tormented the king addressed him thus, "How art thou, Gregory? How bearest thou all that? Hast thou yet any consciousness, or feelest thou yet any pain?" Then answered the saint, "Yes, because I asked the Creator of the world, the Maker and Framer of all things therein, both visible and invisible, and He gave me the strength to bear this torture."

The king seeing that not even these fresh torments could make the saint yield in his valour, gave orders that he should be tried in another way.

He sent to fetch iron nails and had them stuck into the soles of his feet, and taking him by the hand he made him run hither and thither on this and on that side, until the ground was sprinkled all over with the blood that spurted from his wounds. Then the king asked him again, "How art thou, Gregory?" He then answered with joy, "Such torture as this saves a man from everlasting torments, and brings him to his endless rest." Then the king said to him, "I will torment thee here, and thou shalt rest there." And the executioners made him run to and fro incessantly.

But the saint remembering that by such acute torture he was made like unto the Saviour when crucified, whose hands and feet were cruelly pierced with nails, greatly rejoiced within himself; and while thus running to and fro, he in his joy sang this song of the Psalmist, "They that sow in tears shall reap in joy. He that goeth on his way weeping and beareth forth good seed shall doubtless come again with joy, and bring his sheaves with him'." Then the king said to him, "Are these the invisible works of thy God, which thou seest?" S. Gregory answered, "Thou hast well said, these are the invisible works wrought by my God, because the body of God's beloved ones is sown in weakness in this life, being dissolved in the throes of death; but in the life to come it rises again in freshness of life that nothing can impair: it is sown in dishonour, but it is raised in glory.

' Ps. cxxvi. 6, 7.

Therefore, though they weep who sow their seed in the earth, that is, who have to endure the troubles and afflictions that come upon them, because they love and serve God; yet when harvest-time comes, and they carry their sheaves and the rich yield of their labour, do they with 'it receive gladness of heart with joy and pleasures for evermore."

Then said the king, "Now will I torment thee, and thou shalt rejoice." And he commanded the attendants to cuff him, and beat him until he shed a cup full of tears, and his gladness leave him. They then smote him with heavy blows upon the head and beat his eyes repeatedly. And the king began to inquire of him, saying, "Is this joy?" and he replied, "Even so, it is joy, for if the labourer does not bear the heat and burden of the day, and return home sun-burnt and covered with sweat, he will not enjoy the sweet fruit of his labour when the winter comes." The king answered and said, "Work then now, in the torture in which thou art, for anon wilt thou with joy gather thy fruit yonder there." Thus saying, the king commanded him to be put to a fresh torture, which we are going to relate.

CHAPTER X.

Of the fifth, sixth, and seventh torture of S. Gregory, and of the godly words in which he replied to the king's inquiries.

[1] Not only was the king not softened at the sight of so much suffering, but he even prepared to inflict on S. Gregory yet more cruel tortures, in order, if possible, to make him do his will respecting the worship of his idols. He therefore commanded to boil together salt, nitre, and strong vinegar, and all was soon ready; he then placed the saint on his back, put his head in a carpenter's vice, and introducing a reed in each of his nostrils, he ordered to pour through it the horrible matter into each nostril when the saint drew his breath.

Thus, while his head was in the vice they turned the screw with a bar, and poured into his nostrils, by means of the reeds, the hot mixture of salt, nitre, and vinegar, in order that, reaching his brain, it might disturb it; and by thus bringing him to a state of frenzy, to persuade him at last to worship the idols.—What senseless folly, that of idolatry! They were thus trying to bring the saint's mind from its sane state to that of madness, while he, strengthened with almighty power, endured such

---

[1] Agathangelos, Metaphrastes, and Lives of Saints.

horrible tortures and, with God constantly before his eyes, ceased not to confess and to magnify Him. To such a state did their folly bring them, so far had their imagination misled them—poor things!

Here, however, let us notice, as regards what has just been said, that the tortures of S. Gregory were twelve in all, as Nerses Shnorhali also writes; yet if we do not consider the cuffing he received as a separate torment, as some do not consider it, we must reckon the torture of the boiling salt and vinegar separately, and then it becomes the sixth torture after the torture of the vice, which we reckon the fifth. But if we reckon the cuffing separately, making it the fifth torture, as some do, then we cannot reckon the torture of the boiling salt and vinegar by itself, but we must reckon it together with that of the screw as the sixth. Having said thus much on the subject, in order to make every thing clear, we now continue our narrative.

After these things the king commanded a large bag of sheep-skin to be brought, and be filled with soot from a chimney and with ashes of a furnace. They did not fill it tight, but only so as to appear full, and only so as to hinder his breathing, for they put it over his head and tied it round just below his chin, in order that in breathing he might stuff his nose and mouth with the soot and ashes till it reached the brain and injured him; or if it choked him, well and good, let him be choked. And they left him thus six days. But by the grace of Christ the saint remained marvellously well and unhurt, nay, he was even strengthened above his other trials, and with joy glorified Christ God. Tiridates, however, although eye-witness of these wonders, did not yet awake to receive the words of truth proclaimed by the saint, but still continued in his hardened state.

When the six days were over, the king commanded Gregory to be brought to him. He came, and the king said to him joking, "Where hast thou been hitherto? or, where art thou, Gregory?—may-be in that kingdom of which thou speakest, or among those good things which thou art looking forward to receive."

The holy martyr then answered boldly, "That happiness, O king, has not yet come to me, for I am still burdened with the body. But since I have been found worthy to suffer all these things for the name of my God, there truly is and abides for me an imperishable kingdom, in exchange for them all, and after a little while I shall enter into the glory thereof. Then shall every thing be laid bare and naked before that tribunal, when the Word of God shall sit to judge not only the works but even the thoughts of men, piercing even to the dividing asunder of soul and body, in order to reward every man according to his works. Alas! woe is thee, for awful is the lot that awaits thee at that day; awful are the toils that will hold thee, and the torments thou also shalt endure."

Then the king tried again to persuade him, and said, "What is this change that I see in thee,

Gregory? What then has cast thee down, from a life of happiness and state with me, into such dishonour and misery; not only that, but also of rebellion against thy sovereign? Know, however, that abundant gifts and honours are ready for thee, if only thou wilt receive them; if, coming to thyself and repenting of what thou hast done, thou wilt alter thy mind, so will I mine. For it is the wont of great men readily to forgive those that have offended them, when they see them sincerely sorry at their feet, begging to be forgiven. But if, on the contrary, thou wilt still persist in thy presumption and obstinacy, and continue to run after thy mistaken faith and ideas, then will it behove me to avenge on thee the insults thou hast heaped on the gods I worship. By them and by their great power I swear that I shall make an end of thee."

The saint then replied in a clear voice, but with great boldness, and said, "Success in the life that now is, is no sign of happiness, but happiness is rather a want of prosperity therein; for tribulation is but the touchstone that shows openly the real value of Christian firmness by testing it; when a man counts it a great gain to lose his life for the defence of God's honour and for the glory of His name, that he be not found having, in any way, departed from the worthiness of his faith. It matters very little if, according to those who love the present life, they who serve God in spirit and in truth appear to thee vile and contemptible, as they also appear to those who love the world, when setting at nought such things. For if this be judged of according to right, it is both proper and fitting to look to Him who judges, not according to what now appears, but according to what will be revealed at the last day, when Christ, coming down in glory from heaven, shall requite every man according to his works."

And then, showing his kindness of heart, the earnest desire he felt for the salvation of the king's soul, he said, "Oh that thou, O king, wouldst hearken, if it were but a little only, to some of the words thou hearest from me, as it behoves thee to do! for thou oughtest to do something in order to cause God's wrathful indignation to pass from thee. And taking the road to eternal salvation, which I show thee distinctly, thou wouldst then cease to thrust Him away from thee, who desires the salvation of thy soul. But, O king, thou wilt do to me what the spirits of hell tell thee to do, yet shalt thou also behold the help sent me from heaven at the proper time, until thou find thyself more weary of tormenting me than I shall be of being tormented for my love of Christ."

Such boldness of speech on the saint's part only further roused the king's wrath, who ordered him to be given over to yet more infamous tortures, as we are about to relate.

CHAPTER XI.

Of the eighth torture to which they put the saint, and how sore it was; of the questions the king asked him, and with what holiness of soul he replied to them.

'THE king, seeing that such tortures of the body could not in any way bend the saint's will to the unlawful worship of idols, commanded both his feet to be tied together, and boiling water to be poured down into his stomach, in order not only to hurt him, but also to put him to open shame. And the tormentors did as the king commanded them.—Horrible feeling and passion of the wicked, who were not satisfied with only torturing him, but with the torture must also cover him with shame; but he was wonderfully supported in this trial also, wherein he must have died but for the strength vouchsafed unto him from above.

When this was over, the king commanded him to be let down, and he then began to ask him, "Wilt thou obey my orders or not? Wilt thou worship the gods who are the life and support of the world?" S. Gregory answered him, saying, "I worship my God, for He alone is the maker of the world, and on Him it rests. And I place my trust in His Son, Who is One with Him, of equal power

---

' Agathangelos, Metaphrastes, and Lives of Saints.

and majesty; and in the Holy Ghost, Who fills the world with wisdom. I never held by idols carved and made by hand, but only by the true God; neither will I worship any one else as long as there is breath in my body." Then the king began with entreaties to remind him of the greatness and of the supreme honour he enjoyed in the palace. And he then promised to restore him unto his former rank and dignity, if he would but once offer incense in worship to the gods.

To this the blessed Gregory replied, "I offer incense' and sacrifice only to the true and living God, our Lord Jesus Christ, Whom I love. But never will I do so to idols which neither speak, breathe, nor feel; no, not even if thou command that I be made to suffer yet more than I have done hitherto. God forbid that I, who have been made partaker of the intelligent Spirit of God, who have been saved from the horrible bondage of Satan by means of His precious Blood, and who was by Him adopted at the font of holy baptism, should again be brought into captivity to the sworn enemy of man. I once for all detached and severed myself by my vows, in presence of the Angels of God, from the vanities and pomp of the world, and from all

' [Those who would infer aught from this, as to the use of incense in the early primitive Church, must bear in mind that—albeit this purports to have been written by Agathangelos, who was secretary to Tiridates—there is yet nothing to prove that it is not a modern insertion; for Armenian writers warn us that the MSS. of Agathangelos vary very much, and that they should be read with great caution.]

that in which the flesh alone delights, and I renounced them all, and this will I not forget. How then is it possible for me to return to them? But now, put me to every kind of torture, to any thing thy gods tell thee to do; for, however great and terrible they be, they cause me no terror whatever; neither will they make me break my vows, pledged as they were to my Lord Jesus Christ, and kept until this day. Yea, moreover, am I so much more joined to Him, as I become more really partaker of the sufferings and torments He endured for my sake."

The king, having heard these words, became very angry and said, "Since thou hast dared to say of the gods, that they are carved images without life, I will avenge it on thee." So saying, the king ordered the executioners to bring him to another painful torture, as follows.

CHAPTER XII.

Of the ninth, tenth, and eleventh tortures of S. Gregory, and of his words to the king.

WHEN a man is lifted up by power, while he yet is a stranger to the grace and to the faith of Christ, in his heathen worship of idols, and in his thirst for vengeance, no word spoken by man is able to soften him and to bring him to a better mind; but he rather becomes more and more hardened, until he even excel wild beasts and leopards in cruelty. * Such was king Tiridates ere he received the light of grace and of faith. For although he saw the wonderful patience of S. Gregory, and repeatedly heard the witness he bare to the truth, yet never did he reason himself into a better way of thinking. But on the contrary, being yet more irritated, he commanded him to be hung by his two hands to a piece of wood in the shape of a cross; then to tie his hands with thick ropes, and his feet also, like the Saviour Jesus; and then with iron scrapers to tear his sides until the whole place was sprinkled with his blood.

Then the king drawing near said to the saint, "Wilt thou not hearken to me, Gregory, now that thou art in such torments?" The blessed man answered, "I will keep the vows I made when even a child—to worship God and to serve Him, who is able to deliver me out of any tribulation, and to cast thee, who knowest Him not, into torments. And yet thinkest thou to terrify by the threat of torments those who know and serve Him, and thus to sever them from His love and from His service?" Then said the king, "Who is that God of thine who can deliver thee out of my hands, and who judges, as thou sayest, of his own judgment?"

So saying, he commanded a number of iron spikes

* Metaphrastes and Agathangelos.

to be brought, in basketfuls, and to be spread thick over the ground. Then they placed him naked on those spikes, and dragged and buried him in them, and rolled him about, until his whole body was pierced through, and there was not a place in it whole. And the earth that was sprinkled with his blood blossomed and budded forth, not with corruptible, passing flowers, but with incorruptible, unfading plants of faith, and with abundant fruit, as we shall see shortly.

Then said the king to him, "Where is thy God, Gregory, in whom thou trustest? Will he now come and deliver thee out of my hands?" But the saint endured his sufferings with extraordinary patience, and remained alive by the power of God, praising Christ God with unmingled joy; and all his tortures were easier to bear than if they had been a pleasure, by the grace of Christ. After this they again cast him into prison.

The next day they brought him before the king, who said to him, "I greatly wonder to see thee yet alive, still thinking nothing of torture, and to hear thee speak, thou who shouldst have already perished in such tortures as these." So spake the king, because he did not know how the saint could have been healed from within of the wounds he had received with the iron spikes and flesh-hooks. But S. Gregory answered, "My patience in enduring torture does not come from my own strength, but by the help of the grace of my God, and from my efforts to endure, which I have asked Him to enable me to make. So then mayest thou try the servant of God; but thou shalt also know that nothing can separate from His love those who put their trust in Him. For He it is who gives patience and strength to endure tribulations and trials, until the wicked like thee be made to blush for their own vain folly, and be ashamed in the day of visitation and of rebuke."

The king, being enraged at these words, commanded to have certain iron instruments of torture, made like caps, put upon his knees, whereby the knees were made to swell in great lumps, upon which the iron caps were tightened with wedges. They then hanged him thus garotted by his two hands and left him three days in that state, until his knees mortified and dropped off his body. But the saint continued glad and happy, glorifying Christ God. Yet during all this, that rational leopard of a king did not lose the spots of his heathenish cruelty. But on the fourth day he gave orders to take down S. Gregory and bring him before him. The king, however, seeing that the more he tormented him the firmer he was, and that he would rather be tortured than not, was ashamed of himself, especially after the trial of the iron spikes and flesh-hooks to which he had put him, so that, instead of promising him honours and distinctions if he would recant, he now began to revile him, saying: "Where is now thy God, whom thou praisest continually? See thou, Gregory, that thy vain trust in Him has not delivered thee as thou hadst thought it would, neither has it taken thee out of my hands."

The saint replied and said, "See thou, rather, that thy confidence is vain: for thou hast not been able to frighten me with all thy tortures, nor to constrain me to stoop to the worship of thy gods. What thou worshippest is vain and a lie, and the cause of all thy error. Seeing, however, that I am not afraid of any of thy threats of torture, but that, in the strength of my God, I have fought with the enemy who is hidden within thee, and who wars against the truth, and that I have given my body to the fiery ordeal of all those torments—if thou wert not blinded by thy passions, oughtest thou not to understand from this unconquerable strength of mine, which is God's gift, that it is God who is with me, and that it is He who with me also struggles and fights against thee, O king? But He will also crown me after I have endured; one day He will place upon my head the crown of eternal glory with Him. Wherefore is it that I do not care to have my body torn to pieces; for as my outward man perishes, so also is my inward man renewed. Thus are we taught by Holy Scripture and by faith.

"But although He is able at once to deliver me out of thy hands, He does not do it, because He wishes to give me an opportunity of bringing forth fruits of patience; and to thee, one of repenting, ere He cast thee into the torments and the unquenchable fire of hell. For sooner or later does the body of man grow old and decay; but the Maker thereof will one day come to find the sons of men, and once more to renew into life their bodies decayed and mouldered into dust. Those whom He shall find established in chastity, in holiness, in meekness, in humility, and in the fear and service of God, will He then renew, and quicken, and adorn, with a new spirit and a new body. But those whom He shall find in trespasses, in wickedness, in estrangement from God, and in idolatry, although He will also make their bodies bud afresh with life, yet will He cast them, with their new bodies and new spirits, into the unquenchable fire of hell, and into torments that shall never end; yea, and especially those who, like thee, are living in idolatry."

On hearing this, the king became very angry and said, "I care not whether thy God renew thee or not, but for what thou hast just said, 'that He would throw me into unquenchable fire,' will I cast thee into fire that may be quenched; we shall then see what thy God will do."

Then the king commanded him to be again brought to this new and awful torture, the last of all, but also the most horrible, as we are about to relate.

CHAPTER XIII.

Of the twelfth torture to which S. Gregory was put, and how wonderfully the Martyr of Christ remained through it unhurt and invincible. Of the pit into which he was cast to die, and how long he remained in it.

[9] KING Tiridates having heard the Saint say, that the more his outward body perished the more also was he renewed inwardly, and that, like the Phœnix, he came again into fresh existence; and also, that if he, the king, did not turn to Christ, he would assuredly be burnt in the fire of hell that is not quenched—his wrath was kindled against the saint, and he said, "For that thou saidst all this, will I cast thee into burning fire, and thou shalt there be made to know thy deluded state." So saying, he commanded to melt some lead in an iron crock and to pour it upon his body, which was singed and shrivelled all over; but he did not die. Then they proceeded to pour some of it down the mouth of the valiant martyr of Christ; it reached his inward parts, yet withal did it not kill him, by the strength of Christ. Thus was he strengthened with courage and fortitude, until it was to him as if water were poured over his body; and it became evident to all that also in

[9] Agathangelos and Metaphrastes.

this torture the king's madness was being loudly and openly reproved; while the bystanders treasured up in their minds all the saint's words touching the service and fear of God.

Meanwhile the king wondered, marvelled, and trembled at the saint's endurance, and at his being able to live through such awful tortures, and he said to him, "How is it thou hast breath left after all the torture thou hast gone through?" Then the saint answered, "Said I not to thee just now, that thou mayest try the endurance of God's servant, because God gives strength to His servants, and puts to shame those who are without Him in the world, and who, like thee, strive and fight against Him? Because He said Himself: 'I will neither leave thee, nor forsake thee[1].' This, therefore, is the way in which He preserves and blesses His creatures and His beloved ones; He maintains and keeps them in their faith in Him, until He reward them with glory at His second coming."

At the end of two years thus spent in torturing the saint, Tiridates thought it was of no avail for him to talk to him any more. He therefore sent messengers to him promising him both life and honours—for which he did not care—if he would recant; but if not, and if he still continued obstinate, then to tell him, that he would be put to fresh tortures; so as, at last, to overcome and break down his resistance. So anxious were the king and his nobles to bring S. Gregory to the worship of their

[1] Heb. xiii. 3.

gods; not that the king himself should benefit much by it, but that, if S. Gregory was not made to do it, injury might thence accrue to the heathen worship.

At this particular time, however, one of the noblemen, Ardavazd by name, said to the king, "O king, live for ever: that man," meaning S. Gregory, "ought not to live, because he is not worthy of life, nor yet of seeing the light of the sun. For, though he has been with us so many years, yet have we not known who he is, until at last we have found it out. He is the son of Anak, who killed thy father Chosroes, and brought the kingdom of Armenia into captivity and ruin. Now, therefore, it is not fit he should live; for he is the son of a man both guilty and worthy of death."

The king having made inquiries, and having ascertained the truth of the matter, commanded Gregory to be bound hand and foot, and taken to the province of Ararat, and there be kept in the fortress of the town of Ardashat, where he should be cast into a pit, and left there till he died. He then went to his winter quarters, and published an edict throughout his dominions, that whoever was caught unawares dishonouring the gods, should be brought forth with hands and feet tied, and a rope round his neck, and that his goods should become the property of his informer. But the pit in which they had cast the saint was a hole full of stinking mud, used only for malefactors, and therefore filled with snakes and with other venomous reptiles, the mention alone of which filled every one with terror. For when a malefactor happened to be thrown into it, he died that same day on account of the stench of the place, of the filth and mire, and of the snakes and other creeping things that lived therein. But by the grace of God the saint was kept from all harm.

Such was the quantity of venomous snakes and reptiles in that pit, that he sank, and was buried in them swarming and crawling around him. Yet was he in no wise afraid of them; for they, having lost all their cruel nature, did him no hurt. But although, when at first the saint was cast into the pit by the executioners, and fell among the reptiles, they then sharpened their teeth in order to bite him, as they did others; yet when they saw him coming down softly, borne unhurt upon the wings of angels, they trembled at his presence, and were afraid of him. And albeit they only saw the saint come down, and did not perceive his angelic escort, nevertheless were they surprised at feeling deprived of their wonted nature; so that, contrary to that nature, they now crawled near the saint, gently to minister to him, and not to hurt him.—Oh the wonders God can work in behalf of His beloved ones! For the very same venomous reptiles which, thought the wicked king, would at once bite the saint to death, now on the contrary watched over him, and came to lick his feet. He was thirty years old when cast into that pit, and he remained in it fourteen years alive, by the grace of Christ. Those, however, who say that he spent fifteen years in it, reckon the year he was thrown in, and the year he came out; whereas they who write that he only spent thirteen years in the pit do not reckon the last. Thus neither departs from the truth.

According to one account, there was in that fortress a widow woman who believed, named Anna. She received in a vision an order from God daily to prepare a loaf of bread, and to throw it to the saint, whose body was thus supported with necessary food; while he never ceased to praise the most Holy Trinity in company with angels, as if he were in a temple, rejoicing with joy unspeakable in the Divine presence. For every day of his stay in that pit he saw with his eyes open the angels of God, who by their constant attendance upon him evermore gave him fresh strength and happiness, and by the revelation of many hidden things made him glad and joyful in giving glory to God. And there also did he not cease to entreat God in his prayers for the enlightenment of the Armenian nation; and being heard, he was, by the grace of the Holy Ghost, fitted to become the Illuminator of the Armenian race.

What marvellous long-suffering and endurance in that holy Father! It was vouchsafed to him by the Lord as a special gift in answer to his prayers. Thus only was he enabled to exist during those fourteen years in that pit, full of deep slime and mire, and of venomous beasts of all sorts, as if he were all the time in Paradise giving glory to God, and gladdening his inward heart by doing God's holy will.

At the end of these fourteen years, S. Rhipsime

and her companions came into Armenia, when
Tiridates, having made them suffer martyrdom,
was changed into the appearance of a hog. Meanwhile S. Gregory was taken out of the pit through a
revelation from God, and by his prayers restored the
king to his former human form; after which he
enlightened him and all Armenia with the knowledge
of God.

Therefore must we now turn our narrative to
these holy women, S. Rhipsime and her companions,
and in the next chapters tell in detail how every
thing happened.

CHAPTER XIV.

*Concerning S. Rhipsime and her companions; who
they were and whence they came into Armenia.*

HERE must we depart a little from our course. It is
all the more necessary, as by so doing we shall more
fully bring to light the love of God and the circumstances under which it was displayed in behalf of
the Armenian people.

[2] In the days of the wicked emperor Diocletian,
when the Church of Christ was being fed with the
graces of the Spirit, and increased in the midst of

[2] Agathangelos.

bitter persecutions, blossoming like a lily among thorns, there was in a place set apart for the training of virgins given to God, in the outskirts of Rome, a virgin, called Rhipsime. She was born of Christian parents, who, after enlightening her by baptism, had devoted her to God from her birth, and had placed her in that abode, where she grew up in purity and holiness of life, under the fostering care of S. Gaiane, who was at the head of it.

Rhipsime was a maid of royal descent, of a noble countenance, remarkably handsome, and in her life, angelic. Moreover, the community of modest virgins among whom she lived tended to mortify her body to sin, and to make her resemble Christ by taking up her cross in purity of life, and following Him. For, being like them, satisfied with daily food, and clothed in the modest apparel that becomes a solitary life of self-denial, they ceased not to praise and glorify God by their heavenly conduct, cheerful dispositions, and daily prayers morning and evening; thus turning the life of the body into a spiritual existence, and setting the example of a pure and godly life to all who saw them.

About this time Diocletian thought of taking to himself a wife. He therefore gave an order to painters to go round about Rome, and to draw the likenesses of the richest, handsomest, and best grown maidens found therein, and to bring him those portraits, that he might take to wife the one he liked best. His order was at once obeyed by messengers sent round about the country for that purpose; while he who had the management of the business, having heard of the maidens who were in the convent, under the care of Gaiane, hastened to send thither painters, who, having examined them, should make portraits of the best looking.

Those painters went, and entered by force that abode of innocence, where, beholding the ravishing beauty of Rhipsime, they were struck with it, and at once made a picture of her, and brought it to the emperor. When he beheld the majestic beauty of Rhipsime, he at once became enamoured of her, and sent to her an invitation, with the good news that preparations were made for her espousals to him, the emperor. The rejoicings were to last over many days; and ambassadors were also despatched in haste to make the event known every where, that, according to royal custom, they should bring presents and offerings from every quarter, and celebrate the emperor's marriage with every possible mark of public rejoicings.

But what was all that to the holy virgin of Christ, who, joined to Him with all her heart and in the straitest love, had chosen to suffer the most cruel pangs of death, rather than to be separated from Christ and to defile her pure, unsullied maidenhood? No one can tell the dangers to which she and all her companions found themselves at once exposed; we can only relate what is written about it. But when these innocent lambs became aware of the schemes of the old enemy, who lay in ambush for them under cover of the wicked emperor, intending to shoot in secret his arrows on these maidens devoted to Christ, they remembered their vows of purity, the rules of the order they had embraced, and they put on mourning and wept. Then they poured forth their grief in the most earnest supplications and prayers to God, entreating Him to send them help in the hour of need against all the snares and dangers with which they were then surrounded.

And their prayers were after this wise. We will not give them in full, but only in part, that the thread of our narrative be not broken:—

"Lord of lords, God of gods, O Thou eternal God, who madest man out of the dust of the earth, and who hast been, in all ages, the helper of them that put their trust in Thee, help us now, O Lord, in our present struggle, that we may overcome the wiles of the enemy; that Thy great Name be glorified, that the horn of Thy Holy Church be lifted up, and that we also may be found worthy to dwell with Thee in Thy kingdom. Grant that the oil of our lamps may not fail; that the light of faithfulness to our vows of purity may not be put out, and that the dismal night of perdition and ruin fall not on our path of light, lest our feet swerve from Thy pure and holy ways. So let not the eyes of our souls be darkened, and lose sight of the gladdening light of Thy truth.

"Let not the tearing wild beast destroy Thy holy flock; neither let the cruel wolf get the mastery over the lambs that are in Thy keeping; neither let the enemy of our vows scatter abroad the sheep of

Thy holy Apostolic Church. O Lord, our God, who didst send Thine only begotten and beloved Son, who came and filled the whole earth with Thy spirit of wisdom, we have heard that Thou saidst, 'When they persecute you in this city, flee ye into another; and if they drive you from that, seek refuge elsewhere[3];' therefore, Lord, do Thou now watch over us who have taken refuge in Thy holy Name, and defend us, lest we be mixed up with the wickedness of the heathens, and the abode of our innocence be defiled by their lawless deeds. Direct us to do Thy will, and cover us under the shadow of Thy wings, until we reach in safety the haven of Thy rest. And if it be Thy will, give us to drink the cup of martyrdom, that we may receive in exchange for it the crown of life at the just judgment of Thy second appearing in glory. Amen."

Having finished this prayer, the virgins were moved by Divine leading to take counsel among themselves, and they decided on fleeing to a far country; not as wishing to avoid a timely death, but in order that, by escaping from their own many wicked passions, they might keep themselves in innocency of life. So then, while the emperor, who had not the least doubt about the consent of S. Rhipsime, was making preparations for his coming marriage with her, S. Gaiane took her foster-child Rhipsime and her other companions, with priests and others who favoured them, fled towards the East, and taking ship, came to Alexandria.

[3] S. Matt. x. 23.

As to the several stations in their journey from Alexandria until they came into Armenia, both Agathangelos and other historians omit to mention them¹; but the writers of the Lives of Saints in our days speak of several places visited by S. Rhipsime and her companions, some of which we will quote. We are told, that from Alexandria they came to Jerusalem, and that they visited in pilgrimage the principal holy places around the city; but when they came to Gethsemane and to the sepulchre of the ever-blessed Mother of God, they tarried there to pray, when S. Gaiane, taking Rhipsime by the hand, brought her near to the tomb of the Blessed Virgin, and said, "O Mother of our Lord, I commit this one to thee; keep as a deposit this maid, who is wedded to thine only Son, and signed with the life-giving sign of His Cross."

Then the Blessed Virgin appeared to her in a vision, and told her to go to Edessa in Mesopotamia. And while there, visiting the congregations, the Virgin appeared to her a second time, and told her to go into Armenia. And they, coming all together to the eastern parts of the country, went about the mountains of both provinces of Armenia; and halting at several places, they at last came to Valarshabad, the royal capital of the province of Ararat.

---

¹ [S. Metaphrastes does not mention any of these stations; he only says of Rhipsime and her companions that, καὶ οὐκ ὤκνησάν γε, ἀλλὰ μεταναστεύουσιν ὡς στρουθία ἐπὶ τὴν βάρβαρον τῶν Ἀρμενίων χώραν, they tarried not, but like sparrows flitted to the barbarous land of Armenia. S. Greg. Ill. xviii.]

There they built a convent of their own, outside the city, towards the Wine-presses of the vineyards [5], to the north of the eastern side. They had, however, no means of subsistence. But one of them knew how to make glass beads, and another how to weave blankets; so that, taking these things into the city, they sold them, and bought the necessaries of life. And they thus lived away from the dwellings of men, as a small community of nuns, occupied in prayer and praising God.

CHAPTER XV.

How king Tiridates heard of the arrival of S. Rhipsime; what means he used to have her; and how, when taken, she was brought to the king's palace.

[6] WHEN Diocletian heard that Rhipsime and her companions had fled, he became very angry, and sent at once messengers in all directions, as well as ambassadors to divers countries, to see if haply they might find them. One of these came from the emperor to Tiridates at Valarshabad, with letters patent, written as follows:—

"Diocletian the emperor, to our beloved brother

[5] ['i hndzanayargs aikesdanyats, Αηνοί, as S. Metaphrastes, S. Greg. xviii., renders it, was the name of that locality, celebrated ever since.]

[6] Agathangelos, Metaphrastes, and the Lives of Saints.

and colleague Tiridates, greeting: I hereby make known to my brother and ally concerning certain wicked men, Christians, who go about among us, ever given to a false superstition; for their community is always blaming our government; they serve and honour One who was crucified and then died, and they worship a piece of wood; they keep the bones of those who are put to death, and among themselves reckon death for their God an honour and glory. They have blunted our swords, and death has no terror for them. They take no account of the heavenly bodies, of the sun, and of the light of the stars, and teach thoroughly to despise the images of our gods. They have turned away the whole world from the worship of the gods until they have severed men from their wives and wives from their husbands, making them live apart from each other[1]. I chanced to see among them a handsome

[1] [This is a common charge against Christians among the early accounts of the Church; we must, however, here understand, "husband and wife" in the sense of "man and woman." In the Ethiopic account of the martyrdom of S. Peter, we read: "Peter was in the city of Rome rejoicing in the Lord with the brethren, and giving thanks unto Him night and day for the multitude of Gentiles that came to him every day, and believed in our Lord Jesus Christ.

"Among those who thus gathered around him were four women kept by Carpus, prefect of the city, whose names were Acmaba, Acrabania, Caria, and Duras. And it came to pass, that as they heard Peter's teaching, and all that he enjoined in it, and how he exhorted them that they should keep themselves pure and not defile their bodies with sin; they received this commandment with joy, and agreed among themselves that they would give up their former life and altogether abstain from intercourse with Carpus.

maid whom I wished to take to wife; her, too, have they dared to take from me, and to cheat me of her, whom they have accompanied, when she with her foster-mother fled in secret hence to somewhere in your parts. And now, brother, give diligence to find their whereabouts, and to condemn to death her foster-mother and those that are with her; but send her, the handsome damsel, back to me. But if thou delightest in her beauty, then keep her for thyself, for the like of her is not to be found in our land. May the gods grant thee health; with all respect,

DIOCLETIAN."

When Tiridates had read this letter, he gave strict orders that every where in his dominions search should be made for Rhipsime and her friends; and at the same time he despatched ambassadors to every quarter, to say that, if found, the maid and her companions should at once be brought to him; promising to reward with rank and honours the man who found them. Thus commanded he to watch

---

"When the news of this reached him, he was indeed sorry, for he loved them exceedingly. He therefore sent messengers who should follow them and ascertain whither they went; and those messengers found out that they resorted to Peter. There was also a certain woman, named Akistiana, well favoured, and the wife of a minister, Altibius by name. And it came to pass as she went and abode with them and heard Peter, that she also withdrew herself from her husband, who became like a lion, furious against Peter, and commanded that he should be put to death, because he was aware that through his preaching many women had given up their husbands, etc." (Gadla Hawaryāt, ch. i.) Λάγνος γὰρ ὢν οὐκ ἠνείχετο τὰς αὑτοῦ παλλακὰς ἐπιστρέφειν πρὸς Κύριον, says Mich. Glycas of Nero's anger against S. Paul.]

every road in all the provinces. After a few days, however, tidings were brought to the king from the Wine-presses where Rhipsime and her companions lived. For it could not be that the real innocence of those witnesses for Christ should long remain hidden, that their light be covered under a bushel, or be placed under a bed; but rather was it fit that the rich oil of their love for God, that fed in them the wick of faith, should, from a golden lamp set on a golden candlestick, shine all over the world, as it was meet it should do.

So then, after the publication of the king's order, when these things became noised abroad, a band of men lay hidden for some days around the dwelling of Rhipsime and her friends, and at the end of three days brought intelligence to the king of her exquisite beauty, extolled as it was from mouth to mouth; for when she appeared, all men flocked around her, rich and poor together, even the nobles of the realm, all came in crowds to gaze at her beauty. But when the blessed virgins became aware of their intentions, and heard their licentious talk, they poured forth their prayers to God in tears and with uplifted hands, that of His great mercy He would deliver them from the hands of these impious heathens, as He had done before. Then, covering their faces for shame of those who had come in troops to stare at them, they bowed their heads and looked down.

One of those who thus gazed and wondered at Rhipsime's beauty was an intimate friend of Tiridates, to whom he related it. The king then greatly desired to see her; and the next day gave an order that Rhipsime should be brought to the palace, but that Gaiane and the other virgins be kept within the walls of their dwelling. Then were seen golden-decked canopies, with a troop of attendants, issuing from the gates of the palace, and wending their way towards the abode of Rhipsime, until they reached the door of her abode, bringing with them a suit of beautiful and gorgeous dresses, with other ornaments, carried by some of the first men of the land, for her to put on, that she might make her entrance into the city with all due pomp and splendour, and, after her entrance, should then be brought into the presence of the king. For, albeit he had not seen her, yet, from the reports he had heard of her great beauty, he was thinking of taking her to wife.

S. Gaiane seeing the danger that now befell Rhipsime, went to her, and began to say to her, "Remember, my child, that thou didst renounce and despise the pomp and magnificence of the golden throne and the regal purple of thy ancestors, and that thou didst sever thyself from it all; and that to those thou hast preferred the brightness of the kingdom of Christ, who created thee, who keeps thee in life, who shall raise thee again from the dead, and who has in store for thee the unspeakable goods He has promised to those who put their trust in Him. Thou, child, didst despise and renounce thy father's house and thy purple robes therein, for the sake of keeping unsullied the purity of thy maidenhood; why then now wouldst thou throw such a sacred deposit as food for dogs? God forbid, child, that thus it should be! but rather let Him who has directed us from our childhood until this day, make us with thee acceptable unto Himself in His eternal kingdom."

When Rhipsime heard these words and saw the procession and crowd come on her account, she was strengthened by the Holy Spirit, as it were with an armour of strength; and putting on her youthful frame the breastplate of faith, like a valiant soldier clad in his armour from head to foot, on the look-out and ready, she hastened to take refuge by prayer in the help of her almighty and all-powerful heavenly Bridegroom, and spreading her arms in the form of a cross, she began her supplications to God as follows :—

"O Lord God Almighty, who hast established all Thy creatures in order through Thine only-begotten and beloved Son, and who hast adorned and fashioned all things, both visible and invisible, through the Holy Ghost, Thou art He who did create all things out of nothing, and at Thy command all powers, both visible and invisible, do bow and obey. Thou who didst preserve Abraham in the midst of all the lawless nations of Canaan, and who didst keep Thy maidservant Sarah from the shame and defilement of the heathens; who hadst pity on Thy servant Isaac[1], and didst deliver Thy maidservant Rebekah from the wicked Philistines[2], leave us not; let us not go from Thy hand, O Lord,

[1] Gen. xx. 3, 4.   [2] Ibid. xxvi. 10.

we beseech Thee, for Thy great Name's sake. Thou who hast taught us, trained us, and put Thy Word in our mouths, that we might thereby escape from the snares of the enemy, and saidst, 'My Name is called upon you,' and 'Ye are the temples of My Divine Nature, and shall bear My holy Name[1]'—lo! many wicked men are now gathered together against us, to defile Thy holy Name, which is called upon us. Weak and frail as we are, we are yet Thy maidservants, however unworthy we be. Keep and defend us, O tender and pitiful Lord, from the hands of wicked and lawless men. Thou who hast brought us into this great trial, give us to come out of it conquerors in Thy strength; for victory is Thine, and Thy Name will not only bring us out of trouble, but it will also keep us in wisdom and prudence by our trust in Thee. Thus shall we share the inheritance of Thy righteous ones and receive at Thy hands the reward of our work; who establishest every one of those who abide in Thy fear and keep Thy commandments."

While Rhipsime was offering these supplications to God with strong crying, the crowd outside was gathering together on her account. It consisted of a number of the king's officers, who came with great pomp from the Court to lead her away to her espousals with the king; wherefore came they with rejoicings, bringing her the good news of what awaited her, namely, to be the queen of the whole Armenian nation. And they said, "Hail, thou

[1] Amos ix. 12. 2 Cor. vi. 16.

lovely maid, beautiful daughter! for thou art now reckoned to the race of the Arsacidæ, and shalt become the best-beloved of our king! Glorious queen of the houses of Aram! Great sovereign of the Eastern nations! Lo! we are come to lead thee away as the bride of our great and glorious king, like whom there is no one in all the world, under the whole heaven, so handsome and so strong. Make haste, deck and adorn thyself, thou lovely maid, and come to the gilded chariot in which thou art to be brought into the presence of Tiridates, our king. Strip thyself of the mean garments of thine affliction, and put on the regal purple woven with gold and pearls which the king sends thee. Fear not to come into the awful presence of our glorious sovereign, when thou appearest before him in the hall of his palace; for thou hast the wonderful beauty of the gods, excellent as thou art in all respects."

With such words did they come to congratulate her. But S. Rhipsime and all her companions, who, on the contrary, counted all these glad tidings and addresses as the sorrowful news of death and evil, lifted up their voices and wept, and with upraised hands and pitiful sighs entreated God mercifully to deliver Rhipsime from the disgrace and shame of such espousals.

And they all said together, "God forbid that the greatness of this world should seduce us, or that the pleasures thereof should allure us, or that the kingdoms thereof should alarm us, or that persecutions should make us yield, or that sufferings and blows should compromise us; yea, even though our enemies be many, and though they torture us in all manner of ways: shall we then be now afraid of the death you threaten against us? God forbid we should exchange the life eternal that is to come for that which now is and passes away; wherefore, neither afflictions nor sufferings, neither bonds nor tortures, neither fire nor water, neither the sword nor pleasures, neither life nor death, nor any thing else, shall be able to separate us from the love of Christ. We have committed to Him the ward of our purity. We abide in Him; and, delighting in His love, we will abide as we are until we stand without shame before Him in glory."

Then a violent thunder from heaven terrified the crowd, while a loud voice was heard saying to S. Rhipsime and her fellows, "Be strong and of good courage; quit yourselves bravely, for I am with you. I have kept you in all your ways; and after preserving you from all evil, I have guided and brought you to this place, that here also My Name be by you glorified among the heathens of these northern parts of Armenia. I will preserve you from the assaults of the cruel enemy, and ye shall come with Me into My chamber, and receive at My hands the kingdom prepared for you. And thee especially, Rhipsime, according to thy name indeed, together with Gaiane and with thy other friends, have I made to pass from death to life. Fear ye not; for ye shall come to the place which My Father and I have prepared for you; a place of untold joys for you and those who are like unto you." Thus spoke that voice while it went on thundering aloud.

This awful thunder continued until all those who stood there were stunned and terrified at it, while others sought to run away from the place; and many of the horsemen, rushing one against another, unable as they were to master their horses that were prancing and neighing, were trodden under foot and killed. Footmen also, in the general panic and confusion, fell one against another and died. Thus many perished, and a loud wailing cry was raised. Then some of the courtiers, who had heard the words of Rhipsime and her companions, ran and reported them to the king, and told him that the maid would not put on the robes he had sent, nor come. For there were among them scribes learned in the Latin tongue, who wrote down all that Rhipsime and her companions had said. So they brought and read them to the king.

Then he answered and said, "Since she will not come with pomp and magnificence to the palace, she shall be brought by force and introduced into the royal chamber." The king's officers then went and seized Rhipsime, and brought her—now dragging her along, now carrying her in their arms. But she, seeing herself fallen into such great and near danger, cried with a stout heart; and firmly trusting in the help and succour of her Almighty Heavenly Bridegroom, she said, "Lord Jesus, help me; deliver me from the sword, and save me, helpless as I am, from the hands of these dogs." Meanwhile, the crowd that followed blew their horns until the ground resounded under them; and thus did they bring her to the king's palace, even into the royal chamber.

CHAPTER XVI.

How S. Rhipsime, strengthened from above, struggled with the king; how she overcame him; and how gloriously she and her companions ended their course on earth.

[1] BUT when Rhipsime found herself shut up in the royal chamber, she began with earnest prayer to entreat the Lord to come to her aid. "Lord of all powers," said she, "Thou art the true God, Thou art He who did cleave the Red Sea and did cause Thy congregation to pass through it; who madest the barren rock flow with streams of water[2], to give drink to Thy people panting with thirst. Thou art He who did cause Jonah to descend into the depths of the sea, and then did bring him out thence and place him without hurt and whole among the living[4]. Thou art He who did save Daniel when cast as food to wild beasts, and rescued him with glory from their fangs[5]. Thou also didst bring out of the fiery

[1] Agathangelos, Metaphrastes.   [2] Ex. xiv. 2. Numb. xx. 11.
[4] Jonah ii. 1, 11.   [5] Dan. vi. 18.

furnace the three children who were cast into it because they worshipped Thee, so that those who beheld Thy marvellous deeds magnified Thee[e]. Thou art He also who changed into the appearance of a brute the wicked and cruel king of Babylon, and made his abode among the beasts of the field, and gave him pasture among the wild asses of the desert, because he would not learn to acknowledge and worship Thee for all Thy marvellous deeds done in his behalf[f]. Thou also didst twice over deliver Thy maidservant Susanna from death. Thou art the same, and Thy years shall have no end, and Thou, Lord, givest not Thy glory to another[g]. Thou also art glorified all over the world, let not the heathen reproach Thy holy Name; Thou art able to save me now from all defilement, so that I may die pure and innocent for Thy Name's sake."

While the holy maid was yet pouring forth her ardent supplication to God, the king came into the chamber in which she was detained. Meanwhile the king's servants outside began to prepare the marriage feast, to sing songs of joy, and to be merry all over the palace. Outside the palace, in the city also, they hastened to make preparations according to the heathen customs of those days, to celebrate the king's marriage, with the blowing of trumpets and public rejoicings.

But at the same time also the King of kings, the Almighty, All-powerful, and All-merciful Lord God,

[e] Dan. iii. 50.   [f] Ibid. iv. 30.
[g] Hist. of Susanna. Heb. i. 12. Isa. xlviii. 11.

looked upon His beloved child Rhipsime, and heard her prayer, and those of S. Gregory, who, from the bottom of the pit in which he lay, entreated the Lord to strengthen her, and to deliver her from the king's violence, and thus to enable her not to lose the sacred treasure of her innocence, which she had carefully kept until then. So that, when the king thought of having his own way with her, she at once received such an amount of manly strength and power from the Holy Ghost, and fought and struggled like a man with the king. She battled with him, giant-like as he was, from the second hour of the day until the tenth hour, and overcame him.

How wonderful that he—who was known to have such extraordinary strength, who, when among the Greeks, won for himself renown by his deeds of valour, and who, when he came to his own country, regained his ancestral kingdom of Armenia, then under the power of Persia, through his strength of arms and valour in war—should now lie on the ground beaten and overcome by a maid, by the will and in the strength of Christ! It was to show that the strong are not so in their own strength, but that the Lord makes weak the strong men who rise against Him, as the holy Hannah said of old very distinctly.

Then the king, thus beaten and overcome, came outside and commanded that S. Gaiane be taken, her head put in stocks, and that she be thus brought to the door of the chamber. And he put words in the mouth of his officers, and commanded them at once to bring her, that she, from outside the door, should desire Rhipsime to give way to him, and so save herself and her companions alive. Because the king, having become aware that, as Gaiane was Rhipsime's foster-mother, and had taught her to preserve her innocency of life, if only she wished Rhipsime to change her mind, Rhipsime herself would have no objection. S. Gaiane then determined to talk to her, and from outside the door spoke to her in Latin words of comfort that gave her courage. "My beautiful maid," said she, "my lovely daughter, let not thy stout heart give way, which thou hast had from thy childhood; for from thy mother's womb hast thou been devoted to the Lord, and united to God from thy birth, at holy baptism. Be of good courage, and be not shaken from thy hope and trust in Him. Remember that thou wast nourished in holiness and adorned with purity of life. Remember, my daughter, that thou wast espoused to Christ, signed with the sign of His holy Cross, and given in charge to the blessed Virgin. Stand fast in thy purity and innocence, that thou be worthy of the wreath that withers not, and of the marriage feast of Christ. This world is vain and passes away, its promises are but a shadow, and all its pomp is only vanity. Be strong a little longer, and thou shalt see the glory of God. He will keep thee from defilement and be thy support. God forbid, daughter, that thou shouldst lose the inheritance of the life that is with God, for the sake of that which passes away and is not, which to-day is and to-morrow is no more."

When those of the officers who understood Latin heard these words, they smote her on the mouth with a stone, thereby breaking several of her teeth, urging her at the same time to tell Rhipsime to do the king's pleasure. She, however, did not alter her way of speaking. How wonderful that albeit the holy woman had lost so many teeth, she was nevertheless strengthened by Christ to say as distinctly as before, "Be strong, be of good courage, and thou shalt soon see Christ, with whom thou longest to be. Bear in mind the cup of death which we are to drink together, remember also the resurrection of all men; remember the rebuke given to the rich man, and the burning in the endless torments of hell; remember the voice from heaven which thou hast heard to-day with thine own ears; be strong, therefore, for He who will give thee strength, as well as to ourselves, will also make us worthy of the crown and of the rest He has promised, that we be like brilliant lights in His everlasting habitations.

"Remember the Lord, who for our sakes humbled Himself that He might raise us up on high; who shed His blood on the cross, and was put to death for our salvation and in order to give us life. Set Him before thee in thy mind, and call upon Him with thy heart; and behold, He will at once come to thy aid, He will strengthen thy arm as He did that of the stripling David against the lion and the bear. And He who by his hands slew the giant, will also put to silence with David's faith the wickedness of the lawless one with whom thou art at this moment. O thou daughter of prophecy, brought up in righteousness, He who in His mercy and pity has showed us these things to-day, will give thee and us to see Him face to face without shame!"

Thus did Gaiane converse with her foster-child Rhipsime, in the Roman tongue, from the door of the king's chamber. But the officers who stood by and who understood that language, hearing her conversation, pushed her aside from the door. Then the king once more tried to prevail with Rhipsime, and struggled with her from the tenth hour to the first watch of the night. But the holy virgin, strengthened by the Holy Ghost, defeated and overcame the king, and left him on the floor utterly and disgracefully beaten, with his crown off his head and his purple robes torn and in disorder; while she walked towards the door in her own poor garments, all tattered and torn, having gained the victory in her purity, by fighting, in the strength of Christ, her invisible and spiritual enemy, secretly disguised under the form of king Tiridates, until she had fought and overcome him.

Then opening the door of the room, she ran away with all her might, and, favoured as she was by the darkness of the night, she escaped safely through the midst of the city, led by her good angel, and unseen by the crowd of people, of whom no one either took any notice of her or went after her. Thus did she come to S. Gaiane and her companions outside the town towards the Wine-presses, and greeted them with these glad tidings, "Be glad, O ye women, that I have not been humbled, and rejoice, O ye wise virgins; for I have smitten down the giant king, and I have overcome the adversary in the strength of Christ. Now, then, go ye to the city of Rome, and give good news to the Apostles; for this is the day of my espousals. Come and see me espoused to Christ; blow the trumpet and make ready, clothe yourselves in red blood, and bring me to the nuptial chamber, and with me be joined to our heavenly Bridegroom." Having said this, she went over to a high place on the north side, near to the highway that leads to the city of Ardashat; and kneeling down she offered prayers of praise and thanksgivings as follows:—

"Lord God, God Almighty, who is able to requite Thee for all the good things Thou hast vouchsafed unto us? We thank Thee, and we magnify Thy holy Name, for Thou hast kept firm our trust in Thee, and Thou hast saved us alive from the teeth of ravenous beasts, that would have defiled us. What is there in us with which to repay Thee, unless we give ourselves up to Thee, in return for the salvation Thou hast wrought for us? For Thou Thyself, O Lord, madest us worthy, in our service of Thee, to bear Thy Holy Name, whereby Thou hast delivered us. Beside Thee, O Lord, we know no one; and we call upon Thy great Name continually. Now, therefore, is it better for us to die in our innocence, than to lift up our hands to strange gods that are not. We long, O Lord, to come out of our bodies, that we be numbered among the witnesses [martyrs] for Thine only-begotten and beloved Son. Let us only escape from being defiled, and if we have to suffer torments for Thy sake, we are ready to bear them, that we may not lose our reward. And Thou knowest, O Lord, that I never coveted the rewards of this life, because I had an eye unto Thy faithful Word. Look, O Lord, upon Thine inheritance, and upon the works of Thine hand, and direct us to Thy city of Jerusalem above, where Thou wilt gather together all Thy righteous ones, Thy saints, and all those who love Thy Name; and let the light of the Lord shine upon us." Thus did the holy maid Rhipsime pour forth her prayer from her heart burning with love for God.

But ere it was day, some one having told the king where she had fled, he sent at once a troop of officers and executioners, with lighted torches before them. Then coming to her, they bound her hand and foot, and, first of all, sought to cut off her tongue; but she of her own accord put it out. Then they stripped her of her tattered clothing, and striking four posts into the ground, two for the hands and two for the feet, they tied her to them, and placed hand-lamps under her for a long time, roasting her body with the flame. They then thrust sharp flints into her bosom, and cutting open her body, they emptied it out.

But while she was yet alive, they dug out her eyes, and then cut her to pieces limb by limb. For they thought that it was by some magical art that she had been able to baffle the king. They said, therefore, that whosoever resisted or disobeyed him should be treated after this manner.

Thus was the blessed Rhipsime's martyrdom accomplished in Christ. She counted as less than nothing all the pomps of this vain and passing world, with all the glory, luxuries, and pleasures in which women delight, and which she would have enjoyed in the royal palace, and decked herself in the most precious ornaments of a spotless innocence. Thus clad in the pure garments that befit the spiritual espousals in heaven, was she honoured with the valour of a martyr, and in company with angels admitted at the marriage feast of her heavenly Bridegroom above.

S. Rhipsime's companions, having heard of her end, came and gathered together what was left of her remains. But the executioners rose against them and put them all to the sword, in number three-and-thirty virgins, all of whom offered themselves with a willing heart in sacrifice for the Name of Christ, and said, "We love Thee, Lord, for that Thou hast heard the voice of our supplications. Thou didst incline Thine ear unto us, loving God, when we cried unto Thee. We magnify and glorify Thee, O Lord, for that Thou didst not withhold Thy goodness from our unworthiness. O Thou lover of men, Thou hast kept us like the pupil of Thine eye, and under the shadow of Thy wings have we taken refuge from the gathering of evil men. And now we die for the sake of Thy glorious Name." Having said this, they all ended their life together in the Lord.

One of them lay at home sick*, at her dwelling, near the Wine-presses, and could not join the rest. They went and massacred her also, who, when about to expire, said, "I thank Thee, good Lord, that also of Thy bounty Thou hast not left me, because through illness I could not follow my companions, and die with them; but Thou, Lord, who art good and gracious, receive me and mingle my spirit with the band of Thy martyrs, my sisters and companions, who have joined Thy beloved Rhipsime." Having said this, she was put to death, and died in the Lord; so that thirty-four virgins in all suffered martyrdom that day with Rhipsime, whose bodies were drawn asunder, and given for food to the wild beasts of the field and to the birds of the air, but they would not touch them; neither did any smell of corruption come from them. But who among human writers will be able to tell in detail, and sufficiently to praise, all their glorious deeds, their reward for an unsullied life, the white lily of their maidenhood, their crown of martyrdom, the marriage-feast in light, where, in company with legions of angels, they received the

---

* [Her name was Mariamne. A church was reared to her memory under the name of Shoghagath, close to that of S. Gaiane and to that of S. Rhipsime. The church dedicated to S. Mariamne was called *Shoghagath* or "diffusion of light;" a name it has in common with Etchmiadzin itself, "because," says Muravieff (Trav. vol. ii. pp. 29, 67), "from this spot did S. Gregory behold the rays of light as they fell on the seat of Etchmiadzin itself."]

wreath given them at their espousals to Christ their immortal, heavenly Bridegroom, bidden to sit together around His table on seats of untold beauty, that were prepared for them?

Meanwhile the king—who was so widely celebrated for his exploits, who had carried off prizes at the Olympic games, whose gigantic stature and whose manly courage were in the mouth of every body, who had won so many victories this side the Euphrates, and who, after sundry great battles, had by his power alone rescued his ancestral dominions from the grasp of the Persian king—did not seem to feel his shame and reproach at having been overcome and beaten by a young maid, neither did he take it to heart. Yet, having been ravished by her exquisite beauty, he sorrowed at her death. "See," said he, "the witchery of that Christian race: how many they ruin for ever, by drawing them away from the worship of the gods, cheating them out of the pleasures and honours of this earthly life, and are not afraid to die. But especially see their bewitchment of that wonderfully lovely Rhipsime, the like of whom there was not any where in the world among those born of women; see the craft of them who, by their arts, gave her strength enough to get the better even of me!"

CHAPTER XVII.

Of the martyrdom of S. Gaiane and her companions, of the insults they endured, and of the infamous punishment that came from the Lord upon the king and his servants.

[1] The next day the chief executioner came to the king to receive his orders concerning the death Gaiane should be made to suffer. But the king was so possessed with love for Rhipsime, that he had forgotten all that had taken place the day before, and thought she was yet alive. Therefore did he promise rank, honour, and presents to whomsoever could by any means make her alter her mind, and persuade her to come to him. Whereupon the chief executioner answered, and said, "O king, let thine enemies so perish, and they also that despise the gods and set at naught thy commands. For Rhipsime herself is no longer alive; but that witch, who was the cause of the death of that beauteous maid, and two of her companions are still living." When the king heard that Rhipsime was dead, he was again filled with grief on her account; and sitting upon the ground, he put on mourning and wept, and bemoaned her, saying, "I cannot live without Rhipsime."

He then gave orders about Gaiane; and first, that

[1] Agathangelos and Metaphrastes.

her tongue should be torn off with the nape of her neck; and then, that she be put to death by slow torture. "For," said the king, "she dared by her wicked counsel to cause the death of one who was gifted with divine beauty, thus thinking scorn of the favour I had lavished on her; therefore shall she die of a slow death." Then the chief executioner, going from the presence of the king, ordered her to be brought with her two companions in chains, outside the town at the southern gate, near the bridge over the river, where criminals were usually put to death. And in order to ingratiate himself with the king, he prepared to torment that poor woman even more cruelly than the king had ordered. They then drove into the ground four posts for every woman; and while they were being bound, S. Gaiane began to pray with her fellow-sufferers in this wise:—

"We thank and praise Thee, O Lord, that Thou hast thought us worthy to die for Thy great Name's sake, and hast conferred so great an honour on our earthly nature, that we should be made partakers of Thy divine essence. Thou also hast made me to share the same portion with Thy saints, Rhipsime and her companions. I therefore now long to come to them who loved Thee; that I too may follow my daughter Rhipsime and my sisters and companions. But now, Lord, think of us; of us who are thus accounted as sheep for the slaughter, and made to die for Thy Name's sake. Awake, arise, O valiant God! leave us not altogether, O mighty Lord! but help us, and save us because of Thy holy Name. Give us victory over the wicked one, and let him and his fellow workers be brought low in awe of Thy glorious presence."

After this the executioners tore off the garments of those women from them, and tied every woman to four posts. Then they bored a hole through the skin of their heels, inserted a tube and blew through it, and then flayed the women alive, from the feet upwards as far as the breasts. But shrink not with horror, O ye that hear of these things or who read them in books, for albeit they were stripped of the skin of their bodies, they were all the more endued with the divine graces of the Spirit; but rather mark, how little they thought of the most horrible sufferings of the body, and how, when in the midst of them, they ceased not to seek Christ with fervent prayers poured forth from a heart fondly attached to Him, and, with an earnest desire to be with Him, said, "Remember us, O merciful and pitiful Lord, since for Thy sake are we killed all the day long, and are accounted as sheep for the slaughter." But the chief executioner, seeing that to strip them of their skin was to them like taking off their garments, without the least inconvenience to them, who made proof of the utmost courage; and hearing that they spoke of the Lord Jesus, he commanded the nape of the neck of every one to be cut open and her tongue to be torn off through it, according to the king's order, thus striking, as they thought, at the root of their prayers, which they took to be mutterings and charms of witchcraft; they then thrust sharp flints into their bosoms, and strewed the contents of their bodies over them; and ere they were dead they cut off their heads with the sword, and so did they die in Christ.

But if any one should inquire into the number of them, we must remark, that those who left the land of Rome together, and who thence came to Armenia, were more in number than those who suffered martyrdom. These were, together with S. Rhipsime and S. Gaiane, thirty-seven in all. The others, however, had left these before their martyrdom, to go to divers places and to preach the Gospel there; and so did not fall into the hands of the tormentors. Of their company were Nune and Mani. When they came to the hills of Taranaghi[1], Mani went to the mountain of Sebuk, where she led the life of an anchorite, and died at rest in the Lord. But S. Nune came to Georgia and turned the Georgians[2] to the faith of Christ through her preaching and the wonders she wrought.

S. Rhipsime died among her companions on the twenty-sixth day of the month Hori of the Armenians, that is, on the fifth of October according to the Roman reckoning; while S. Gaiane and her two companions died to the glory of Christ our Lord on the

---

[1] [The province of Taranaghi is in the Higher Armenia, and in it is Mount Sebuk, on which S. Gregory the Illuminator retired from the world and was buried. Géogr. of Vartan. p. 430, ed. St.-Mart.]

[2] [For some account of S. Nino, Nina, or Nunia, see Hist. of the Georgian Church, p. 17 sq.; also Feasts of the Georgian Church, p. 8. sq.; and Hist. of Georgia, vol. i. p. 60 sq. of text. Also, Socrates' Hist. Eccles. Lib. i. c. 10; Sozomen. Lib. ii. c. 8.]

morning following the death of S. Rhipsime. The Greek Church keeps the feast of S. Rhipsime and her companions and of S. Gaiane and her companions all together on the same day, the 30th of September; but the Romish Church on the 29th of that month.

Tiridates continued six days in the deepest grief after the death of Rhipsime, on account of her exquisite beauty; after which he gave himself up to hunting for a time. Every thing was now ready for the sport; the nets were spread, the snares were set, and other toils prepared and arranged for the king's chase in the royal domains called Shemagan. But as he got into his chariot to leave the city, a chastisement fell upon him suddenly from the Lord. An unclean spirit smote him and thrust him out of the chariot, and the king began to tear and devour his own flesh, raving mad. And suddenly he was like the king of Babylon, changed from the form of a man into that of a brute, not, however, of a graceful one, but into the vile appearance of a wild boar; the snout, the mouth, the tusks, the ears, the feet, and the mane were all those of a wild boar. He went, therefore, and mixed with other boars of his own species; and once with them in their cover of reeds, began like them to eat grass, and, naked and foolish, to roam and beat about among the mountains and on the plains. They tried to keep him in confinement within the city, but could not by reason of his savage disposition and ferocity, rendered far worse by the evil spirits that had taken their abode within him, and wrought in him.

What awful sight, that of king Tiridates, thus bringing upon himself the state and condition of a wild boar, by reason of the unlawful passion he cherished within himself for the maid of Christ, Rhipsime, and then mercilessly gave cruel orders to put her and her companions to death with awful tortures! For this reason did it righteously come upon him from God the Lord of all, to be humbled, degraded, and made to take the form and appearance of a wild boar—a terrible warning to those after him who would sin in like manner. And if any one should inquire into the reason of all this, he will be made to understand it from the example of the like awful punishment sent upon the king of Babylon, as told by Daniel the prophet; historians telling us plainly that what befell king Tiridates was but a fresh example of the same judgment; the like of which is also told in the divine songs still made in memory of him. Let no one imagine that with the outward transformation of these two kings their guilty spirits were also changed into those of dumb animals, for this could not be. Let us, however, return to our narrative.

But many of the men of the city and others who belonged to the army, who had joined or assisted the king in putting the martyrs to death, were all driven so mad with divers diseases brought on by evil spirits, that they took to gnawing their own bodies. And all the king's familiar friends, his servants, and his officers, were smitten with plagues, so that the distress and affliction of the king's house were exceeding great, by reason of these chastisements; and wailing and woe spread all over the country. But the loving and merciful God, who makes all such bodily afflictions to turn to the health of the soul, did not keep His anger long, but, having regard to the misfortunes of those who were thus afflicted, was moved with pity, and warned in a vision the king's sister to bring S. Gregory out of the pit, and through him granted them the healing of all these plagues, and to the whole country of Armenia the light of the knowledge of God, as we shall relate in the next chapter.

CHAPTER XVIII.

How S. Gregory was brought out of the pit by a divine revelation. How the king, while in the form of a boar, came and fell at his feet, he and they that were plagued with him. How the saint healed them all, and gathered together the relics of the holy martyrs.

[*] KING Tiridates had a sister called Chosrovitukht. Of her Moses of Chorene writes that she was modest and well-behaved, like one of the virgins of old; and that she did not, like other women, let loose her tongue, although she was not a Christian. And yet, from innate delicacy, she did not marry,

---
[*] Moses of Chor. ii. 79 and Metaphrastes.

but continued a virgin; and for this reason she did not share in the plagues that fell upon the king and his house. And above this, she was thought by God worthy of being the first to receive the glad tidings of the general cure of all this affliction in a vision she had from Him, and in which she was told to fetch out of the pit the holy Father Gregory through whom they should receive the health of their bodies and the light of their souls.

She then came to the governors of the city and told them the vision she had had, saying, "I had a vision last night. A man in a bright light came to me and said, 'There is for you all no hope whatever of relief from the plagues that afflict you, except you send to the city of Ardashat, and bring thence the man Gregory, who is kept there a prisoner. When he comes he will show you the cure and healing of your diseases.'" When they heard this they began to laugh at it, and said, "How can this be? May be thou also art gone mad. For lo! this is the fifteenth year since he was let down the deep pit, in which not even a bone of him could now be found. For the very first day he was let down, he must have died, from the snakes and other venomous reptiles, as well as from the deep mire of that hole."

The same vision appeared to her a second time, but with repeated threats that if she did not at once give the message, greater sufferings and plagues should fall upon the people and the king, yet more horrible deaths and divers other tortures. Again then did Chosrovitukht relate the words of the angel in great fear to the same governors of the city. Then they sent the principal man among them, one called Oda, to the city of Ardashat, to bring thence S. Gregory. And when he came to the city, the chief men thereof came out to meet him, and inquired of him the cause of his coming. To whom he replied, "I come to fetch Gregory, a prisoner in this city." But they wondered greatly, and said, "Who knows whether he be yet alive; for it is now a long time since they cast him into the pit." Oda then told them the vision and the circumstances thereof, at which they all were greatly astonished.

They then came to the house in which the pit was, and brought ropes long and strong, which they let from above down into the depth of the hole. And Oda cried with a loud voice, and said, "Gregory, if thou art yet alive in the deep below, thou shalt now come out; for the Lord thy God, whom thou servest, has commanded us to bring thee out." Then the saint, hearing these words, stood at once on his feet, and taking hold of the ropes, pulled them. Then they above, thereby understanding that he had heard them, hauled him up and out of the pit. Finding his body had grown brawny and black, they soon washed him, and put on him suitable garments. And with joy did they then bring him to Valarshabad, where the chief men of the city awaited him outside the walls. And when they saw in the distance Gregory with the men who had gone to fetch him, and the multitude which escorted him, they went forward to meet him.

Then did one witness a marvellous sight. The king like a boar, and others possessed with devils, with many of that city and of the nobles thereof who were raving mad, were seen running together to the same spot to meet him, driven as they were to do so by the devils. And falling down before him, they wallowed, foaming and tearing their own bodies. And the king, under the form of a boar, rushing forward, grunting, roaring, wallowing, and foaming at the mouth, was awful to look at, when at the coming of the saint he shrank up his snout, stuck up his bristles, and ran forward on all fours with the rest. The saint, however, had pity on them, knelt down on the spot, and prayed for them, and they were at once delivered from the devils, and returned to their former senses. And he commanded them to clothe themselves, and to cover their nakedness, because when of another mind they wore no clothing, covering themselves only with shame.

The king, however, was not at once restored to his former state by the saint; but when rescued from the violent hold of the devils, he only gradually returned to a sensible state, and recovered his sound mind. Then they put garments on him to hide him from the gaze of the vulgar. He was yet, however, lying before the saint like a boar in body, that same king Tiridates, who always was haughty, stern, proud, and to others terrible; trying to kneel before him, but unable to do so in his present state, his limbs not helping him thereto. But he stood before S. Gregory respectfully, ashamed of himself, and tormented with the remorses of his conscience. He tried to entreat him with his voice, but could not, as he was not able to articulate distinctly with the voice not yet restored to him. All he could do was to express the feelings of his heart by his tears, until he roused the saint's pity, and with his moanings induced him to obtain his healing through his prayers.

Then the princes and nobles, coming with the king, embraced the feet of S. Gregory, and entreated him, saying, "Forgive us all the evil we have done thee." But he, raising them and making them stand upright, said to them, "I also am a man like you, and I have a body like your own. But ye, now learn to know God your Creator; Him who made the heavens and the earth, the sea and all that in them is, the sun, moon, and the stars, and all other things. He alone is able to make you whole." He then began to ask them where they had put the bodies of the witnesses [martyrs] for Christ. "What witnesses meanest thou, lord?" said they to him. "The witnesses for God," answered the saint; "whom ye put to death with cruel torments." Then they showed him the spot where the remains of S. Rhipsime and her companions were thrown. He then gathered together their relics from the place where they had been slain, and found that by the power of God those remains had been kept free from corruption, though there were nine days and nine nights since those bodies were cast outside the town, where neither the beasts of the field nor the birds of the air had come nigh them.

They then brought fine linen and rich clothing, with which they covered them. S. Gregory, however, thought the dresses brought by the king and others unfit to cover the bodies of those holy virgins; but he clothed them in their own tattered garments that were heaped up in one place, saying to the king and to his attendants, "So shall they remain, until your clothing be worthy of such bodies." He then carried them to the Wine-presses, where their convent stood, which he then made his own residence. And there, when night came, he watched in prayers to God, that He would vouchsafe to the king and to the whole people a sensible mind, to understand the words which he would thenceforth speak to them, to the salvation of their souls.

CHAPTER XIX.

How S. Gregory comforted with words full of hope the king and the people who, for fear of God's plagues upon them, were now at the Saint's feet. How he prayed them to turn to God, to repent, and with an obedient heart to hearken to the words he was prepared to speak to them.

'THE next day S. Gregory proclaimed throughout the city the coming predication he would hold during

' Metaphrastes and Agathangelos.

sixty and more days, in order to instruct the people and to prepare them for holy baptism, and to teach them more fully the mysteries of our Christian faith. Then, when they and the king were gathered together around him, they fell on their knees, and with tears besought him, saying, " Forgive us all the evil we did thee, and implore for us thy God, that we perish not." Then he at once began to speak to them words fit to enlighten them, a few of which we will now give as briefly and as clearly as we can, so as not to interrupt the thread of our narrative.

The saint then said to them: "Ye said, 'Implore thy God.' He is the Creator, all-powerful, infinite, immaterial, who, willing only what is good, at one word of command called the world out of nothing into being. Acknowledge Him, that ye may be healed of your past sufferings, and be released from this chastisement which in His mercy He has sent upon you as a warning, according to the words of the wisdom given of God, that 'Whom the Lord loveth He chasteneth, and scourgeth every son whom He receiveth.' For He in His loving-kindness calls you to become His children; and His only-begotten and beloved Son is not ashamed to call them His brethren who turn unto Him and worship Him. And the Holy Spirit will give you the earnest of His love, and delight your hearts with joy that shall never cease. But this, only if ye turn and walk according to His will; and then will He give you everlasting life.

"Ye rightly call Him 'my God;' for those who

know Him not, though they be His creatures, are nevertheless strangers to His love. But they that fear Him are brought nigh Him; He watches over them and takes care of them. May be ye will say, Where does He keep them that fear Him, since those who have fallen into our hands were tortured and died, and we have judged and condemned them as we liked? Know ye, therefore, that God has willed that man's rest should be in death; and at His second coming will He appear to give good things to them that love Him.

"But ye are yourselves witnesses of how firm He kept His martyrs through the power of His divine nature; so that even the many tortures they suffered could not make one of them double-minded or make her waver an instant. He also delivered the holy Rhipsime and her companions from your foul purposes and lawless deeds. And as regards myself also, He counted me, unworthy though I be, worthy to suffer for His holy Name's sake, and gave me patient endurance; until He bring me to His heavenly inheritance, which you will also come to know, so as to receive the same blessing through the love and mercy of Christ.

"Know Him, then, who has called you out of darkness into His marvellous light; draw near unto the Throne of grace, and receive mercy at His hands. Renounce every superfluity of naughtiness and malice, and wash yourselves in the water of life, that ye may be fit to put on the vestments of light."

Then addressing himself to the king, he said:

"Thou knowest thyself best the amazing strength of thy frame, and yet how thou wast defeated and thy strength made of no avail, by one young maid; because she was kept by the power of Christ, who is Lord of all. And as regards myself, thou also knowest that this is now the fifteenth year since I was cast into that deep, dark, and filthy well, where I existed in the midst of snakes and of other loathsome reptiles. But through the strength and power of the Lord I feared none of them; neither did my heart fail me once, because I put my trust in God, the Creator of all things.

"I know that ye did all this through ignorance; but now be turned unto the Lord and learn to know Him, who will have pity on you, and will give you life. Then those you put to death will be your advocates, because they are now alive. And learn to know God, for He is Lord of all; and from henceforth give up the worship of images of wood and stone, gold, silver, or brass, for they are vain and worthless. I did not say this to you before, because of the error of your ways; for a thick covering of the darkness of the shadow of death lay over the eyes of your understanding, so that ye could neither perceive, bring to mind, nor know your Creator.

"But I will not cease to entreat the Lord for you night and day, that ye may not perish, but that of His great mercy and long-suffering He may forgive you your trespasses. In days of old He allowed men to walk in their own ways, but now He has begun to call you to His glory, that ye may inherit the life everlasting that passes not away. Wherefore has He also sent unto you His beloved faithful witnesses [martyrs], who, after having witnessed for Him, set the seal of their death to the firm, unshaken reality of their faith; whose praises are heard even among you, from those who are alive unto God, and who speak in favour of them that possess the good things; because they died for God's sake, and for that reason are able to turn the death of many into life.

"But we have been reconciled to God with them through the death of His Son. Because the Son of God died in order to turn the mortal state of His creatures into immortality. So they died as witnesses to His divine nature. Not indeed, that God was not able to give us life without His death; but in order that by thus lowering Himself, He might magnify His creatures in His abasement, and exalt their degraded state by becoming like our own selves. Neither was it that without the death of those witnesses He would not be faithful and entitled to belief, but that through their death He might magnify those that loved Him.

"Likewise did He keep the breath in my body, albeit I suffered and endured more tortures than the human frame is able to bear. For how was it possible for human nature to endure such torments even one day? or could any one exist even one day in that pit, where I stood buried in a mass of snakes and other reptiles that crawled about my body, entwined themselves around me, and clung to all my members? But the wonderful mercy of God kept me in life through it all. Yea, and even that of which ye were not worthy, the word of healing and of help to both souls and bodies, do I now administer among you.

"For I have already prepared the help I am about to bring to you. Begin at once to feed on the heavenly words you hear. For if you hearken to the words of truth from the Creator of all things, ye shall be saved, and sanctified with but little chastisement; ye shall be endued with everlasting life; and the words I bring you and the circumstances of my life will be sown in you for your help and comfort. But if ye will not listen to the words of life I preach to you, God's vengeance against you shall destroy you altogether by the most awful plagues."

When they heard these words, they, all together, with the king, put their hands to their necks and rent their garments, saying with one mouth, "We were perishing in our ignorance and in ways of darkness; can there then be a hope of pardon left us, that all these our many sins be forgiven us?"

S. Gregory replied to them and said, "The Lord is loving unto every man, and long-suffering, of abundant mercy and kindness unto all who call upon Him; and He forgives those who pray for forgiveness at His hands."

Then they said, "Tell us, we pray thee, how we may entreat the presence of our Creator; and tell us plainly whether, if we truly repent, He will turn and receive us for our repentance's sake, and make for us a place of conversion; or whether all hope of life in Him be not cut off from us? But wilt not thou then remember against us all the evils we did thee; and wilt thou teach us in the right way, or wilt thou not cherish a rankling hatred for us, so as to cast us away from the right way?" Thus was there a general lamentation and weeping, because they could not altogether shake off from themselves the sore plagues with which they were afflicted, which were the workings of evil spirits within them. For if at any time or any where they should thus be freed from their plagues, then the devils falling upon them would drive them to tear their own bodies among themselves with their teeth.

S. Gregory, hearing the words they spake, melted into tears; and placing before them both his own free pardon for what they had done to him, and God's promise that "He will not keep His anger for ever," he encouraged them to turn from their former evil ways and to repent of their having put the holy martyrs to death; showing them the enormity of their sin. Then, bringing the matter before them, he said, "Because of the death of those blessed saints, whose blood has flowed upon your land, does God now visit you and make inquisition for it; but He, the bountiful God, will grant you forgiveness, if you repent truly of what you have done."

After this, alluding to his own office as he had received it from God, he said, "Since the matter is not about myself, and it is not in me to hide from you any thing, let me tell you, that while in that deep pit, I saw every day a vision with my eyes open—an angel of God constantly strengthening me, and saying, 'Be of good courage, stand firm, for the Lord God has preserved thee, and has accounted thee worthy to be His minister; so that albeit thou enterest with others into the work of the Lord, thou shalt receive the wages of blessings that shall never grow less.' For ye cast me into the deep pit of a horrible death, but by the will of God I came out thence whole. In saying this, however, I take no credit to myself, but I say it because it is impossible to hide the marvellous works of God. For it is not hidden, but rather plain to all, and told among all of you, that He brought me alive out of death—me whom you thought to have been dead long since, as ye testify yourselves.

"And ye that were dead in your trespasses and sins, shall now be brought through death unto life; inasmuch as it has been given me to announce to you the will of God concerning you, and to bring you into the way of truth, which is, to renounce altogether the vanity of your worship of gods of wood and stone, of gold, silver, or brass, that are of no avail and useless, and to turn unto the living God, who made the heavens and the earth, the sea, and all that in them is; to turn unto His Word, His only-begotten Son, and unto the Holy Ghost both living and quickening, who will cleanse and purify you of all your past worship of idols.

"But if I see you willing and ready to turn to God, I will begin and with all my heart teach you about the Creation, how well and how good the world was created by our beneficent God, and how every thing in it was put in order by Him. How the Son of God came into the world in a body, and what He did, what sufferings He endured in the flesh, and how He also died in the body; how He rose again, and how He went up into heaven also in the body, and how He is to come at the end of the world, in a new body and in the glory of the Father, to judge the world. I will also tell you how it behoves us to walk in the commandments of God, fleeing from all evil and doing good, until we reach the good things promised us. All this will I tell you in detail and without weariness."

Then, having thus told them beforehand what he was going to do, in order to prepare them to yield themselves obedient to the words of life, he commanded them to continue fasting for sixty days; in order that, by thus patiently subduing the body, they might better prepare themselves to receive the grace of God.

CHAPTER XX.

Of the Saint's discourses to the king and to the whole Armenian nation during those sixty days and more.

* S. Gregory, having thus made known his intended preaching, gave notice to all those who

* Agathangelos and Metaphrastes.

gathered around him that they should prepare themselves, and give diligence to incline their ears to the teaching he was going to impart to them during many days. And there in his abode at the Wine-presses, he taught those who came to him, during sixty-five days, all that God did during the six days of the creation, and what was made on every day, in order. Not in dark, involved sentences; but discoursing on those subjects at great length in plain words, he made the multitude acquainted and familiar with the inspired words of Holy Scripture and with God's many works of righteousness. And thus did he from day to day, and all day long, teach the crowd that flocked to the door of his house at the Wine-presses, thronging and crushing one another in their eagerness to hear him speak.

He first made a beginning of his teaching by telling them "that there is one God, invisible, uncreated, eternal, incomprehensible, and in His essence infinite, who is alone in His nature, and before whom there is none else. That He is the Maker of all things both visible and invisible." And at the same time he gave them to know the most holy Trinity, threefold in Persons, but one in essence and substance, the Father, the Son, and the Holy Ghost, who made the heavens and the earth out of nothing, and all sorts of beings that are in them, both spiritual, intellectual, and material.

"He created man out of the dust of the earth, and of His goodness made him like unto His divine image and similitude, placing him at the head of

His works, through his reason and self-command. And He gave him also graces and immortality, and placed him in the garden of Eden, to keep and to till it. He commanded him not to eat of the tree of the knowledge of good and evil, in order that he might become fit to enjoy the highest glory through his ready obedience to God's commandments. But of his own free will having readily yielded to deceitful words, he transgressed the commandment of his Creator and Benefactor. And being thus deprived of the quickening graces of God's nature, he and his children fell under the power of death, being taken captive by Satan, and subjected to the bondage of sin.

"But the all-merciful God did not neglect or cast off His creature thus fallen; but, like a father moved with pity, He inquired after His child thus gone astray, and was pleased to send His only-begotten Son, who is one with Him, in order that, by taking upon Himself our likeness in perfect humanity, He might blot out the guilt of our trespasses by a wonderful purpose and counsel. Wherefore, after giving His law and commandments to the house of Israel, He sent them from time to time prophets and wise men, who should repeatedly announce His coming, and who should prepare for it His own race; whence He, the Word of God, was to take His flesh. Then in due time the Only Begotten came down into the womb of the Blessed Virgin Mary, and took upon Himself our nature, by marvellous counsel. And being made true man like unto ourselves in all things except sin, He was born of her in a pure, unsullied birth, being conceived by the Holy Ghost."

The multitude, hearing all this with attention, marvelled and wondered; and, being filled with joy, glorified God. But after telling them of His miraculous birth of a Virgin, he also told them of His other counsels for our redemption; of His works; of His sufferings and death; of His resurrection and ascension, all in order. And he thus taught and informed them, by explaining to them the mysterious purposes of God for our salvation, in words suited to their intelligence.

He also related to them the coming down of the Holy Ghost upon the Apostles; their acts, and the trust committed to them. He likewise preached the glorious second coming of our Saviour at the end of the world, when He is to come in the glory of the Father to judge the quick and the dead, and to give to the righteous the everlasting life promised them, but to the wicked the never-ending torments that are reserved for them. He thus taught them in his exhortation the principal points of our Christian religion; and having thus made them thoughtful and attentive, he further instructed them in other matters connected with the worship of God. For greater details, and for S. Gregory's full instruction, we must refer our readers to the chapter of Agathangelos on Tiridates; that should, however, be read with caution, discerning what is true from what is not, by the comparison of several originals.

But not only were the inhabitants of the city who thus came to hear S. Gregory's instructions struck with awe at the power of God, but others also from distant cities who heard of all these marvellous things, became obedient to the Faith, and hastened to the sight of the miracles that were taking place, and to give ear to the quickening preaching of the Gospel. Then both the king and his nobles, who listened day by day to the words of life, and who received it with all readiness, offered themselves to do every thing that the man of God should require them to do. Most of those who came to him were also instructed in the truth delivered by Christ, taught, as they were by him, not generally in the whole, but, as much as possible, one by one. And all the sayings which he uttered through the grace of the Spirit, and offered to the people, were in accordance with the things spoken of God; the interpretation of the words being by him ascribed to the power of the Holy Spirit.

When he had finished his public homilies in the ears of the king and of all the people assembled, he began to urge them to build temples, in graceful words of exhortation, which were briefly these :—

He said, "I have now set before you, and in your hearing, the whole of God's message to you; and I have hidden from you nothing in general: but, on the contrary, I have told you, from beginning to end, of what profit it would be to yourselves. Now come, let us gather together and bury the treasure we have in these relics of the martyrs;

for from them shall be vouchsafed unto you the healing of all. Let us give them a resting-place by building over them a chapel and a temple in which we may daily offer together prayers unto God, first for His reconciliation to us, for the peace of the country, and for mercy in faith and love; and with it for life, and for the kingdom of God.

"That ye may be set free from the bondage of works of darkness in which you live, and that ye may receive the divine glory in light, through their prayers and intercession with God. And that they may release you from the plagues that are come upon you, you being through them reunited to God; that He who dwells in those saints may therefore have pity on you for the sake of your repentance, of your obedience, and of your confession of the Faith; showing your profession of the Christian religion by fasting, so that ye become fit to receive the washing of Holy Baptism, and to obtain the portion of saints, and the honour of the Cross, which is foolishness to to them that perish, but to you who have been found is wisdom and salvation. And that ye may also come to the divine marriage feast, to eat the flesh of the true Lamb of God and to drink His Blood, so as to become partakers of His sufferings, that ye may also share in His glory.

"But now it is eventide. Go, take rest in sleep; and to-morrow set about building resting-places for the saints ye put to death; that instead of the dwellings of clay ye will now rear for them, they may prepare for you dwellings of light in the kingdom of God, to which we hope to come through their intercession, there to dwell with them in the reunion of the kingdom of Christ. Unto whom be glory and power, now and for ever, world without end. Amen." Having said this, he dismissed the crowd.

But, while the multitude that had not been afflicted with plagues from above came and went as they liked, the king, who was not yet cured of his boarish appearance, and those who with him had also been punished by God, never parted from the saint, for fear of the plagues that yet rested on them. But they continued night and day at the door of the saint, among the vineyards, covered with sackcloth and sitting on ashes, after the example of the Ninevites. And thus did they fast sixty days, according to the saint's commandment.

CHAPTER XXI.

Of the vision seen by S. Gregory, and by him told to the king and to the whole multitude; and how he entreated them to build a temple to the holy virgin martyrs.

'ON the morning following the expiration of the sixty-five days, at daybreak, came the princes and

' Agathangelos and Metaphrastes.

nobles, together with the king and all the mixed multitude of people, and they fell down before the saint, earnestly beseeching him to procure for them the healing of their plagues. Women also, and young children as yet without sin, came, troop after troop, and entreated him in the same way. For as we said above, they had been beaten with the rod by the Just Judge on account of the murder of the holy virgins, and for having tortured the man of God as they did.

But among them the king had especially been singled out, by being transformed from the likeness of man into that of swine, his whole body being, as we said, covered with a boar's bristles, his nails like claws, his teeth like tusks, and his feet like the cloven feet of a hog; while his face, being turned into a snout, gave his features a most revolting appearance. And so he continued to be until the sixty-five days were fulfilled, wrapped up in sackcloth in the midst of the crowd around him, that flocked from all parts to S. Gregory's gate. For he had as yet received from the saint only the cure of speech and hearing, and of his inward senses of mind and intellect; so that, while still like a boar in outward appearance, he was yet able to hear and to speak with intelligence.

What awful and wonderful sight, to see that same king, the once haughty, gigantic Tiridates, who loved to display himself in the pomp of his royal estate, who had brought to his feet the blessed Gregory, and had treated him like the worst of criminals, binding him and commanding him to be tortured bit by bit; thus behaving towards him in the most insolent and overbearing manner—to see him now, looking up to the saint as to his lord, and to see how he seats himself on his knees at the saint's feet in the most humble, cringing attitude, in the form of a slimy, disgusting boar, covered with dirt! He weeps incessantly, bathing the saint's feet with his tears, and entreating him, with supplications, sighs, and groans, to cure him. Yet S. Gregory does not at once hearken to him.

But when the crowd assembled began with tears to entreat the saint to grant healing to their king, he answered them, and said, "I also will, like one of yourselves, pray for the relief you ask, while ye, on your side, shall pray the Lord with all your heart to send you the healing you need. Only be diligent in building the convent, and give rest to God's martyrs, that they also may give you rest from the sufferings that shall come upon you, and deliver you from the bitter and terrible condemnation kept in store for you, which is yet to come; and at last make you worthy of the kingdom of Christ." Then they at once said to him, "What is thy will, lord? Command us what to do, and we will do it."

He then told them the vision which we are going to relate. But ere we begin it, we wish the reader to know that, concerning this vision and the interpretation thereof, several trustworthy writers, both among ourselves and other nations, relate some more and some fewer particulars; therefore do we think best briefly to tell that in which they all agree, or at all events coincide, rather than exclusively to follow one account. And if some one should prefer any one particular account to the short extract here given, the best way is for him to read that, and not this.

Then said the saint, "Come now, brethren, let me tell you the manifest love of your Creator towards you, which He has revealed to me in an awful vision. How the Godhead stooped down to His witnesses [martyrs]; and their immeasurable exaltation, whereby they have been raised to the unspeakable and incomparable kingdom of heaven. How it was revealed to me in an ineffable and marvellous vision that they would be to you harbingers of life, whereof I only gathered a few details. Well, then, last night, while ye were buried in sleep after your labours of the day, was I alone watching, deeply pondering over the unexpected, unsearchable and wonderful mercy of God towards you; over the way in which He now visits you, and the manner in which you should be taught out of the inexhaustible treasure of His divine counsels. I also took into consideration the love of those martyrs for you, while taking in hand this work of love, and the unspeakable bliss prepared for them in return for their sufferings.

"Suddenly there came a tremendous voice like the roaring of thunder, a dreadful noise, like the waves of the sea clashing one against another. The firmament then opened into the depths of the heavenly mansions, and a man in the semblance of light came down, called me by name, 'Gregorios!' and I, looking, saw his figure, and fell to the earth trembling and half dead. He then said to me, 'Look up, and behold the wonders I show thee.' I then looked and saw the firmament opened, and the waters that are above it rent asunder with the firmament itself. On either side stood, visible to the eye, masses of water like deep valleys and high mountain tops, and other things which no tongue can tell.

"Then a light, shed from above, reached to the earth. And in that light swarms of bright beings with faces of man, flitted on two wings, their wings being like unto fire. As in the sunbeams of spring, or in the ray that comes in at a window, we see particles of light play up and down, so did those luminous beings fill the whole space, like a dust of light, from heaven to the earth.

"Then, behold, an awful figure of a man, tall and stern, whose presence was of light, and his descent from above, grave and majestic. In his hands he held a large hammer of gold, and he, like a swift eagle, came soaring and flying down; and many others came after him. And he came and alighted near unto the bottom of the ground in the midst of the houses of the city, and then with his hammer smote a large space of the ground, until the heavy blows resounded into the very depths of hell. And the whole earth looked to the eye as if it were one level, even plain.

"Then I saw, in the midst of the city, near to the king's palace, a round pedestal of gold, in size like unto a large hill, and very high. And upon it a pillar of fire, high unto the heavens; and on the top of that a capital of cloud, and a cross of light on the top of it. And, looking, I saw three other pedestals, one on the spot where the holy Gaiane suffered martyrdom with her two companions; and one on the spot where the holy Rhipsime suffered with her thirty-two companions; and another near the place of the Wine-presses, where one of those holy women suffered, who was detained there by sickness. Those pedestals were red, of the colour of blood; and the pillars that rested on them were like clouds; and on the top of those pillars were crosses of light, after the pattern of the Cross of our Lord. Those three pillars were all alike, but the first was higher than the rest.

"Then I saw that above the crosses were remarkable arcades that joined them one to another, and above them again, the appearance of vaulted clouds; a marvellous fabric of God's building. And inside that vault, above the arcades, I saw those thirty-seven martyrs clad in brilliant white garments, which I cannot attempt to describe. And on the top of the building I beheld a throne of fire, marvellous and wonderful to see, reared by God, with the Saviour's Cross above it, whence beamed forth a light spread abroad throughout the heavens.

"That pillar gave a light that streamed down upon the pillars of the vaults, and poured forth an abundant spring of water, that flowed and spread all over the ground, as far as the eye could reach, until it become a full sea, and the whole landscape appeared blue of the colour of the sky. And I saw a great multitude of tables of fire, with a pillar upon every table, and a cross of the same material on the top of it. And they were like stars in multitude; they appeared so, and glittered as much.

"Then I saw a flock of innumerable goats of a black colour, which, passing through the waters, returned and met together; but they turned their black colour into a kind of white, and their fleece in general shone with light, until brilliant rays actually darted from them. And while I was looking, the flocks suddenly brought forth, and multiplied, and filled the place; and the young that were born shone like their parents, and these again brought forth and multiplied exceedingly.

"Some of them strayed to that side of the waters; and those young became tawny wolves, and rushed among the flocks, and began to tear them in pieces, until much blood did flow. And while I looked, I saw that some in the flock grew wings, and became winged; and flying upwards, they were mingled with the hosts of angels of light. But some were torn in pieces by the wolves. Then suddenly there arose a flood of fire that took and carried away the wolves; and I looked on, and stood wondering.

"Then the man who had at first addressed me, and who showed me these things, said to me, 'Man, why wonderest thou, and why understandest thou not the marvellous things of God?' Then said I, 'How, Lord?' And he answered, 'This vision has been shown thee, that thou shouldest understand it. This, namely, that the heavens are open, know thou, means that the gates of Christ's loving-kindness for His creatures are now open. And the voice like the roaring of thunder that was heard, means, recollect, that the rain of God's mercy and pity is now falling upon the earth. But the opening of the heavens signifies that God's mercy and pity was for a time shut up towards His creatures because of their transgressions, but that afterwards it over-abounded, so that His righteousness overcame, and was as it were marvellously opened, until the unspeakable grace of the Holy Ghost rained down in infinite goodness, for the salvation of all men.

"'Then as to the waters, which at first were firm and solid, being parted hither and thither, it means that nothing can stand in the way of, hinder, or cheat, those who will rise upwards from this earth to heaven; especially martyrs, as were those holy virgins. For those holy martyrs, who have just borne witness for Christ, came from the north countries; for they came by themselves, and showed the right way to others. But now the light that came down upon this place is the preaching of the Gospel, which also fills the north country. And the luminous beings with two wings, that came down in swarms, signify the company and fellowship of angels both with God's martyrs and with other men; who longed to see flowing into the dust the sweet rose-like blood of the holy virgins, and who from henceforth are to mingle with men, by dwelling with them in great numbers. But this man, of a noble and awful countenance, whose presence is all light, who holds a golden hammer in his hand, and with it smites the earth, represents the searching character of divine efficacy and energy, and the all-powerful effects of the Word of God, whereby the earth trembled and shook. This awful display of God's power threw down, and brake, and levelled to the earth the idols of man's error. And that the earth resounded at this, implies the assent of obedience and service to the Word of God.

"'The golden base is the rock of firmness that abides unshaken; and the pillar of fire set on it is the Catholic Church, that gathers together all congregations into oneness of faith under the shelter of her wings. And the capital of clouds is that which will bear the righteous when they shall spread their wings and rise upwards to meet the Lord in the air at His second coming. But the Cross of light that stands above, is the badge of the great Pontificate [Patriarchate of Etchmiadzin] that carries about with itself in the midst of the congregations the image of Christ, the Son of God made flesh, as High Priest, who gave Himself up in sacrifice on the table [altar] of the Cross for the sake of men. And that place shall be a temple unto God, and a house of prayer offered up by all believers, and the seat of the Pontificate.

"'But the three bases, which are red, of the colour of blood, are thus marked with the sufferings of death endured by the martyrs, who by their death have raised a stay for the confirmation of the true faith, with their blood. And the pillars are of cloud, because a cloud rises lightly and swiftly into heaven. And the cross betokens the sufferings of the martyrs, whose sufferings resemble those of the Saviour. But the first cross that was shown thee, has the merits of the sacerdotal office, magnified in the Cross of Christ. And the three crosses, mark the place of rest of the holy martyrs, that on the spot where they were slaughtered and their blood was spilled, a convent should be raised as a resting-place for their bones. But the reason for which the first pillar is the highest is this, that the honour of the Catholic Church is greater and higher than all the elevation of any saint. And the arcades that connect the pillars together, represent the mutual communion and unity of the Catholic Church.

"'And as to the vault [or pavilion] above, it represents the city of common gathering in the kingdom of heaven. And as to the martyrs thou seest there, know thou that death is only for a moment, but that their existence in life is for ever, glorified as they are in the glory of the Son of God; wherefore is the figure of this cross stamped on their persons. And the throne thou seest above all, is the throne of the Almighty Nature of the Godhead exalted on high, for He is the Head of His Holy Church, and the giver of all good things.

And the light that surrounds the cross is God the Holy Ghost, who glorifies the Son.

"'Then as to the light that shines between the four pillars, and as to the abundant spring that flows at their feet, it means that from the Catholic Church, the grace of the Spirit brings forth the fountain of Baptism, in order to wash the defilement of both body and soul. And that this water spread abroad abundantly over many places, means that many congregations are to be saved by Baptism. Then, that all the fields appeared to thee sky-blue, is intended to represent that the earth is to become heaven by the intercourse of angels with men. But as to the multitude of [holy] tables of fire which thou seest, they truly represent the [holy] tables of God, which dispense propitiation unto all; and the reason for which they appear to thee of fire is, that the service of the Spirit is to be with glory. Then the pillar by the side of every table shows the service of the prayers of the priesthood. But the crosses of fire on the top of them mean that by the fire of the Most Holy Spirit, the bloodless sacrifice which is offered in holocaust, is performed in remembrance of Christ and to His glory, who was crucified for the sake of men, that His Holy Name be glorified all over the world. And that there was, as it were, a multitude of stars, means that the services of holiness are like stars in multitude.

"'Then with regard to those large flocks of black goats, which after going down into the water thereby became white, behold there the grace which the great power of God is about to bestow by means of the priesthood, by the hands of which God's right hand shall cause to flow the fountain of Baptism for the propitiation and remission of the sins of many sinners; and that their luminous fleece was bright and glistening, means that those who are baptized are to be clothed in light. Then that they brought forth other flocks of goats, and multiplied and covered the land, means that in process of time the doctrine [or preaching] of believers shall increase; then a fresh birth unto newness of life takes place, and the grace of Baptism is thus multiplied.

"'And that some of those goats passed over to that side of the water, to the same side whence they had come, means that in after time, some of the wicked and transgressors shall depart from the truth, and renounce their anointing with the Chrism of their vow of holiness; and many shall deny those vows. And the lambs that become wolves and tear to pieces the holy lambs, represent those who, from among the congregation and from the order of priests who turn from the Truth, become wolves and shed the blood of lambs; that is, they disturb and destroy the order of the priesthood and the congregation. But those of the lambs, that is of the congregation, or of the priesthood who with singleness of heart endure unto the end, take wing and rise to the kingdom of heaven; while those who be of the mind of wolves, or who share in their work of devastation, shall be with them cast into fire unquenchable.

"'But thou, be strong and of good courage, and also be wary; for a work is now come to thy hand to do, that will readily do great good, so that thou, entering into the labour of other true labourers, mayest receive as thy wages the incorruptible reward of Christ. Behold it is committed to thee by the Lord Jesus Christ. Be careful and let a temple be built in the name of God, on the place that was shown thee, where the pillar of fire rested on a base of gold; also a chapel to the martyrs on the spot where they were slaughtered and where they began their existence above, putting their trust in God. So that the wounded may be cured, and the preaching of the Gospel may abundantly prosper; and that the people may steadily, from day to day, reach unto the perfect stature of faith in Christ.'

"When the angel had said these things an earthquake took place, and towards the morning the vision disappeared." And here S. Gregory made an end of his account of the vision and of the explanation of it told him by the angel.

Certain historians, however, after relating the vision of that heavenly landscape, add, that other pillars of cloud did appear to the saint, and a capital of light on every one of the pillars made it a remarkable spectacle; and they say, moreover, that those pillars represented the going up from earth to heaven after the resurrection, inasmuch as such progress is straight and lightsome, while the capital of light on the several pillars is intended to remind us of the dwelling of the righteous, and of the brightness to which they shall be taken up to meet the Lord at His second coming. But this is the same thing that we have related from Agathangelos, that above the crosses were arcades connecting them together, and over them the appearance of a kind of dome and other things, which he makes to rest upon it, but which he does not fully describe.

CHAPTER XXII.

Of the activity with which the people who were enlightened by the Illuminator set about building the Convent of S. Rhipsime, and of the quantity of gifts and of other offerings they brought to the sacred remains of the martyrs; and how the Saint restored at once the senses to the king who still had the appearance of a boar; of the care with which the sacred relics of the holy martyrs were laid in separate chests and placed to rest in their tombs; and how, after all this, the king was perfectly restored to his former state.

[a] It was marvellous to see the submission of the king, of the princes, and of the people, who had just been enlightened, and their readiness to obey the orders the saint gave them. They watched attentively every word and every order that issued

[a] Agathangelos and Metaphrastes.

from his lips, and did it at once. And they not only brought offerings, but also their own persons to the service of the saint, whom they truly knew, believed, and loved for the sake of his teaching. For after he had told them his wonderful vision in the spirit, and the marvellous and mysterious meaning thereof, that foretold in general what would befall them, he commanded them earnestly and diligently to set to work at the building and resting-place of the martyrs, according to the heavenly vision.

The saint began to speak with the king and his nobles and the people, and said, "God Almighty, the Creator of all things, who is All wise, and who heals all sickness, has given you warning that He will draw nigh unto you in His divine goodness. Wherefore has He shown you, through us, the way of life and the means of salvation, at the same time granting you the forgiveness of your sins, and also giving you beforehand, in a vision, knowledge of what is to come, that His will be fulfilled in you. Now, therefore, make haste to obey His orders; come, let us build the resting-place of the martyrs, and there lay them in peace, that they also may renew you altogether." Having said this, he commanded that the materials for the building be got ready.

Then the whole multitude being filled with joy at these words, ran about in all directions, every one to prepare materials according to his rank and ability. Some gave the wood, others the stone, others the bricks, others the lime, and others again something else that might contribute to the building. They brought it all, and laid and heaped it up where he told them; while he, S. Gregory, directed as architect the work according to the pattern he had seen in his vision, and taking in hand the measure used by builders, he traced the foundation of the edifice, thus showing the plans thereof and directing the workmen. And the whole people hastening willingly to give what help they could, put their hands to the work, and pursued it with diligence. Even women, being well disposed towards it, took in hand such work in the building as was suitable for them according to their power.

The king, however, and his nobles with the people did not merely defray the expenses of the workmen, and the hire of labourers, and of other gifts, but they also devoted themselves to this holy work as part of their worship and service of God, wishing with warm love for it to have a share in it, and to contribute to it after their power; nay, they counted themselves happy if they could do aught to gratify the martyrs by building them a place of rest. And thus men and women of every rank and quality generally, offered themselves, working at the building with faith and fear, so that not one of them should be shut out of the grace of salvation, and thus be deprived of healing.

And the three churches of the martyrs were raised. One to the north, on the eastern side of the city, where S. Rhipsime suffered martyrdom with her thirty-two companions. Another on the south side of that of S. Rhipsime, on the spot where S. Gaiane and her two companions died. And the third nigh unto the Wine-presses, where was the convent of those virgins; of which one of them was left there by reason of her sickness, and suffered martyrdom like the rest. And when these temples were built, they finished, and trimmed, and adorned them with gold and silver, and lighted them with candles, and candlesticks with lights burning, and furnished them with various other necessary and precious utensils.

Then S. Gregory commanded them to put the remains of every one of the martyrs into separate wooden coffins in the form of chests, firmly nailed together, giving them, himself, the proper height, width, and length. When they had made them after his directions they brought them to the door of the Wine-presses and laid them before the saint. He then took them and brought them himself inside, not allowing any one to come in with him; "for" said he to the people, "it is not meet that ye should come near and touch them, for ye are not yet healed, neither are ye yet cleansed by Baptism." Thus did he alone lay every one of the sacred remains into their respective chests clad in their plain clothes, and signed them with the sign of the cross.

When the saint thus began to clothe the sacred relics in their own garments, both the king, his nobles, and great men, with freedmen and their attendants, brought every one sweet-scented oils and perfumes, with threads of various colours, silver tissues, and golden stuffs, wherewith to wind the relics of the saints. The queen also and her royal damsels, with noble ladies and daughters of the great men of the land, were eager to bring together purple, gold, mohair tissues of various colours, and garments of the whitest wool, to clothe the saints withal; and laid them in heaps at the door of the Wine-presses.

S. Gregory came forth, and when he beheld all these gifts he rejoiced exceedingly over the faith and devoted love of the people; nevertheless, did he not allow them to come near the relics of the martyrs, but said to them, "Have I not just told you, that until ye are cleansed by baptism, it is not meet that ye should draw near to them? but your readiness to help is all in favour of your salvation. And now let all this that is brought out of the royal treasuries abide, until the good Providence of God shall provide for you pastors and doctors, fathers with bishops and their elders [presbyters], and all the ecclesiastical orders, whereby to enlighten you. All this, however, will come in for the service of the glorious [holy] table of God, through the establishment of a Patriarch. Now however, let us lay every separate remains of these holy martyrs apart and at rest."

Then the king, drawing near to the saint, entreated him with tears to grant him the healing of at least his hands and feet, that he might be made worthy to work, however little, at the resting-place of the saints; because he then still had the appearance of a wild boar, except that he could speak. Then S. Gregory, having pity on the king, hearkened to his earnest entreaties, and going to the sacred chests containing the bones of the holy martyrs, there knelt down and offered supplications to God the Lord of all, and the giver of all good gifts. Then, lifting up his hands towards heaven, he prayed for the healing of the king through the mediation of the holy martyrs. And in order that his prayers might surely be accepted, he told the people to do the same as he did.

Oh the wonderful power of God! for no sooner had the saint ended his prayer, than a marvellous work was being accomplished. For in the twinkling of an eye the king, who was thus plagued with the appearance of a boar, shook off from him his tusks and hoofs, and was thus at once partly restored to his former figure, by being stripped of a boar's tusks, features, and stiff bristles. So that according to his request he might labour with his hands and take part in building the resting-place of the saints; and he thanked the Lord for so great a relief and comfort which he had received from Him, through the prayers of the Illuminator.

Then the king asked S. Gregory what he had better do. The saint then gave him the size and measure of the chests containing the bodies of the saints, in order that, going into the temple, their resting-place, the building of which we described above, he might dig a place for every one of them there within, and thoroughly make it ready. But the

s

king besought in favour of his own wife, queen Ashkhen, and his dear sister Chosrovitukht, that they also might be allowed to take part in the work; to which the saint agreed, telling them to come and help the king. The king then took a spade and a mattock, and dug a resting-place for the holy martyrs, according to the size of every chest; while his sister Chosrovitukht and Queen Ashkhen, receiving into their robes the earth dug up by the king, carried it outside. Oh the power of faith in Christ and of love for Him! See that great king Tiridates, strong, stern, imperious, terrible, and haughty. See how meekly he stands in the graves which he digs for the tombs, digging, delving, and shovelling the earth, like a labourer, and watering the ground with the sweat of his brow and with tears drawn from within, from his innermost contrition of heart. At the sight of which the multitude of princes, nobles, and common people alike did wonder, and set it to themselves as a good example to follow. But let us continue the thread of our narrative.

Thus was the resting-place of S. Rhipsime prepared in order on the right-hand side. After that they went on with the tombs of the other thirty-two holy martyrs, in the place where their blood was spilt, in the church built for them, on the spot prepared for the table of Christ, which was not yet set up. For S. Gregory had not yet taken holy orders, though he was building the church, and could not, of course, set up the [holy] table. They did the same with regard to the chests containing the relics of S.

Gaiane and her two companions, in the monastery at the south side of the city; and they prepared a place for the one who suffered martyrdom alone at the Wine-presses, in her own mortuary chapel.

Then king Tiridates asked permission of S. Gregory to go and bring very large stones from mount Masis[*]. And having found some huge, hard, broad, and long stones, he brought them rough, for the use of the temple; not indeed by placing them upon wagons, or by dragging them along by machinery, but he slung them upon his huge, giant shoulders, and thus brought them all the way to the temple, one by one. The king brought eight columns; and in one of the churches of these virgins he set up four of those columns at the entrance of it, in order to adorn the doorway, to make amends as it were for the struggle he had in his room with S. Rhipsime, who through all-supporting Grace got the better of him, and did such wonders. Unto whom the king offered the labour of his own hands, as it were a crown of victory to her.

When the chapels were finished, the saint, accompanied by a large crowd with lighted lamps, and with great pomp, gave the people to carry the chests which they brought to the church prepared for them; he then laid every one in the place made ready for it, and did every thing else relating to them according to the pattern shown him in the vision.

---

[*] [Mount Masis is the so-called Mount Ararat, on which the Ark is said to have rested, according to Armenian tradition.]

And he then sang this hymn in praise of those virgins.

"O God, great and glorious, who sheddest Thy light on Thy saints, and on those that are at rest, we take the sufferings of Rhipsime and her companions as a propitiation for us in Thy sight. And over the resting-place of every one of them we have marked the holy sign of the cross." Then setting up a cross inside every one of the three churches on the place of the holy tables, he said, "Before this life-giving sign only shall we worship Thee, O Lord God, Creator of all things. Behold, firm pillars have been raised to Thine honour. These are pillars that bear the weight of the salvation of him who wrought them. Behold, I have set up these three pillars, and the fourth pillar of life, that brings you near unto God. Now, go ye, surround with honour the hallowed spot pointed out in the house of the Lord."

Then the king with the saint and the whole people went all together to the place of the pillar of fire on the golden base, that was shown to S. Gregory in the vision, as we reported above. And having surrounded that spot with a high wall out of honour for it, they made it fast with gates and bolts. And there the saint set up the sign of the Saviour's Cross, in order that whosoever came thither should fall on his knees and worship the Almighty God and Creator of all things.

Meanwhile the hearts of the people were day by day more and more enlightened by the preaching of

God's service; they renounced the vain worship of their lying idols, the work of their own hands, and with their whole heart were turned to the worship and service of God; while they vied one with another in their earnestness to fast and to pray, and with their hearts to yield obedience to the divine teaching they received from S. Gregory.

But when the resting-place for the remains of the holy martyrs was finished, and the whole people stood together within the place of worship, the house of God, the saint began to speak to them, saying, "Kneel down, all of you, in prayer in presence of the Lord, that He will heal you of your plagues;" and they did so. Then S. Gregory, himself kneeling down with them, continued in prayer to God, and with earnest entreaties and supplications, prayed for the healing of the king, who hitherto was only partly restored to his former appearance, from that of a boar. Oh, marvel! for it happened that while he was in prayer and in tears with the people, the king shook off his body, all at once, the whole skin of the boar he had on him, with his hideous tusks and bristles. His wonted face and countenance returned to him, and his body and flesh became as soft and tender as those of a new-born babe; and he was thus completely cured, and his body made sound; at the sight of which, all were filled with joy, and blessed and glorified God for it [1].

[1] [Sozomen, who relates the deeds of Nina or Nunia, in turning Iberia to the faith of Christ, says (Hist. Eccl., lib. ii. c. 8) that

Likewise, those among the people who were blind, halt, sick of the palsy, lepers, scurfy, gouty, who had the dropsy, and were possessed with devils, were all severally released and cured of their plagues. But the most wonderful part of it is this, that through the prayers of the saint they were not only healed of their bodily infirmities, but were also cured within of their spiritual diseases. And thus they exchanged their inveterate evil habits of sin and of error, in various ways, for a modest and correct behaviour, and orderly conversation, to the astonishment of all who saw them, as Metaphrastes tells us.

But our Saviour Christ had opened the fountain of the knowledge of Him to the holy Illuminator, that he might satisfy those who panted and thirsted after true divine teaching. One might then witness the heartfelt joy of all at the surprising sight of what then took place. For the country, which, as yet, was not well informed respecting the divine wonderful operations, mysteries, and counsels of God and the doctrine of Christ, at once became wise by better acquaintance with all these, and learned in all the sacred traditions of the Christian

the Armenians πρότερον χριστιανίσαι, were made Christians before that. Λέγεται γὰρ Τηριδάτην τὸν ἡγούμενον τούτου τοῦ ἔθνους, ἔκ τινος παραδόξου θεοσημείας συμβάσης περὶ τὸν αὐτοῦ οἶκον, ἅμα τε χριστιανὸν γενέσθαι, καὶ πάντας τοὺς ἀρχομένους ὑφ' ἑνὶ κηρύγματι προστάξαι ὁμοίως θρησκεύειν. He does not even allude to S. Gregory; but very properly remarks that the conversion of Armenia may have first begun from the intercourse between Armenians and the inhabitants of Osrohene (the land of Edessa).]

orders and service of God. While from various parts of Armenia crowds of people came and flocked around the saint, when they saw that the grace of the preaching of Christ's Gospel had burst forth from the province of Ararat, and from the royal city, over the sons of Haïk, over the children of the house of Thorgoma[2].

CHAPTER XXIII.

How King Tiridates, together with S. Gregory, destroyed the temples of devil-idols in the land of Armenia, and determined to raise in their places temples to the true God. How the Saint drove away the devil when he rose up against him; and how he continued to shed abroad his light, by turning to Christ the whole Armenian nation through divine signs and the preaching of the Gospel.

[3] WHILE king Tiridates was by the Divine Will and chastisement humbled and broken in the outward appearance of a wild boar, yet, though being as such apparently without the use of speech, he, nevertheless, after his senses had been cured of the plagues inflicted on them, was able to attend to the teaching and discipline of the saint, and to understand it thoroughly. Thus did he receive into his heart and mind the truth of our holy faith, growing wiser and

[2] [Togarmah.]   [3] Agathangelos and Metaphrastes.

better for all the divine words of teaching which he heard from S. Gregory. After hearing of the Unity of the Godhead in three Persons, and all that our Redeemer did and wrought for our salvation, together with the graces and gifts of the New Covenant conferred upon us by Him, when told him by the grace of the Holy Spirit through the saint's preaching, they were all by him, as it were, written down and painted in distinct and bright colours in his mind, as a kind of intellectual Gospel.

For, according to the testimony of ancient historians, we are told that no sooner was the king cured of those plagues by the prayers of S. Gregory, than he at once became acquainted with God, his Creator and Saviour, by whose rod he was made to suffer such things. And thus, sincerely repenting of his sins in his inmost heart, by God's great mercy vouchsafed unto him, he turned to Him, and clave to Him: his humility, the rivers of tears he shed, and the sackcloth and ashes on his body, showed his conversion and repentance, being visible signs of the unseen work that was taking place within him.

As his understanding became enlightened and clear by his faith in God, when he heard the word of life, while at the same time his heart was being kindled with love for Him, he wept incessantly over his former wicked ways, having especially present to his mind his struggle with the beautiful maid Rhipsime, his putting the holy martyrs to death, and the sufferings he inflicted on S. Gregory. Thus humbling himself to the lowest depth, he, with his whole heart yielded unreserved obedience to the Gospel of Christ, and burned with desire to do only that which pleased Him, and to spread the glory of His holy name.

Wherefore, as soon as he was completely recovered, he would brook no delay in doing all he could to establish the worship of God in every part of his kingdom. He called his governors and princes to hold counsel concerning the honour and worship due to the true God, to take measures for the salvation of the whole people, and to do all that was requisite, in order that every subject of his realm should be exhorted to turn from his heathen creed to the faith of our Saviour Jesus Christ, and to uprightness of life.

With the consent of all his nobles, he determined first of all to forbid, by an imperial edict throughout his dominions, the worship of the idols called gods, both of his ancestors and of himself, as well as to demolish, cast down, destroy, and wipe off the land of Armenia all temples of idols, as well as the idols themselves, and to leave none remaining; then, in the place of those temples, to raise churches to the honour of the true God, Jesus Christ. And instead of the carved images of the gods, to set up our Saviour's Cross, according to S. Gregory's orders; that no one put any obstacle to the treading under foot of the last remnant of idolatry, or hinder in any way the freedom of God's worship. So that all people, being thus encouraged, should be able, through the preaching of Christ's Gospel in all parts of his dominions, to attain unto the perfect service of God.

The pious king Tiridates, having settled and devised all this in council with his governors and princes, set to work at once with S. Gregory to put it into effect. He prepared himself, and got ready, with many of his grandees, to go the round of the provinces of his kingdom, and to do what he had determined. He went out of the city of Valarshabad with his nobles and a suitable retinue of soldiers, together with S. Gregory; and marched until he came first to the town of Ardashat, there to demolish and destroy the idol-temple of Anahid.

But as during their progress they came to an idol-temple called Herazmwin-deghi, and set at once to pull it down and to destroy the idol, lo, a troop of devils, under the semblance of a large army of cavalry and infantry, armed with shields and other weapons, set themselves in battle array, and with spears and flying banners rushed against the king and his attendants. But at the sight of the Cross of Christ they raised a loud cry of fear, and fled; while S. Gregory and his men went on intending to destroy this temple of the goddess. For the men who accompanied S. Gregory were armed with the Cross of Christ, and in the strength of it prepared to demolish the temple.

But when they arrived there, they found opposition got up by the devils, who would hinder and fight them. Showers of arrows, stones hurled thick from the top of the building by those men flew in all directions, so as well nigh to terrify the new believers. S. Gregory, seeing this, came to the door of the temple, and, raising his hand against the tower in which they were, made the sign of our Saviour's Cross, and in a moment the whole building of the temple shook on its foundations, crumbled, and fell to the earth; and the timber thereof suddenly caught fire and burnt, by the power of the sign of the Cross. And the smoke of it rose up in a mass to the sky, and spread abroad like a large cloud.

Then all the devils, being put to flight before S. Gregory and his men, were seen putting their hands to their necks, smiting their foreheads; and setting up a hideous howl, cried, "Woe be to us! woe be to us! woe be to us! Jesus, the Son of Mary, the daughter of man, has driven us out of the whole country! and now, after being bound, are we put to flight! But now, whither shall we flee? for His glory fills the earth. Let us then go to the north side of the heights of Caucasus; may-be we shall be allowed to dwell there. And let us do our utmost to abide as we are; for, without rest, thus to beat about the air, driven, severed from the abodes of men whom the lust of doing our good pleasure destroys, we could not endure to live." Such words did they shout before all, who, hearing them utter such things, were thereby confirmed in the faith. Suddenly, however, the host of black devils became invisible in that place, and, like smoke, vanished in the air.

Meanwhile the men who were with S. Gregory set to destroy and raze the remaining foundations of the building; then they distributed among the poor, the destitute, saints, and widows, the hoarded wealth of the temple. But they devoted to the maintenance and service of the new church the landed estates of the temple, the servants thereof, with their priests and the fields belonging to them. And S. Gregory, having taught them all, and the people in general, the holy faith and laws of Christ, established them in the true worship of God, and settled the various places where churches should be built.

He did not, however, set up any where tables of the Lord, because he had not yet received the honour of priest's orders; but he marked out by walls the place of the Lord's house, and set up a cross in the place where the table should be. And not there only, but in all the cities of Armenia, and in villages, small towns, and hamlets, did he mark the place of the Lord's house. He also set up the figure of the Cross at the opening and entrance of roads, in streets, market-places, and where ways met, and then made a proclamation to all men to beware lest they worshipped any one but the Lord God, and serve Him alone; an order which king Tiridates himself confirmed. Then, having commended them to the grace of God, and taking with him the king, he went from place to place throughout the land of Armenia to sow the Word of Life.

Thence they came to the province of Daranalia, that there also they should destroy the temple of the idols. In Tortan also was there a temple dedicated to the white devil Belshamen[4], which they destroyed first, and brake in pieces the image; and, spoiling it of all its treasures of gold and silver, they distributed them among the poor; but the landed estates and vested property they consecrated to the Church, which they went about to build, and where they also set up the all-saving sign of the Cross. Then the blessed Gregory, beginning at once to preach the Gospel, taught the whole people of the province for many days, with the assistance of the king, turning them from the worship of devils they had inherited from their fathers, to obedience of the Faith, and to the worship of the One God, Father, Son, and Holy Ghost. And the grace of the Lord made his work to prosper in their eyes, in that he confirmed the words he then preached by signs and wonders from God. Meanwhile unclean devils, who dwelt unseen inside their temple, came out thence; and after appearing among the people under various forms more or less hideous, horrible, deformed, or grizzly, were driven to flee thence into the lands of barbarians.

After having set them right, and established them in this way, he came to the fortress of Ani, where there were mausoleums erected to the former kings

---

[4] [Belshamen or Beelschemin (Ba'al shamayim) properly "the lord of heaven," was the name of an idol of the sun, commonly worshipped in Syria, especially at Haran, as Jacob Sarugensis tells us in his treatise on the fall of idols. Ass. Bib. Or., vol. i. p. 327.]

of Armenia. There they threw down the temple of the idol Aramazda, which is called the father of all other idols; and he planted there the Cross, and dedicated to the service and maintenance of the Church both the town and the fortress thereof. Then, after having taught the people in the true worship of God, they came thence into the borders of Egegheats; and having reached a certain town called Erez[3], they rushed at once to the temple that was the original place of worship of the kings of Armenia, and began to demolish it from top to bottom.

But there also did a terrible sight present itself. For a host of devils in the shape of soldiers, armed with shields, fought those who came near, and made the hills resound with their loud shouting. But by the invincible power of the Cross of Christ they were put to flight and destroyed. But as they were running away, they brought down a lofty wall of the place that was tottering and falling. Nevertheless, those who were with S. Gregory and the king rushed to destroy that place; and, strengthened by the Cross of Christ, they set to work, and brake in pieces the golden image of Anahid, then destroyed the temple, levelled it with the ground, and, taking all the spoil thereof of gold and silver, dedicated it all to the wants of the Church.

Then, after having established the people of that place in the Christian faith, they crossed the river

---

[3] See chap. vi. p. 139.

Kail [Lycus], and demolished entirely the temple of
Nane, the daughter of Aramazda, that was in a town
on the other side. But having taken all the treasure,
as well as the idol Anahid, they dedicated it to the
use and maintenance of the church which they
determined to build there, and left it in the place
for that purpose. After which, S. Gregory sowed
the seed of God's Word among the people during
many days, turned them all to the true worship of
God, and bade them abide firm in the faith of Christ
and in the keeping of His commandments.

Thence he came to the province of Tertshan[6], that
there also he might accomplish his Apostolic mission
and teaching, and work signs, in order to deliver
the people from the savage customs of their satanic
state of existence, and make disciples of the heathens
of those parts; that he might turn their heathenish
ways into the discreet doings of men loving God,
and set them all in order, after making them docile
and obedient to the teaching of the Gospel. He
then came to the temple of Mashig [Mithra][7], the
son of Aramazda, situated in a village called, in the
Parthian language, Pagayaridj. He threw it down,

---

[6] [Tertschan, or Terdschan, was one of the eight provinces of Higher Armenia (Moses Chor.). It was also called Athakh. Vartab. Vartan Geogr. St.-Martin Mem., vol. ii. pp. 360, 434.]

[7] [Besides the usual treatises on the worship, &c., of Mithra, see especially "Mithra," by Dr. F. Windischmann, in Abhandl. für die Kunde des Morgenl. 1 Band, No. 1. Justin Martyr tells us that the worshippers of that god imitated several Christian ceremonies, especially those of Baptism and the Eucharist. Apol. pro Chr., ii. p. 98.]

and destroyed it completely; but as to the hoarded treasure found there, he distributed it among the poor and the destitute, and dedicated the site to a church. And, having confirmed the people of the place in the knowledge of the Truth, the saint went on his journey.

Thus, whithersoever he went with the king and his nobles, did he pull down the temples, break in pieces the idols and all the carved or molten images, the work of human folly and ignorance; and the temples where the souls of men were ruined, and all manner of wickedness, transgressions, and sins perpetrated, did he break, pull down, demolish, and exterminate, until he left not a trace of them. And he taught and confirmed in the faith of Christ those who before had been living in all manner of abominations.

In this way did S. Gregory go on with the work of enlightening every place by God's kind care and the help of the king, who did with a good heart whatsoever he could by law, as we said above. For, albeit the king did not wish to tyrannize over the people, and make them yield to what was not as yet law of the realm, he still forbad every where, by stringent orders, the worship of idols called gods, and the vain superstitions of his ancestors, destroying alike idols and their temples, and commanding every one to lend an obedient ear to the preaching of the Gospel.

Then he also did that which must have been well pleasing unto God, as well as a welcome sight to angels — wherever he came with the saint Illuminator, he became himself a preacher of the Gospel, by telling of his former ignorance, of his evil doings, of all his cruel treatment of others through unbelief, and of the punishment he had suffered from God on account of it all; how he had been changed into the form of a wild boar, how he had been turned to God in consequence of it, and how he was restored to his former state by the prayers of S. Gregory, with the other wonderful circumstances we have detailed already; all of which he told, confessing them before all the people with the utmost humility, to the astonishment of every body. And with this he earnestly exhorted them all to hearken diligently to the preaching of the saint; at the hearing of which, the people, being seized with astonishment, were ravished in their minds. And, according to the prophecy of our Saviour, having found relief, they listened in faith to the preaching of S. Gregory; not only by their outward attention to his words, but also by receiving it with their whole heart.

Meanwhile the various tribes of Armenia were being instructed by all the great and wonderful things S. Gregory did; for king Tiridates not only destroyed the temples of idols, broke up the idols and forbad their worship, as soon as he was turned from his gross, heathenish habits to the Gospel of Christ, but supernatural signs and wonders were also wrought by the saint and Illuminator in the name of Christ. At the sight of which the people said, "In truth, being softened in our manners by the saints who teach us the way of salvation, it becomes us to give ourselves up to it all."

For S. Gregory, while teaching the people through the Holy Gospel to turn from their vain worship to the easy yoke of the service of Christ, persuaded them, not only by word of mouth, but also by signs and miracles, drawing the people to the faith of Christ by the cure of divers diseases and sicknesses which he wrought in the Saviour's name, whereby that name and the power of the Cross were greatly honoured and magnified.

And thus was it that, not by stern orders from the king, but by the power of our Saviour's Gospel, and by signs done in His name, together with the inward efficacy of divine grace given to the converts, the work of the Gospel was firmly wrought, whereby our whole nation was turned to the faith of Christ by S. Gregory. But as the saint came out of the pit in the year of our Lord three hundred, and our illumination came from him, therefore was that also the first year of the illumination of Armenia. He was then himself about forty-four years of age when he was brought out of the pit.

CHAPTER XXIV.

How S. Gregory was chosen by king Tiridates and all the princes of the realm to be bishop of all Armenia, in consequence of a revelation. How he was sent to Cæsarea to seek imposition of hands; by whom he was consecrated; and how he then returned.

As S. Gregory spread the knowledge of the Gospel according to rule among the new converts, he did not do so merely by preaching to the people in general, but according to the heavenly knowledge he had inherited from his childhood, and which had been increased in him by the gifts of the Holy Ghost, he instructed the principal people by special teaching, placing before them the writings of learned men, which he explained to them. Among these was the king first and foremost, and his household after him; then next those of the Arsacidæ who showed disposition to be taught wisdom, with the attendants at the palace, together with the freedmen and the great men of the court, were by him instructed in the rules of divine doctrine and of the Church. In order that henceforth they should no longer judge of how things should be by civil laws and rules only, but according to what is right in the sight of God; and that in all respects they should diligently hold by the Christian faith, and be zealous for the honour and for the name of our Lord and

Saviour Jesus Christ. Hitherto, however, S. Gregory had not deemed himself worthy to receive the most honourable office of the priesthood; but as it was no longer possible to hide the necessity of having common priests and a patriarch for the spiritual wants of the nation, he made the king acquainted with it. "I must tell you," said he, "to bring from one of the neighbouring Christian nations a priest who shall enlighten you, and be your shepherd."

The king, his queen Ashkhen, and his sister Chosrovitukht, having discussed the matter as regarded S. Gregory, said among themselves, "We must lose no time in seeing that he receive holy orders to administer to us the sacraments of the Church, and be the chief pastor who shall feed the whole nation." The king then sent an order to all his princes and nobles to meet him in the province of Ararat, in the city of Valarshabad, whither he returned, to the seat of his kingdom, after his tour through the provinces.

Thither came all the governors of provinces, with the nobles and great men of the realm, to the king. He called them together into the council-chamber, and said to them, "We must have a chief patriarch and spiritual pastor, who shall enlighten us, and direct us in God's ways. Let us make haste, and choose S. Gregory, the guide to life given us of God, to be constituted our pastor, who shall enlighten us in the laws and precepts of God our Creator, and renew us with the baptism of the holy font into newness of life."

Having heard this, the whole council, with one heart, one mouth, and one voice, chose him for the Primacy. But, when he heard of it, he declined to take upon himself the office of Patriarch, saying, "I am not sufficient for so high an office; it is beyond all expression honourable and sacred; seeing the Patriarch stands as mediator between God and man. Seek ye now some one worthy of it, and you will find him."

Meanwhile, a vision appeared to pious king Tiridates, in which God bade him not tarry in putting his counsel into execution. He saw an angel of God, who spake to him, saying, "Ye must without delay appoint S. Gregory to the Patriarchate, that he may enlighten you through baptism." At the same time an angel of God appeared also to S. Gregory, bidding him in no wise to resist or gainsay the choice of him to the sacred office. "For," said the angel, "it is commanded thee by Christ." The saint therefore yielded at once, and said, "The will of God be done!"

Then the king, filled with awe and with joy, undertook and determined with every precaution to send S. Gregory to receive imposition of hands. He called together his princes, and desired them to appoint and prepare chief men who should accompany S. Gregory on his travels, and bring him to Cæsarea of Cappadocia, called Majag in the Armenian tongue, to the Patriarch S. Leontius, to be by him ordained and consecrated Patriarch of the whole of Armenia.

He then caused to be written letters patent to this effect: "Having gathered together from the writings of various historians, we order at this time the present decree: "Lost, as we were formerly, and shrouded in the thick gloom of ignorance and brutishness, we could neither distinguish the truth, nor come to know God the Creator of all things. Although God in His infinite mercy had sent us this sun, the great Gregory, and had shown us the holy virgins [Rhipsime and her companions], that from them we should learn His infinite goodness and love towards men, yet we, through our own folly, became enraged against them, and tortured them to death; but this Gregory, being strengthened with God's invincible power, continued in life, in spite of our fury and wicked devices against him.

"And now, not only have the depths of God's pity and mercy not set us aside, lost, as we thus were; but in order to teach us wisdom in our foolishness, He wrought such wonders in connexion with the virtuous conflict [of those holy martyrs], and so chastened us, that our king was turned into a hog, and fed with wild beasts. But now, having had pity on us through the intercession and the prayers of those holy virgins and glorified martyrs, He healed us all by the hand of this Gregory, who suffered martyrdom; and He scattered the thick darkness that covered the eyes of our souls, and brought us out into the light of truth, to the holy faith, and to the knowledge of Him.

"But because he was found the greatest of all

martyrs, therefore was the vain conversation and degraded habits we had learned of our fathers removed from among us by him, through whom God taught us all His faith, and commanded that we should walk after His will, giving him to us for chief guide, until He clearly gave us the direct order that we should set him up over us for our first pastor, inspector, and teacher in the Truth. And this is not our own decision only, but it has been so ruled by a divine vision from above.

"Wherefore, trusting in the help and acceptable prayers of your holiness Leontius, Archbishop of Cæsarea, and of the whole clergy there assembled, did we through the mercy of God commit ourselves to your prayers.

"From king Tiridates and all the forces of Greater Armenia, and from queen Ashkhen, and from the royal maiden Chosrovitukht, greeting. For this reason have we sent unto you some of our chief men and some of the most honourable princes of our great country, that they may tell you all the wonderful things of God which have been wrought among us in this land. Therefore have we also desired them to bring to you the holy confessor Gregory, with credentials from us to your holiness, in order that, according to the gifts of the spiritual grace of Christ transmitted from Him, you may set him over us to be our pastor, the healer of our plagues, our teacher and guide in the divine truth, as it has been commanded of God. And for us, pray ye, that God make us worthy of His mercy, teach us to walk uprightly in His holy ways, and let the proofs of His love abide on us. Farewell in the Lord."

Such was the tenour of the letters patent sent by Tiridates to Leontius.

These also were the princes whom the king ordered to accompany S. Gregory. The first was the governor of the madhouse; the second, the governor of the hospital; the third, the chief of the royal women's household; the fourth, the chief of the royal knights; the fifth, the commander-in-chief of all the armies of Armenia; the sixth, the governor of the Kurds; the seventh, the governor of the province of Dzoph; the eighth, the governor of the Karkars; the ninth, the governor of Ereshdun; the tenth, the governor of Mog; the eleventh, the governor of Sun; the twelfth, the governor of Dzok; the thirteenth, the governor of Udatzi; the fourteenth, the governor of the province of Zarevanht Her; and the fifteenth was the governor of the land of the Ardzrunians.

These fifteen princes, being ordered by the king, made preparations to accompany S. Gregory to Cæsarea. They took with them gifts and offerings of gold and silver, horses and mules, and costly apparel of divers sorts and colours, for the ornaments and service of holy places, and of the houses of God in the parts to which they were sent; as well as gifts to all the churches in the places through which they passed.

They brought S. Gregory in the gilded coach of

the palace, drawn by four white horses, accompanied by all the fifteen princes, in coaches, on palfreys, and a suitable retinue, and troops with banners of every rank. They started first from the province of Ararat, from the western side of the city of Valarshabad, and came into Cappadocia, formerly belonging to Armenia, to Cæsarea, then under the dominion of the Greeks; for in those days the country west of Armenia formed part of the kingdom of Greece. Wherever they came to, from city to city, they met with the greatest hospitality.

And great were the rejoicings of the Christians, who flocked to the sight, when they heard of the wonders wrought by God, and of the salvation that had reached the converts of Armenia; being thus honoured as they went along, until they came to the metropolis called Cæsarea, but in Armenian, Majag. There they met S. Leontius, Patriarch, and the clergy of every degree, and divers orders of angelic ministers. And, having saluted them, they told them all that God had done for them, and presented the king's letter to the Patriarch.

He welcomed them with gladness and with rejoicings in the whole city. He took the letter; and, having read its contents, was filled with joy, and gave glory to Christ; while all men in the city made preparations for a public feast, and honoured S. Gregory in a manner befitting his holiness, praising him for the valour and virtue with which he had borne his conflict as martyr; and they glorified God.

Likewise did all the principal men of the city vie one with another in doing homage to the saint and to his escort. Having ascertained the office and dignity of every man separately, they treated them all accordingly, after the custom of believing Christians towards those who give them advice in the Gospel, showing them every respect and attention. Thus was the blessed Gregory magnified of all, as well as honoured, praised, and glorified, as he deserved to be, for the name of Martyr he had won for himself.

Many bishops were also invited, and gathered together at Cæsarea, to lay hands on S. Gregory; and, according to the Holy Gospel, they laid hands on him, S. Leontius being at the head of them. And with great pomp and solemnity they set him Patriarch over the whole of Armenia.

Then, not many days after his consecration, S. Gregory was dismissed with great honour, and with the display of all the ecclesiastical pomp the city could afford, carrying letters from S. Leontius, and accompanied by all his retinue of princes, to return to his post as Patriarch of Greater Armenia, commended, as he was, to the grace of God. He and his suite returned to their hosts the most humble thanks for all the unspeakable gifts they had received from them. And, taking leave one of another with a parting embrace, they separated and left.

Thence they came straight to Sebastia, and tarried there certain days, where S. Gregory, seeing a number of dear brethren, persuaded them to come with him, that he might ordain them priests for his own country. Of them a great multitude followed him, so that he left the place and took leave of the Bishops, of the princes of the land, and of the people, with great pomp and splendour, and went on his way.

Wheresoever they came they stayed some little time; and wherever they passed, crowds of people and of the clergy flocked to see the living martyr for Christ, S. Gregory, and receive his blessing. And they said one to another, "Come, let us go and see S. Gregory, who is just arrived; he is the man who endured suffering so many years for the sake of Christ, and who, being found a faithful martyr, has won for himself the name of Confessor." Thus, under the Lord's guidance and protection, did they pass through many places with spiritual joy and gladness, until they came back into Greater Armenia.

CHAPTER XXV.

Of the wonders wrought by S. Gregory after his return from Cæsarea, with the power of the holy Cross, against the assaults of devils; how many idol-temples he destroyed; how many people he enlightened with holy Baptism, and who they were; and of the strange things that took place at the arrival of the relics of the holy Precursor [*S. John the Baptist*] and of the martyr Athanakini, which S. Gregory brought with him from Cappadocia.

⁸ WHEN S. Gregory, the Sun of Armenia, returned to the borders of Greater Armenia, from his journey to Cæsarea, he learnt that in the province of Taron there was an idol-temple of Vahevahian left standing. That temple, which was full of silver and gold, gifts and offerings brought to it by the kings of Greater Armenia, was the place of sacrifice of those kings, situated near to the town of Vishab, at the foot of the hills of Karki, on the river Euphrates, where the temple looks as if standing against great mount Taurus. The place was also called Hashdishad, by reason of the multitude of sacrifices offered there. And in that temple there were three idols, to which God's people, ignorant of the truth, still sacrificed, together with some of the new converts. The first was the god Vahevahian, and for this reason was the temple called after the name of this god, the temple of Vahevahian⁹. The second idol was the Mother of Gold (Wosgimair), whence the statue or image thereof was called "mother of gold;" the third idol was called Asdeghgan, called the Mother of Hercules by the Greeks, that is Aphrodite.

With S. Gregory were certain relics of S. John

⁸ Agathangelos and Metaphrastes.
⁹ [Indjidj., Anc. Geogr. p. 93, says that Vahevahian was the generic name for a large temple; and that in this one, situated in Duruperan, there was a statue of Hercules. *Hashdishad* means a place of sacrifices; and *Asdeghgan* is Astræa.

the Baptist, and of Athanakini, Bishop of Sebastia, who, with ten of his disciples, suffered martyrdom under the cruel emperor Diocletian, on the 16th day of July. When he came in front of the temple he wished to bring those relics upon the highest part of the temple, in order thus to destroy it, and in the place thereof to build a chapel as resting-place for the remains of those saints. But when they came near to the river Euphrates, about the distance of two horse-gallops, where through a small valley they had to cross a little water, the mules of the chariot which contained the sacred treasures stood fast, and could proceed no further. At this moment an angel of the Lord appeared to S. Gregory, and said to him, "The Lord's will is, that the saints should abide in this place." Then he marked out in that place a spot for a church to the memory of those saints, and blessed it; and the company that was with him proceeded at once to build it. And there he laid the relics of those saints to rest.

But while they were busy in rearing the chapel, S. Gregory gave orders to the soldiers and to the princes who were with him, to get to the top of the idol, and to beat it down with hammers. They went to the temple for that purpose, and sought to find the door whereat they might go in and break down the image; but they could not find it, as it was hidden from them by devils. They then tried to beat an entrance from the outside, and thus get inside; but this too they could not accomplish; for no iron could be found there for the work.

The princes then came in haste to S. Gregory, and told him every thing. Then he, taking with him the emblem of the Cross, went and stood in the valley over against the lofty walls of the building, and said, "Thine angel, O Lord, shall drive them away." Oh the power of the holy Cross of Christ! For hardly had the living witness of Christ ended these words, than a mighty wind burst forth from the wood of the cross, which he held in his hands, and rushed straight at the mountain, and smiting against the buildings of the temple, demolished them altogether: so completely was that temple destroyed, that no trace of it could be found, neither of stone nor of timber, neither of the gold nor yet of the silver thereof; neither could one tell at all that a building had ever stood there.

But also the multitude of the heathen priests, who had armed themselves against the men sent to dismantle the temple, said, "Better it is for us to put ourselves along with our idols than to witness their ruin;" so that they too were so thoroughly destroyed, that of their bones not one has yet been seen. And many people in those parts who saw the marvels that had happened, were taken with awe at the power of the Cross, and were thus turned to the faith of Christ. To them said S. Gregory, "Now see yourselves, what has become of your shameful idols; for they were naught; but from henceforth serve the Lord God who made heaven and earth."

Then the saint went up to the place where the idol-temple had stood, and gathering together the inhabitants of the land, he preached to them that Christ is God, and turned them all to the true worship of God; he also laid there the first foundations of a church, and set up the table of the glories of Christ [the holy table]. And having made a font, he first enlightened with Baptism those who had come with him from Cæsarea, the princes, governors and other nobles of the court, and the soldiers; and after them the inhabitants of that province. He spent there twenty days, and baptized more than nine or ten hundred thousand people. But, as this may to some persons appear hard to believe, it must be remembered that S. Gregory had with him many priests, and that there was nothing amiss in their baptizing [as well as he]. On the holy table, also, of the chapel reared as a resting-place for the relics he had brought with him, did he offer the Divine Sacrifice, distributing among the congregation the quickening Body and Blood of Christ.

As regards those relics, we are assured by men of those days and by historians, that S. Gregory left only a portion of them in the chapel he built there, and that he brought the remainder away with him, and placed in the great church which he built over the spot where the idol-temple had stood. For the angel who had said, "It is the Lord's will that the saints abide in this place," did not mean that the whole of the relics should for ever remain at the place where the mules had stood fast, but only until the idol-temple was destroyed and the church was built in its place; and that they then should be there deposited for good, as it was right to do. And so did the saint. For it was impossible to build a suitable and proper church in the space of twenty days; inasmuch as in that time, the saint could only trace the foundations of the church and bless them; and under a temporary shelter set up the table, make a font, and baptize a multitude of people. But he offered the life-giving Sacrifice in the chapel built there for the relics, where the baptized people communicated, as Agathangelos tells us plainly concerning those same relics, although he omits to relate one by one all that we have here told in detail [1].

Afterwards, when the church dedicated to the holy Precursor was finished, there they finally placed the relics, and commanded the people of that place to keep that same day, the 7th of Sahmni, according to our reckoning, in memory of the holy martyrs [S. John Baptist and S. Athanaki], that is the 16th of October of the Roman Calendar. Hither flocked for that purpose people from all parts of the country, regularly every year; and there is a convent also dedicated to the holy Precursor, built by S. Gregory; also another convent named Klaga-hoshi, after a disciple of the Illuminator, who is the founder of convents, and was appointed Father of that one by S. Gregory himself. It is also called Inn-

[1] [This convent was finally built by a Syrian called Zenob, during S. Gregory's lifetime. All Zenob's successors in that convent of Surp-Garabied, or S. Precursor, were Syrians until the end of the sixth century.]

agnean [of nine eyes, or springs], on account of the nine springs that rise close by [2].

And at the first great solemnity held in honour of these relics it happened, as we are told in the song of the seven holy Grass-eaters [3], that S. Gregory, taking the relics of the holy Precursor, proclaimed with them greeting from the Lord to the province around, with prayers to this effect.

"Let the right hand of the Lord be over this province, to preserve it from enemies, lest they should have dominion over it, and to keep it from schisms and dissensions." At that moment a voice came from heaven, "Thy prayers shall be heard." But if any one should in his mind say that this promise does not seem to have been exactly fulfilled, for that enemies of the faith have held, and now do still exercise dominion over the country, to this we reply, that, as regards such promises of God, it behoves us to understand, that the words of the promise fix deep in the heart the certainty that the promise will be granted, albeit not in the very words of it, which, in my opinion, imply that the saint's prayer should be fulfilled on those who in that country led a pious life, as we gather from several places in Holy Scripture.

---

[2] [This convent, situated in Taron, is also called *S. Garabied*, or S. Precursor, and is celebrated throughout Armenia, being the one first founded by S. Gregory.]

[3] [The relics of these seven *Khodadjaragagn*, who originally came from Rome, are also preserved in the convent of S. Garabied, according to Vartan, Geogr. p. 430, ed. St.-Martin.]

After this beginning, S. Gregory went round about all the provinces of the kingdom; and every where, in cities, towns, and villages, he set up churches, with a table in every church, and baptized; and ordained priests and other ministers for the wants of the congregations. And having appointed and located them, he enjoined to them the care of their flocks in the faith and in the commandments of our Lord Jesus Christ, to the salvation of their souls.

CHAPTER XXVI.

How and when S. Gregory baptized king Tiridates and his house, and all his army, with the princes and generals thereof. Also concerning the wonders wrought from the Lord on the occasion of that solemnity.

[1] WHEN S. Gregory, on his return from Cæsarea to Armenia, went into the province of Taron, and there enlightened the people, king Tiridates took his queen Ashkhen, his sister Chosrovitukht, and as many of his princes, nobles, and of his soldiers and attendants as were willing to accompany him, and came to Valarshabad to meet the saint. He first came to the small town of Bakvan, which in the

[1] Agathangelos.

Parthian language is called Titsavan, and there awaited him a whole month. For S. Gregory was meanwhile going about from place to place, filling the country with churches, priests, and ministers, settling and establishing ecclesiastical orders of men, and baptizing a great many people.

At last S. Gregory came to the king, accompanied by the great men who were with him, and an immense crowd of people who flocked to him from all quarters, and went about with him; some for the sake of being cured of their diseases, and others in order to hear the word of God. For he sowed broadcast the word of life, both himself, and the ministers of the gospel who were with him, and whose names it would take too long to mention. Of whom the blessed Father, having commended some to the grace of God, came to a place at the foot of mount Nbad[s].

Then the king came with all his suite to meet him on the banks of the Euphrates, where they were all filled with joy at again meeting together. The pious king and the holy Father fondly embraced and warmly greeted each other, and filled each other's hearts with happiness, in the interchange of mutual expressions of humble love and affection. And the good king Tiridates, laying himself humbly at the feet of the holy Father, promised for himself and for those of his kingdom, to yield themselves obedient to his rule and govern-

[s] [Mount Niphates.]

ment, and to fulfil his wishes in Christ Jesus; and they returned to the town with great rejoicings. He then told the king and his nobles all that had happened to him in Cæsarea and during the journey until that day; all the marvels God had wrought, all the conversions of peoples to God, his enlightenments through holy baptism, and through the preaching of the gospel, exactly as they took place, did the saint tell them to the king one by one; when all who heard it were filled with joy, and gave thanks to the Lord. S. Gregory then delivered to the king the letter of greeting he had brought him from S. Leontius. The king read it, and both he and his nobles were made glad by it. It ran thus:—

"Unto you who have been chastened but cared for, wounded but kindly healed, tormented but subdued, lost but found, gone astray but returned, respected and beloved; to Tiridates, king of Greater Armenia, to Ashkhen his queen, and to the royal maid Chosrovitukht, and to all the multitude of people that are in that country, Leontius, Archbishop and Metropolitan of Cæsarea, and the whole Clergy of the holy Church, Bishops, Presbyters, and Deacons, and the Christian laity, send greeting.

"We have returned thanks with unfeigned joy to Christ's eternal glory, for the salvation that has come to you from God, as we have been informed; as well as for the holy martyrs who are in the midst of you, and who have been glorified in your country, that you, considering the end of their walk on earth, and becoming followers of their faith, should be glorified with them, and be crowned with the same crown as they.

"Because the Maker of all things, who, as regards all countries and all people therein, is of His goodwill pleased that all of them should receive the adoption of sons, warns them all, that they cease altogether from works that cannot profit them, so that He may give them comfort, and that He may give rest in His kingdom to all that travail and are heavy laden; for His yoke is easy and His burden is light. He protects His own, spreads His wings over them, and teaches them; that He may make all worthy of His rest.

"Wherefore has He added you to the rest, unworthy as you were, in order that you also being taught from within, should be able to appreciate that which is worthy in itself. And inasmuch as ye did not understand that which is of man in humanity, He has made you acquainted with what is not human; and whereas ye were in pitiable ignorance, He has established you in knowledge that shall endure for ever; for the Stone which the builders rejected is become for you the head stone of the corner.

"For ye have reconciled Him with tears, whom ye had angered by your sins; and He, who to you was darkness, because your eyes were blinded, has opened them and has enabled you to see clearly. He has removed from you the darkness of heathenism, and has clothed you in bright light. For while in darkness of ignorance ye boasted in your ruin, He gave Himself to you for wisdom; and gave Himself to you as the one who found you [wandering].

"But we heard of your being thus found, and we whelmed you into billows of love with unceasing and unspeakable thanksgivings; and over and above this we blessed our Lord Jesus Christ with unceasing tongues for the marvels He had wrought on your behalf; we also praised God the Father Almighty, for that He vouchsafed unto Gregory the unspeakable gift of His Holy Spirit, whereby ye also may become worthy of the favour of a greeting in the kingdom of heaven. And though far [absent] in the body, yet near [and present] in the spirit, do remember us in your prayers, for the salvation granted unto you; especially when ye shall gather together for the feast in memory of the saints.

"And the evidence of this will remain established in the midst of us both; for by restoring the benefit of the priesthood to your country, it will continue firmly united to us of the Church of Cæsarea, where the imposition of hands had been prepared for you, and through which unspeakable gifts shall be bestowed on you, by means of the renewing grace of Baptism, and of the saving Cross, and of the quickening Body and cleansing Blood of Christ. Other blessings shall come down upon you through the increase of the priesthood, whereby ye will be raised and mixed up with the continued prayers of the servants of Christ. Farewell in Christ, and rejoice evermore in the salvation of the Lord."

But, after the reading of these comforting lines from S. Leontius, as the heart of the king was burning with desire for the new birth of holy Baptism, as also did the hearts of those who had come with him to meet S. Gregory, the saint could hardly find time from the crowd around him to make the due preparations for this holy sacrament. He then came and stood in a public place, where flocked to him all those who accompanied the king and belonged to his household, as well as many others, to whom he began afresh to teach the most holy mysteries of our Christian faith, and the efficacy of the cleansing rite of Baptism, and of other holy sacraments of the Church; making them intelligent in all such matters by his Apostolic teaching.

At that time S. Gregory commanded the soldiers encamped around the king, and in general all others, to continue fasting and in prayers for thirty days; that they should be in a fit state to receive the grace of this holy sacrament. Then, together with the ecclesiastics he had brought with him, to whom according to his custom he gave the preference, he spent that day in strict fasting, in prayers, and in floods of tears. And thus, humbling and mortifying himself with untiring efforts and labour, in order to become the bringer of good things to the land of Armenia, he received from God grace sufficient for the due enlightenment of the people, to purify and perfect so great a multitude through the new birth, by Baptism, and to join it in one mystical Body of the Saviour; which, even now, unto this same

Saviour, as unto one Head, is fitted, joined, and established, and increases from day to day throughout the whole world, in the Lord.

When the days of fasting and all the preparations were completed, at the dawn of day, S. Gregory took the king, with his queen Ashkhen, and his sister Chosrovitukht, and all the great men of the realm, with the soldiers in camp, and brought them to the banks of the Euphrates. And performing the ceremonies ordered by the Church, he baptized in the name of the Father, and of the Son, and of the Holy Ghost, first the king, then his queen, his sister, the great men of the court, his suite, and in general all the people that were there with him.

At that moment a great marvel was wrought by the Almighty Lord God.

For when the people went down into the water of the river Euphrates, the stream rushed by with a murmur and roaring of the waters, as Euthymius writes. So that all the bystanders so wondered at the sight that they stood on the point of running away, and the holy Chrism poured by the Illuminator, surrounded every one of those who had been baptized; while a bright light like unto a pillar of fire was seen to rise into the air over the river, on which rested the base of it firm and standing, and on the top of the pillar a figure of the Cross also of light. So bright was that pillar that the light thereof dimmed that of the sun. And those who were baptized on that day were about one hundred and fifty thousand.

And they all then dressed in white, inasmuch as, having been born anew, cleansed, enlightened, made like unto angels and adopted children of God, they should be made heirs of the light of the Gospel. And having received the grace of the Spirit as an earnest of the glory that awaited them, they, being adorned, gladdened, and made to blossom, should bring forth in Christ the sweet-savoured fruits of faith, hope, and charity, which being shed abroad in their hearts were confirmed by the Holy Ghost. And being thus filled with joy, they might become lamps in the House of the Lord only just set up; where the saint, offering the divine oblation, gave them the communion of the life-giving sacrament of the Body and Blood of Christ.

He then changed the name of king Tiridates into Johannes; and having tarried eight days there, by the river Euphrates he baptized the whole people, which of the royal camp alone could not be less than four hundred thousand. And if any one should wonder at so great a multitude being baptized in so short a time, let him turn back to the sixteenth chapter of our narrative, and he will then see how that might take place.

This extraordinary and wonderful baptism happened in the year of our Lord 302, in the first year of the enlightenment of the country by our Holy Father, Gregory the Illuminator; and in the eighteenth year of Tiridates, sovereign king of Armenia.

CHAPTER XXVII.

Of the schools founded by the Illuminator, in which pastors were taught and multiplied under the protection of the king; and of the number of places wherein the preaching of the Gospel prospered; of the many churches built and provided with ministers; and of the convents filled with monks, and how he succoured them when they were in difficulty.

*AFTER the great solemnity of the baptism of the king and of the multitudes of people, the Illuminator of souls visited every part of the kingdom of Armenia, in order to fill every place with Christian teaching and doctrine, to build churches, and to ordain ministers for the confirmation of the new converts in the faith of Jesus Christ. Meanwhile pious Tiridates, for his part, was doing all he could to settle the maintenance of ecclesiastics and to provide for their income; for, having now withdrawn his mind from earthly cares, he fixed it only on divine things. He also gave orders to the people to worship and only to serve the Maker of heaven and earth; and gave all diligence to augment the number of ministers of the table of the Lord in every place, to the confirmation and increase of the service of God.

S. Gregory, on the other hand, did his best to

---
* Metaphrastes and Sozomen.

come to every place of the kingdom of Armenia, to lay the foundation of churches, and to multiply worthy priests and clerks. And consecrating Bishops from place to place, he put every one of them in a diocese defined by himself. He guided and directed them all in his precepts by a faithful and true conduct, and by watchful care to prove themselves good inspectors of their enlightened flock. And he advised the pious king, who was on intimate terms with him, to establish schools from place to place, with fixed incomes, and to command that in every district the children should be gathered together and instructed in the pious writings of wise and good men.

And taking a number of rough country boys, he cast them into the crucible of instruction for a spiritual life; he taught them in the Holy Scriptures, and rubbed off their minds the rust of vice and of evil habits, by the heat of divine love. And from that time such was the eagerness of some to withdraw from the habits of their fathers, in order to devote themselves to God's service, that they might say, "I have forgotten my people and my father's house."

Then the good king, having taken upon himself to do so without delay, commanded that in the several provinces and districts of his kingdom young children should be gathered together according to S. Gregory's directions, and be brought to school; to be taught letters by faithful and wise teachers set over them. Besides this, he directed that the children of the foul race of heathen priests be also brought under the same instruction; and he fixed the amount to be paid for it. He ordered them to be divided into two classes, the one to be taught Syriac letters, the other Greek writings.

They were taught to read books, and profited in the knowledge of the Holy Scriptures, in the writings of the Holy Fathers, and the canons of the Holy Church. And it was marvellous to see how those, who a short time before were empty, worldly, and rough, soon became spiritual, attentive to the word of God, instructed in the writings of the Prophets and of the Apostles, and inheritors of the Gospel; and how, by the grace of Christ, they became skilled in all the commandments and precepts of God.

And this was all the more marvellous to behold in the case of the sons of heathen priests, whom S. Gregory made his special pupils, and whom he formed in the fear of God and the knowledge of Holy Scripture, whom he trained in the government of a spiritual charge, until they became fit to occupy the rank of Bishop and to receive consecration at his hands.

Of these was one of the name of Alpheus, who was appointed Bishop of the parts about the Euphrates. The second is Euthalius, who became pastor of Pasen[7]; the third, Pasos; the fourth, Moses; the fifth, Eusebius; the sixth, Johannes;

---

[7] [A district of Ararat.]

the seventh, Akabes; the eighth, Ardites; the ninth, Arages; the tenth, Antioches. All these were from among the sons of heathen priests, who after having been taught and trained by S. Gregory, were by him chosen for Bishops in various places, for the purpose of spreading abroad the preaching of Christ's Gospel. Besides these were many others whose names we cannot give in detail. For all those whom the holy Patriarch consecrated Bishops over the wide extent of the Armenian kingdom were more than four thousand in number. But as to the presbyters, deacons, readers, and other ministers of the Church, they were without number. And he made Balbus, a man true and pious, inspector [Bishop] of the king's household and attendants at the palace.

But great was S. Gregory's care to train his clergy in innocency of life; to be holy in conversation, gentle in words, not covetous, not vainglorious, patient, feeling, instant in prayer; so that they might be without reproach or blemish in their walk through life, amid the people around them; pleasing Christ in their service of Him, so as to recommend Him among the nation. He often reminded them how it became them to have their conversation in the world, who ought to carry holiness like life in their heart, and the word like purifying fire in their mouth.

Having founded many monasteries in various places, he made monks of those whom, being adorned with the rank of an angelic life and conversation, he trained in obedience to superiors, poverty, endurance, watchfulness, silence, earnest prayer, and constant praises and thanksgivings; wishing that those who thus submitted themselves, and who in the secluded life of a convent devoted themselves to Christ, should be like the angels in heaven. Likewise did he settle that virgins whom he blessed should live soberly, in secluded nunneries, and should agree together in holiness of life after the example of S. Gaiane and of her companions, who excelled in purity, and received the crown of martyrdom as well as of virginity and chastity, more spotless than white lilies.

After the chief schools of every province were built, other smaller ones were also established in every city, through the Patriarch's forethought, and by command of the pious king; and in them were trained in every quarter youths who showed disposition for letters, from among whom should be chosen, some to be clerks, and others to be employed in some kind of service. And when the Illuminator went about preaching in cities and towns, those whom he exhorted sent their children to schools thus established, in order to be taught.

The first object of the holy Patriarch after his return to the royal city, Valarshabad, from the great solemnity of baptizing the people in the Euphrates, was to build there a magnificent temple to the name of the Only Begotten Son of God; the site of which he had consecrated with holy oil and surrounded with a wall, and marked by a cross, at the time he built the church in honour of S. Rhipsime and her companions, as we mentioned above. And he called this temple ETCHMIADZIN [i. e. "the descent of the Only Begotten"], in consequence of the divine vision he had, in which the Only Begotten Son, descending from heaven to the earth, marked the spot by smiting it with his hammer of gold, which resounded aloud into the very depths of hell. Then S. Gregory arranged that the festival of the Holy Church should be kept from year to year, as the table of feasts after the festival of "his coming out of the pit" shows clearly. Likewise also in the city of Ardashat, and in other cities of every province, did he command churches to be built, and appointed to them priests and ministers.

Thus did the saint labour to spread all over Armenia, from end to end of the kingdom, the work of preaching the Gospel of Christ. From the city of Saghadats unto the country of the Chaldi, unto the Gagharshtsh, unto the frozen borders of Maskt, unto the gates of the Alani, and unto the borders

---

[It was first called *Shoghagath*, i. e. diffusion of light. See, for an interesting description of it, Muravieff's Travels, vol. ii. pp. 40, sq. Speaking of the impression the place made upon him, he says that "one's veneration for it is yet increased when one calls to mind the tradition that the throne of the Only Begotten (the altar of the Church) is reared on the same spot as that on which Noah offered his first sacrifice" (p. 54). It is, however, at a considerable distance from Nakhitschevan, so called, they say, as being "the first descent" of Noah from the hills of Ararat. See note to Introduction, p. 5.]

[Now a district of Georgia.]

of the Caspian Sea, unto the land Phaidagaran[1] of the kingdom of Armenia. And from the city of Amthats[2] unto that of Nisibis, and then on to the borders of Assyria, towards the land of Nor Shirag, and towards the Kurds unto the fortified country of the Marats, as far as the house of the Prince of Mashtin, and unto the Aderbadagan did he extend his preaching. Thus did he bring many to the faith of Christ from among Persians, Assyrians, Medians, and Chaldeans. And, added to this, though he had given in charge the wide sowing of the word of life to many of his own priests, yet did he consider that it behoved him to fulfil in this respect the duties and pattern of a faithful steward, and attend to the ministry himself.

At all seasons, and in all weathers, in summer and winter, by night and by day, untiringly and earnestly in the ways of an evangelist, on this side of the country and on that, rushing with irresistible force against adversaries, before kings and princes, and before all the heathens, did our Illuminator carry the saving name of Jesus; and enlightening every soul with the knowledge of God, by the new birth of Baptism made them children of God.

Many prisoners also and captives, and others who were being tormented by tyrants, did he rescue with great display of the glory of Christ; many unjust bonds for debt did he also tear up and destroy; many also who were afflicted and who lived in con-

[1] [A province of Greater Armenia.]
[2] [Tigranocerta.]

stant fear did he comfort by his teaching; and by placing before them the hope of the glory of God, of our Lord Jesus Christ, well established in their souls, did he bring them round to unfeigned joy. And with untired efforts labouring as he did at the Word of life, did he turn souls from the vain worship of idols to the service of God, and to the hope of the kingdom of heaven.

Oh the wonderful Apostolic life of our holy Illuminator S. Gregory! So remarkable was the holiness of his conversation, and so powerful was his preaching, that the hard hearts of stone of men given to sin melted into floods of tears, and were confirmed in uprightness of life, in repentance, and in the true worship of God. But who would be sufficient to tell the number of those who devoted themselves to the service of Christ, not only by keeping His commandments, but also by taking up the cross in closer fellowship with Him, in the many monasteries built by S. Gregory both in inhabited and in desert places?

After all these things he went about visiting his wide-spread flock, by going the round of the provinces, where he quickened and comforted many who hitherto had been hardened in sin, by his exhortations and the hope of eternal blessedness in store for them. While at other times he, without respect of persons, applied the painful cautery or gave the bitter medicine to those who loved sin, in order to cure them of it, when they obstinately persisted against the threats of the bonds that awaited their souls in hell; and thus did he rescue them from death. He also took especial care to efface all remnants of evil habits and customs from among the people, and instead thereof to establish and strengthen godly ways and conversation, to fear God, and to lead a holy and pure Christian life; such was his object in public, and especially in his preaching. So that at the coming of the Chief Shepherd and Lord of all, he might stand before Him with a clear countenance, like a good servant, together with the flock he had fed, sanctified, and enlightened; and for this receive the crown that fadeth not away.

CHAPTER XXVIII.

In what manner S. Gregory, the Sun of Armenia, tended his flock without in any way neglecting his own salvation; how, without diminishing aught in his care of them from the requisite work, did he retire from the crowd to give himself up to a close and secluded life.

To those who can shake off their outward cares in leisure, the love of God becomes easy; not so, however, to those who are always occupied. For this reason, must those who have the care of souls and who minister the Word of life, at times seek rest away from the scene of their labours, and remain alone in solitude with Christ; in order that their mind may there be refreshed from a multitude of cares, and thus dwell quietly on the thought of God's nature and attributes; and that the heart be kindled and strengthened with His love, which is the best motive for exertions in His service. There also, in retirement, may the man of God, through the teaching of the Holy Ghost, learn in the study of the Holy Scriptures every thing worth knowing, and thus increase his own light.

By these means, his mind being further enlightened, and his heart again kindled with greater love for God and the brethren, does he profit both for his own inward benefit, and for the guidance and feeding of his flock. For inasmuch as he is called upon to direct others in meditating upon God and in learning to love Him ardently, must he especially take care lest himself be found deficient therein; as "the chosen vessel" makes known to all pastors, in his Epistle to the Corinthians (1 Cor. ix. 27). So also did the Prophets of old, the same Apostle, in his Epistle to the Hebrews, telling us, that those of whom the world was not worthy wandered in desert places and in caves of the earth (Heb. xi. 38).

But why mention the Prophets, when our own Lord by His word and example exhorts us to the same, as it is written of Him (S. Luke v. 16), that He retired to desert places, and there remained praying? Likewise did He withdraw His Apostles from their work among the multitude and frequently retire to desert places apart, saying to them, "Come ye yourselves apart into a desert place, and rest awhile" (S. Mark vi. 31). So also did the Holy Fathers who succeeded to the Apostles, enjoin the same things by rule and example to their disciples.

Wherefore did our blessed and saintly Illuminator, entering into the deep intention of such measures, apply to himself and follow the example handed down by the Saviour, His Apostles, and the Holy Fathers; and not only did he submit to it himself, but he enjoined the same to his disciples. From time to time he retired from the world, and taking some of them to every monastery, he went into the wilderness and there spent some time as a hermit and anchorite; and living there from day to day on herbs of the field, he gave himself up to self-denial and hard living; remembering the words of the Apostle that, "When I am weak, then am I strong" (2 Cor. xii. 10), and also, "Most gladly, therefore, will I rather glory in mine infirmities, that the power of Christ may rest upon me" (ib. 9).

There was he in constant communion with God, according to the words of the Spirit of Truth spoken by the prophet Hosea, "Behold, I will allure her and bring her into the wilderness, and speak comfortably unto her" (Hosea ii. 14). Thereby afflicting his body, did he prepare his heart through the quickening of his spirit, for the song of Psalms, of praises, and of giving of thanks, to the glory of God. There did he find strength and courage for the patient daily leading of a holy life, so as to attain unto the eternal bliss and happiness made by Christ the end of our walk on earth. There did he remain to burn with the spirit of God's service, and of devotedness to Him.

There did he abide to continue daily in earnest prayer, in earnest entreaties, in elevation of mind, in enlightenment of thought, in heavenly visions, and in the company of holy angels; there to supplicate his God with acceptable words, and requests agreeable to Him; and there to offer in reconciliation, prayers and supplications unto Him for the life and salvation of all. Thus, while in the body, did the saint spend days of seraphic existence[3] in desert places, on the banks of the Euphrates, among mountain fastnesses, dwelling in caves and holes of the rocks with the great Elijah and S. John the Baptist. Being himself a zealous promoter of such good works, he first of all set the example of them in his own life.

Then some time coming down from those hills, he would go and visit the hermits his disciples, comforting and encouraging them with words of divine love, and pouring forth unto them the remembrance of inward consolation and goodness he had received

---

[3] [In this mountain, Mount Sebuh, to which Tiridates came to visit S. Gregory, and in which is found the saint's tomb, is also a convent of the Seraphim, respecting which Vartan tells this legend: "God sent a seraph to the earthly cherub (the Illuminator), who was then in a deep valley and was on his way to Jerusalem, going thither on his knees. The seraph came to prevent him from going; and in after time, the Vartabed Johannes Bluz, when on the top of this mountain, had a vision of the Illuminator who told it him." Geogr. p. 432.]

from above during his solitary life in the mountains. Thus did he come to the help of all the Churches by Christ's mercy, feeding them with words of life, and by the ministration of the holy sacraments. He thus visited them repeatedly, without delaying to reach to them all the help they needed. And whithersoever he went, did he with open mouth and with a doctrine full of good fruits, sow the Word of life in the hearts of the people, supplying the wants of their souls with counsel and advice suited to every one.

By means of such existence did the saint never forget his own spiritual life; and having to preach to others, he first looked to himself, mindful of the words of the Apostle, "Lest that by any means, when I have preached to others, I myself should be a cast-away" (1 Cor. ix. 27).

He made the object of his life, what S. Luke writes of the Saviour that "He began both to do and to teach" (Acts i. 1); which is the rule prescribed to all Vartabeds [doctors] who wish to be called great in the kingdom of heaven, according to our Saviour's words (S. Matt. v. 19).

But we must now say one word of the wise expedients he used in order to do so much without neglecting his own spiritual improvement, or diminishing aught from his care of the Churches, but on the contrary, himself setting a beautiful example. He fixed upon the spot in the wilderness of each district which he chose for his retirement; and came to it in turns and thence fed his flock. And to whatever district he came, he spent as many days as he could in desert places, giving them his directions; and then passed on to another district and there provided for its wants in the same way; and so on throughout the country.

Neither did he abandon the care of his flock when he retired alone into the wilderness; for he had appointed many Bishops and presbyters in every diocese, as we told above (see ch. xxvi). Nor yet was it that he never stayed in inhabited places, but that he did not continue there; for he oftentimes came to towns and villages to look after his flock and to supply the wants thereof.

Then was the saint the beloved and great wonder of the land of Armenia. For in like manner as Moses with the prophesying bands of Israelites, and S. Paul with his legions of evangelists, spread the life of the Gospel over the world, calling into existence a flock wherever he went, so also did our Illuminator wake up and quicken all people by enlightening and renewing them through his preaching in our mother tongue of Armenia. And as from year to year he saw the loving piety of his flock increase through the number of presbyters and of Bishops which he ordained and established in divers places, so also did he more and more lead a retired life.

Still the various Churches of the country were eager to have him by them, on account of the abundance of spiritual grace that dropped from his lips, and of his bright and marvellous works. No one more so than pious king Tiridates, who always longed to hold intimate intercourse with him, as we are going to tell more in detail.

CHAPTER XXIX.

How and for what reason S. Gregory, after having provided the country with abundance of spiritual pastors, retired into the wilderness; and how, at the request of the king, he consecrated Arisdaghes his son Bishop in his stead.

THOSE who wish to advance in the ways of godliness, ought especially to take care to keep at the greatest possible distance from the seductions of vain glory, which is ever trying to lead us astray from good works. Such men, in order to increase the love for God in their mind, sever themselves more and more from the world and its vanity, from its petty cares, and from the multitude that hinder the mind and heart from holding intimate communion with God. And this shone brightly in the Illuminator, as his historians tell us.

'For after having scattered from the land of Armenia the gloom of ignorance and heathenish superstition with the light of the knowledge of God, and after providing all parts of the country with Bishops and vartabeds [teachers and doctors], drawn

---

' Agathangelos, Moses of Chor. ii. 88, S. Metaphrastes.

by the sweetness of God's love, he went among high mountains, there to give himself up altogether to such holy contemplations. There he increased his bodily fastings and privations, lest he should let pride get the better of him, from the recollection of the wonderful endurance with which he had formerly borne his unexampled sufferings, and from the thought of his apostolic deeds for the conversion of the country, accompanied with wonders wrought by the grace of Christ. In this wise did he limit himself regularly to fast forty days, until the day he was called by Christ to his rest. So, at least, write Agathangelos and Simeon Metaphrastes.

Meanwhile the Church which S. Gregory had planted, and which had tasted the blessing of his spiritual oversight, ill brooked his absence from her. But especially king Tiridates, who, living apparently as sovereign in his palace, nevertheless led therein, in deep repentance, the life of a hermit, and always longed to have S. Gregory with him. And he often asked him to come to him; yet the saint would not consent.

But the greater time he thus spent in solitude, making his visits fewer and fewer, the more did the Churches in general long to see him. They felt as if they were being deprived of their devoted pastor, who was to them like the Saviour, and as if they were growing faint thereby, as the like of him was nowhere among them. For none of the many spiritual pastors and vartabeds he had ordained all over the land bare greater comparison with him, than the stars of heaven do with the sun in brightness.

Meanwhile, Ardavasd, commander-in-chief of all the Armenian forces, who got information about the sons of S. Gregory, told of them to the king, who, hitherto, had had no knowledge of the matter. Notice, then, I pray you, the virtuous conduct of S. Gregory's sons, who, though they knew their father to be so remarkable and to have reached so high a degree of exaltation, nevertheless did not wish to intrude themselves upon him, in order to seek honour to themselves; as he also did not call them to himself, unless so moved by God.

He then had two sons, as we briefly mentioned above (ch. iii.); the eldest of whom, Vrthanes, was married when a layman, but had afterwards been called from choice to the holy and pure life of a presbyter. But the younger son, Arisdaghes, had from his childhood embraced a life of solitude, having attached himself to the hermit Nichomachus, with whom he spent his life in the wilderness, in a separate cell, however, living on herbs, clad in a coarse cloak, and patiently bearing heat and cold in that retreat; denying himself the necessary sleep by standing on his feet, satisfied as he was with an occasional stretch on the bare ground.

Thus did he mortify his body by continued endurance and self-denial, which enabled him to abide firm in the grace of Christ, against the temptations and assaults of spiritual enemies; being in prayer day and night, and spending his time in reading the holy Scriptures and in praises and thanksgivings, fed and supported as he was by meditating on the mysterious dispensation of the world's redemption through Christ. So that, after some years of such holy life, when he had subdued all the lusts of the flesh, and had altogether put off the old man and had put on the new man, had now arrived at being above passions and temptations, and was governed by a firmness that resided in his will, he became a remarkable instance of a life spent for God, to all who beheld him, as well as of evangelical teaching to those whom he had drawn to him and taught. For he brightly shone of all the graces of the Spirit, and was perfected in the keeping of God's commandments, until he was like a star in the lustre of his heavenly life, presenting to all a pattern of holy conduct and conversation.

Meanwhile the king, when he became aware of the holy life of S. Gregory's sons, was filled with gladness. He at once chose three men from the most honourable of the land and sent them with a letter into Cappadocia, requesting that the two sons of S. Gregory be brought to him without delay. Of the men thus sent on this errand, Ardavasd was the first, inasmuch as he had the command of all the forces of the realm. Another was Dodjad, prince of the province of Ashods[1]; and the third was called Tad, the king's messenger.

When they came into Cappadocia they found

---

[1] [In Ararat.]

Vrthanes at Cæsarea; but Arisdaghes was in the wilderness. He, however would not leave his solitude, until a great many Christians said to him that it were better he should go and do the work of God's labourer, than continue thus in solitude alone. He then consented to go to the king with the princes sent to fetch him; and the two brothers then departed from Cæsarea.

When they were brought in presence of Tiridates, he greatly rejoiced; and went himself with them to look for S. Gregory, whom they found in a desert place of the province of Taranaghi, on a mountain called Manyea-Arèk, after the virgin Mani, who had lived and died there in the Lord, as we related above (p. 217); and the king then asked the saint to consecrate his son Arisdaghes in his stead, according to that which is written, "instead of thy fathers thou shalt have children" (Ps. xlv. 17), saying, "Since thou lovest a retired life and wishest not to abide among us, we pray thee to consecrate thy son instead of thyself."

The holy Patriarch heard the king's request; and having come down from the mountain, he called together a synod of Bishops and priests, and consecrated Arisdaghes Patriarch of all Armenia, in his place; for he was most like his father in his whole conduct. Then S. Gregory went with him the round of the whole country, refreshing and encouraging the flock to abide firm in the commandments of God, and in the true service of Him; and then returned to his favourite abode in the wilderness.

After this, Arisdaghes, who was like his father in many respects and in the lustre of his doctrine, went about like him, enlightening, tending, and providing for the Church in the place of his father; being praised of all; to the infinite comfort of king Tiridates, who himself grew in grace and in the fear of God from day to day, setting a glorious example of holiness of life to all the princes and nobles of his realm. He took an oath of all men, both small and great, who were in any way connected with him in the government of the kingdom, that they would ever maintain this firmly established, namely,—" to believe in their Creator with a single mind, to love Him with their whole heart, to keep His commandments, and to obey Him, frankly and unreservedly;" an order which they hastened to fulfil to the utmost of their power.

CHAPTER XXX.

How it came to pass that S. Gregory and King Tiridates went to visit Pope Silvester and the Emperor Constantine the Great; and of the great joy they felt at meeting together.

[a] ARMENIA had now been converted eighteen years, and every thing was being done by good king Tiridates

[a] [Agathangelos, Anuals of the Armenian Church preserved at Rome, Legends of the Saints, and S. Metaphrastes.]

for her spiritual welfare, when news reached him of all the wonderful things done by the Emperor Constantine, and of his conversion to the faith of Christ; for all of which Tiridates returned thanks to God with great joy, because the whole earth was being filled with His glorious name. And he desired to see the Emperor who had just embraced the faith of Christ, and to rejoice with him.

He then formed plans for his journey. He would take with him the great men—S. Gregory the Illuminator, with his son Arisdaghes, and the Bishop Alpheus the Great; and of his army, four prefects of the palace, called intendants. The first was guard over the borders towards the parts of Shirazan; the second, guard towards Assyria; the third, guard towards Albania; the fourth, guard towards Media; the governor of the madhouse, the knight who placed the Crown on the king's head, the great chamberlain, the chief of the Magi, and a large retinue of other officers of State besides. .

With them he left the province of Ararat and the city of Valarshabad to come by slow marches to the borders of the kingdom of Greece, and thence to pass on to Italy. He was welcomed every where with the greatest honours, wherever he came on this journey from city to city; until, having travelled by land and water, he arrived in Italy, in the province of Dalmatia', in the royal city of Rome.

' [A term which formerly had a wider meaning than at present; when Latin was also called "Dalmatic" in Armenian.]

When the news of his arrival were brought to the palace, both the Emperor Constantine and Pope Silvester rejoiced greatly at hearing that Tiridates was come; they greeted him with all due honour, and prepared a palace for his abode during his stay in the universal city.

There was he treated according to his rank by the Emperor, whose guards of honour did duty on Tiridates. They visited each other frequently, and also Pope Silvester, with whom they held sweet intercourse; those three conversing together wonderfully in all humility on sacred subjects, like the angels in heaven.

The Christian Emperor asked our king Tiridates the particulars of his conversion to the faith of Christ; Tiridates then gave him a full account of all that happened to him, and of the wonderful endurance of Christ's hero S. Gregory, during the untold tortures to which he was put; also how Rhipsime, in her own natural strength, had overcome him, Tiridates; and the martyrdom of all her fellow-virgins. He also told of God's judgments upon him when he was changed into the form and likeness of a wild boar, giving full details of it all, without counting it a shame for him as king; but with the deepest humility and boldly did he tell every thing, to the glory of Christ. And how he had been healed of such a plague by the prayers of S. Gregory, to whom he now pointed, and whom he called by name, saying at the same time, "This is the man through whom we have been made to know of God's mercy towards us; he is the benefactor of the whole land of Armenia; he is the man who, tormented by us with untold tortures, endured them all with wonderful patience, and lived through them; he is the man whom we cast into a pit full of snakes and other reptiles, and who remained in it fourteen years, preserved by God from all harm, and who, when come out thence, wrought many wonders among us, and enlightened us all."

And many more things of the same kind did Tiridates tell the Emperor; the saint's endurance and patience, and all the signs he wrought. At which the Emperor was greatly surprised, and threw himself at S. Gregory's feet to receive his blessing; thus giving him all due honour as to Christ's Confessor. Likewise did Constantine show great affection for Tiridates, as for his beloved brother in the Lord.

And they made the Faith which is in Jesus Christ the bond of union between them, whereby their brotherly love might continue firm and unshaken. So also did the Armenian and the Roman Patriarchs; after which, the two emperors turned to tell other things of mutual interest to them. For when Tiridates had done relating the martyrdom of Christ's maidens, the Emperor Constantine also began telling him of their holy life, and of the good deeds and innocence of which they shone while they were yet in the neighbourhood of Rome. And he thus proved to him that they were of a noble family after the flesh, according to the information he had received of them.

He also told him of all the good deeds he had done for the service of God, and the strength he had received from Him, wherewith all the enemies of the Truth were by him overcome and brought low; as well as the light of grace, and the marvellous signs by which he had been converted to Christ. And he said to him, "Knowest thou, brother, that God is manifesting the power of His mercy to the whole earth? So that all creatures should know Him, and praise His truthfulness; for such worshippers does He seek." Such and like discourses full of grace did the two sovereigns hold together in humility, thereby stirring up the love of their hearts towards each other, as did also the two holy Patriarchs during many days.

After these things, when on both sides they had in every respect fulfilled the desire of their minds, the august Emperor, in company with the great men of the realm, took leave of Tiridates, who, having received a blessing from the holy Patriarch, left Rome with great pomp in the royal carriages emblazoned with gold; and, being escorted by the noblemen of the city, they went on their way, being honoured and courted in every place through which they passed. Thus did they reach at last the province of Ararat and the city of Valarshabad, the resting-place of the saints, where they gave thanks and praise to Christ for their prosperous journey and return home.

The following letter, however, shows with what royal pomp and splendour the holy Emperor

Constantine treated our king Tiridates, and also with what spiritual gifts Pope Silvester enriched our new Patriarch S. Gregory, as well as the bonds of love and friendship that were knit between them. The letter briefly read as follows:—

Letter of friendship and of mutual union between the Emperor Constantine and Pope Silvester, and king Tiridates and S. Gregory the Illuminator.

"[1] By the will and power of the co-eternal Holy Trinity, of the incomprehensible Father, and of His Only Begotten Son our Saviour Jesus Christ, and of the Holy Ghost, giver of life and liberator of men, this our imperial contract shall, through God, remain firm and unchangeable, drawn, as it has been, by command of the ever-victorious Emperor Constantine the Great, the august king of kings, universal ruler, and supreme director of the unconquerable power of Rome; we who, by the power of the true God govern the world, from the ends of the wide ocean to the outgoings of the sun, by the invincible power and glory of the Cross of Christ."

Letters patent were also written by order of the great Pope of Rome, Eusebius Silvester, sitting on the throne of the Apostles Peter and Paul, to wit: "I who have power, through the keys of heaven, over all nations from east to west, to bind and to loose, in heaven and on earth, and am supreme commander over the universal Church of Christ.

[1] Agathangelos.

"Whereas, being moved by the Holy Ghost, the great Johannes, otherwise Tiridates, king of Armenia, came to visit us, together with the living martyr and great Confessor of Christ, Lord S. Gregory, Illuminator of the whole East and North, our dear brethren in Christ, and true friends of our high power, and trusty counsellors of our inmost thoughts, heirs and princes in all the kingdom of the Arshagunians. They spent some time on a visit to the lordly residence of the Pope, who is heir and successor, both east and west, of the holy chief Apostles; of the illustrious Emperor Constantine, lately won to the faith of Christ; of Helena his queen, and of their royal children.

"Whereupon our royalty, which is established in God, greatly rejoiced, and we went forth with great pomp and royal pageant to meet the royalty of Ararat and the hosts of Ashkenaz; and we honoured one another, and worshipped together our immortal Lord and King Jesus Christ. Then, after mutual salutations, we went to the church of the holy Apostles, and there worshipped together their relics, giving glory to Christ, who crowns His saints in heaven."

Then after other words he said, "And by the will of God, as well as by the intercession of the Mother of God, of the holy Apostles, and of all the saints, the two kings and the two Patriarchs and the two nations of Rome and of Armenia, with one mouth, with one thought, and with the same breath, declared themselves each brother of the other; to which effect we have made a treaty and confirmed it by an oath for ever between us, in presence of the glorious Cross of Christ; between us, the valiant Latins on the one part, and the unconquerable descendants of Thorgomah on the other." Such were the terms of the treaty.

As to the authenticity of this treaty, not only do our own annalists and historians attest it, but writers also of other nations. Our Patriarch S. Nerses Shnorhali, in his history of the antiquities of the nation, agrees on the terms of the treaty between the two sovereigns. Likewise in the Menologue, in the life of the Illuminator, on the 18th of November, is the same thing told. So also Nicephorus, a Greek historian (lib. viii. c. 35), relates that S. Gregory came with king Tiridates to Constantine the Great[b]. But a certain monk named Gravina, in the 8th chapter of the first part of his

---

[b] [This interview between S. Gregory and Pope Silvester and the Emperor Constantine at Rome is borrowed from Agathangelos (pp. 651 sq. ed. Ven.), who, says our author, is to be read with great caution, as the various MSS. of him differ greatly. But it is note-worthy that neither Eusebius, Socrates, Sozomen, nor Theodoritus even mention S. Gregory, much less this visit, although Sozomen speaks of the conversion of Tiridates (lib. ii. c. 8), and Theodoritus of Pope Silvester (lib. i. c. 3); neither does Simeon Metaphrastes, who gives at length the history of S. Gregory, say any thing of this journey to Rome, though he speaks of the friendship which existed between Tiridates and Constantine. Nor yet does Cedrenus, who mentions Pope Silvester and S. Gregory, giving an account of his being taken out of the pit (λάκκου, hole), say any thing of this interview ; nor yet Moses of Chorene, who speaks of Tiridates' journey to Rome (lib. ii. cc. 80, 81).

history of Armenia, writes at length on the subject. After mentioning other matters, he affirms that, "between Constantine the Great, S. Silvester, and king Tiridates, and S. Gregory, there was a great love and friendship; a thing made plain in an old copy written in the midst of Armenia, in which is given the letter of love and friendship between Constantine the Great and S. Silvester on the one hand, and king Tiridates and S. Gregory the Illuminator on the other."

CHAPTER XXXI.

Of the reason for which S. Gregory, when summoned to the Council of Nicæa, did not consent to go himself, but sent his son, S. Arisdaghes, in his place. Of his feelings at receiving from his son the decrees of that Council, which he caused to be published throughout Armenia by Arisdaghes; and of what took place afterwards.

[1] IN those days appeared at Alexandria the profane

On the other hand, Muravieff (Trav. vol. ii. p. 38) says that, according to Armenian tradition, Tiridates went to meet Constantine at Constantinople. With all this, nevertheless, Michael Tchamitch not only says in his history of Armenia (vol. i. p. 408) that S. Gregory went with Tiridates to Rome, but that he was consecrated Patriarch of all Armenia by Pope Silvester; and at p. 636 sq. of the same volume, he quotes several Armenian authors to that effect.]

[1] Moses of Chorene, ii. 86. Legends of Saints, 19th of Nov.

Arius, who taught that the Son of God is not coessential with the Father, but that He is a stranger to Him and created; that He was not begotten of the Father before the worlds, but came into existence in after time, and is not equal, but inferior to the Father. And in order to refute and drive away such wicked heresy from the Church, Pope Silvester, having taken counsel with other patriarchs, gave orders to call together a council of bishops in Nicæa, a city of Bithynia.

Then the pious Emperor Constantine made all necessary preparations for the council, and wrote letters to all quarters of the earth according to the directions of Pope Silvester, inviting the patriarchs of all those places to come together in the said city. Thither came Bidion and Vegentius presbyters from the city of Rome, who had been consecrated bishops by Pope Silvester; Alexander of Alexandria, Eustathius of Antioch, Macarius of Jerusalem, Alexander of Constantinople, and other bishops from other parts.

Thither also came the Emperor himself, to give help and countenance to the fathers there assembled, and waiting on their orders with all humility. Then came a letter from the Emperor to Tiridates, asking him to take S. Gregory and to bring him to the council. Tiridates himself, however, would not consent to come, as he was then in fear of danger for his kingdom from the princes of neighbouring states. S. Gregory also would not come, lest he should receive yet greater honours from the bishops assembled, on account of the name of Confessor he had won for himself, and of the apostolic works he had wrought.

But they two sent Arisdaghes with a letter, telling the real state of the case, and their reasons for not coming, who, arriving at Cæsarea, took with him Leontius and came to Nicæa, where three hundred and eighteen bishops assembled against the heresy of Arius in the year of our Lord 325; when they anathematized and excommunicated him, and the Emperor banished him into Media.

When the business of that synod was completed, Arisdaghes brought away with him the twenty principal canons thereof, and came to his father and to Tiridates, in the city of Valarshabad, and there laid those decrees before them; whereat they both greatly rejoiced. S. Gregory took them up and read them; and setting to them in words the seal of his approbation said, "Now let us praise Him who was before the worlds, worshipping the most Holy Trinity and the Godhead of the Father, Son, and Holy Ghost, now and ever, world without end, Amen [1];" words with which he enlightened and adorned the land of Armenia. And as to the presence of Arisdaghes at the Council of Nicæa, not only do the chief ecclesiastical writers bear witness to it, but his name is found in the acts of that council [2].

[1] [These words of S. Gregory are added to the Nicene Creed when said in the Armenian Church.]
[2] [The names of Leontius and of Arisdaghes are found in two lists of the bishops present at Nicæa, which are not generally

Here may we mention that our saint Illuminator did not exert himself for the good of his flock by the word of preaching only, but also by writing. For, according to Agathangelos, the learned secretary of king Tiridates, S. Gregory wrote many homilies[1], deep allegories, pleasantly and agreeably written, and framed with the power and the flowing energy of the prophetical writings, confirmed by witness from the Gospels, full of all the sweetest flavoured fruits of the Spirit, and withal written in the most classical and becoming style.

All of which he wrote in various ways and making use of familiar examples for the use and benefit of this present life, and also about the resurrection from the dead, and other mysteries, in easy words to be understood by men of simple minds, especially by those who are occupied in worldly callings, likely to wean them from the love of this world, and to encourage them in keeping God's commandments, and strengthen them in the hope of the good things promised by God and laid up in store for them. So that our holy father Gregory of Nareg, Superior of convents, in his exposition of the Song of Songs, often quotes from the holy Illuminator's homilies.

known—(1) in Zoega Codd. Sahid. p. 245, where we read of ΛΕΟΝΤΙΟC of Cæsarea, and of ΑΡΙΚΗC of Armenia; and (2) in the Syriac Analecta Nicæna, ed. H. Cooper, pp. 11, 12, where we have Leontios of Cæsarea and Aristagius of Armenia. But as these two lists do not quite agree, Aristeus of Armenia, mentioned in the Sahidic fragment, may be for Aristagius of the Syriac list; and Arikes also answer to Akrites of Dispont.]

[1] [These may one day be published in English, if God permit.]

Of him also is the beautiful and spiritual address on Rhipsime and her fellows, which is said aloud at the public morning prayers, and begins with, "O Great God," &c.[5]

S. Gregory still occupied the supreme rank in the Church and ruled her thence without relaxing in

[5] [This prayer or address is as follows: "O great God, mighty and glorious, who enlightenest the saints, and who abidest among them, we take the sufferings of the Apostles as an intercession for us. Hear us, we pray Thee, O Lord, and have mercy upon us.

"Thou, who art incessantly blessed and praised among the watchers on high, make us fit worthily to worship Thee in company with those heavenly hosts. Hear us, we pray Thee, O Lord, and have mercy upon us.

"We bless Thee with united love in remembrance of Thy holy martyrs who followed Thee, Lord, in the way of light; Who for our sakes didst give Thyself to the sufferings of the Cross and to death. Hear us, we pray Thee, O Lord, and have mercy upon us.

"Longing as they were only to fulfil Thy good pleasure, they gave themselves up as victims for the sacrifice, to bear witness to Thy love, breathing forth the sweet savour of Thy divine nature. Hear us, we pray thee, O Lord, and have mercy upon us.

"They purified themselves as temples of Thy holy Name, by cleansing their mind and thoughts in Thy holy fear; and they then took rank among the spirits of Thy watchers on high. Hear us, O Lord, we pray Thee, and have mercy upon us.

"Through the intercession of the holy Mother of God and of John the Precursor, of S. Stephen Protomartyr, and of the holy apostles, prophets, and martyrs, and of S. Gregory our Illuminator.

"Through the intercession and prayers of the saints (N. N.) whom we this day commemorate, and for all Thy saints, O Lord, who have been gathered together in Thy love, remember the souls of our departed, and visit them at Thy second coming.

"Hear us, O Lord, we pray Thee, and have mercy upon us. Amen."—Jamakirk, p. 235, ed. Const. The last two clauses are a later addition.]

any way, giving all diligence to exhort every one to keep God's commandments, to eschew evil, and to give themselves to good works. Night and day, occupied as he was in things belonging to God, did he continue instant in prayer, in fasting and watching; and by the example of his own life and by his preaching did he instil into all men the commandments of God, and earnestly to abide in them; he neither gave sleep to his eyes nor rest to his temples until the day that he found his rest in the Lord.

Likewise did king Tiridates, both by the example of his own good life and by his laws and edicts, teach and press upon every one, both small and great, to worship God and to serve Him, directing his people withal to a due observance of His commandments.

Our holy Illuminator paid great attention to the reading of the Holy Scriptures, giving his mind with due care to the words of both the Old and New Testaments. Regarding the study of which he says, speaking of the first, "Blessed is he whose delight is in the law of the Lord, and in His law will he exercise himself day and night. And he shall be like a tree planted by the water-side, that will bring forth his fruit in due season" (Ps. i. 2, 3). And as regards the New Testament he said, "Give attendance to reading, to exhortation, to doctrine. Neglect not the gift that is in thee, which was given thee by prophecy with the laying on of the hands of the presbytery. Meditate upon these things; give thyself wholly to them; that thy profiting may appear to all. Take heed to thyself, and unto the doctrine; continue in them: for in doing this thou shalt both save thyself and them that hear thee" (1 Tim. iv. 13—16).

And thus both he and the king, and all his disciples, spent all the time they could spare from other holy occupations in reading the Holy Scriptures, whereby they profited, and wherein, like flowers, they blossomed, delighting in the reading of all that tended to inform them in good and holy deeds. He wrote letters to S. James, Patriarch of Nisibis, requesting him to compose homilies on faith, love, and other virtues. So that not only did he devote himself to the pursuit of such studies and knowledge as he had learnt from his infancy at the feet of his teacher, and had thus grown up diligent in secular knowledge and in the instruction of the Holy Scriptures; but also, besides that, was he filled with all manner of spiritual graces that adorned him, and in his letters did he always inquire as to the humility of the heart; thus perfecting his own humble conduct in life by what he heard that of others to be.

CHAPTER XXXII.

Of the side of the wilderness in which S. Gregory exchanged this life for the next; and by what sort of people his body was found and unwittingly covered with stones; when and where it was made known whose body it was, and where it was laid to rest; and in what parts of the world the relics of his saintly body are now to be found.

'WHO, then, is able adequately to set forth all the saintly life of our holy Illuminator? No tongue however skilled can do it, nor yet can the thickest volumes contain an account of all that he did. But we, after having told in a few pages the fragments that are left of his inexhaustible doings, must now finish our narrative by telling a few particulars of his death.

After he had provided for the spiritual wants of his flock, and had enlightened the whole of Armenia, he left the world and retired, as we said before, into a solitude of the province of Taran; and led a solitary existence there in a noble mountain, in the caves of Manyea, and gave himself up to a life of good works of which we told a few particulars.

But while he remained there, he yet sometimes

* Legends of Saints; Moses of Chor. ii. 88; and Metaphrastes.

came from the mountain to visit his flock, to confirm the converts in the faith and in innocency of life. Then, after Arisdaghes came back from Nicæa, S. Gregory spent some little time with him, and then returned to his wilderness, and after that showed himself no where; while Arisdaghes governed the Church of Armenia in his place.

Then, after having lived a length of time out of sight of men, but in company with angels, his mind withdrawn from things of the world and his inward man strengthened by prayer, his thoughts dwelling on high, in unspeakable meditations on heavenly things, enlightened by the revelation to him of things hidden and of unsearchable mysteries, he lived refreshed and quickened every day at the sweet spring of God's unspeakable love. And having thus run the course of his life on earth, while keeping the faith, and earnestly longing with an affectionate heart for a sight of God's countenance, he at last, full of good works, exchanged this miserable existence for the life that never ends, among the angels above, whither his Saviour beckoned him to come.

But the saint, whose cell was a hollow in a juniper-tree, there gave up his pure spirit; and his body remained some time in that cell, where shepherds found it by accident. Not knowing whose body it was, they covered it with a heap of stones; and in such a shroud did they wind up the priceless treasure of which they were not aware. And it was well they did fall in with it, albeit they knew not who it was.

For as shepherds were the first to find and to welcome our Saviour, the great and true Shepherd of the sheep, so also were shepherds thought fit company for His disciple, as Moses of Chorene remarks.

Now, however, my words are to the shepherds, in those of a certain wise writer: "What do ye there, O ye shepherds of dumb animals? do ye thus honour the chief shepherd of a rational flock, on whom even angels wait? He is a shepherd whose body ye see there, but his sheep are sensible and can speak; their pasture is heaven, whence he used to feed them with the bread of immortality, and lead them beside the murmuring streams of the water of life that flows in Paradise. Ye cover him with a heap of stones as if he were a stranger, him, the sun of a thousand rays. Ye hide him as if he were one of your own selves, while the Creator of all has ranked him among angels, apostles and prophets, martyrs and patriarchs, vartabeds and anchorites. Yet blessed are ye, that ye have been thought worthy with your hands to bear the chief shepherd of our spiritual flock. Blessed are your eyes, that beheld and looked upon this sun in his splendour. Blessed are your arms, in which ye have carried him who is raised among the heavenly hosts. And blessed are your nostrils, that have smelled the spirit that is in him."

It was so willed by God's Providence, that his body should thus remain several years hidden from the sight and knowledge of men, after the manner of that of Moses, lest he should be worshipped instead of God by the new converts, as Moses of Chorene thinks. But when, after many years, the faith of all the people had been strengthened, the body of the saint was shown to a hermit called Kamig, who took it and laid it to rest in the village of Thorkan', to the glory of our Saviour Jesus Christ.

Our thrice blessed Illuminator S. Gregory took his seat on the throne of the Patriarchate of Armenia in the year of our Lord 302; and lived thirty years in that high office. For, from the beginning of his taking holy orders, in the eighteenth year of the reign of Tiridates, until the forty-sixth year, when S. Gregory no longer appeared among men, are reckoned about thirty years; therefore was the year 331 the last of his Patriarchate. He was, as Moses of Chorene, relates, Parthian by birth, of the province of Balkh, and of the distinguished and royal race of the Arsacidæ. He rose to be the true Orient in the East of Armenia, like an intelligent sun and a spiritual brightness, in the depth of the wickedness of idolatry, the source of blessedness and of edification for us all. A divine palm-tree, indeed, planted in the house of the Lord, and that blossomed in the courts of our God. Spread abroad as he was among so many peoples, he gathered us all into one, unto the glory and praise of God.

But after some years, when the independent king-

' [In Taranaghi, where, on Mount Sebuh, is the tomb of S. Gregory. Vartan, Geogr. p. 432, ed. S. Martin.]

dom of Armenia began to fall, it pleased the Providence of God to order that the relics of S. Gregory should be removed to Greece, in the days of the Emperor Zeno, who reigned in the year 474 of our salvation; and thence, after a long time, to Italy. So that, as when the saint was in the body, his endurance and the apostolic graces of his works were a help to very many; so also, after his spirit had left his body, was he still to be a help through the wonders wrought by his relics, famous throughout the world, to the glory of Christ our God.

The removal of those relics happened thus: the Greek Emperor Zeno having heard that the remains of our Illuminator S. Gregory had been discovered, sent in search of them, and desired they should be brought to Constantinople, a portion of them being left in Armenia. All that was left us is two fragments of his arms, of which one is now in the city of Valarshabad, in the Patriarchal Church of Etchmiadzin, and the other in the Church of S. Sophia, in the city of Sis. They are both set in gold and silver[a].

But as to the remains that were brought to Constantinople, in the Menologue for the 18th of November, it is said, that in the days of Sambat or Ashod, who then ruled over Armenia, they were

[a] [According to Vartab. Vartan (Geogr. p. 420), S. Gregory's body was brought back from Constantinople and placed inside the well in which he had spent thirteen years of his life. Over this well is a church built, called *Khorvirab*, or "Deep well;" it is situate some thirty miles from Etchmiadzin. See note, p. 48.]

brought back among us, after having been demanded of the Greek Emperor. In the course of time, however, when the Saracens got possession of the country, certain pious monks from fear of the infidels, took those remains and brought them westward to Italy. The greater part of them is laid in the Cathedral of Neridon[*], where they work miracles, especially in granting rain in times of drought. For this reason have they chosen our S. Gregory the Illuminator for protector of their city; and from year to year they hold a festival of eight days in honour of him, on the thirtieth day of September. Those sacred relics were brought thither by priests and by holy virgins who were expelled from the East by Constantine Copronymus.

But the venerable head of the saint, the chains with which he was bound, and chips of the staves with which he was beaten, are religiously kept in Neapolis, in the convent of noble virgins and in the church built to the memory of S. Gregory the Illuminator; where they work wonderful cures on the sick and infirm, who in faith even once touch those chips, which have an extraordinary virtue of healing all manner of sickness, and of driving away devils. Those remains were brought thither also by faithful virgins, for the sake of those who fled from the East when driven thence, as Cardinal Baronius tells us.

The life and deeds of our Sun, S. Gregory the Illuminator, have been handed down not only by

[*] [Νήριτον (Nardo) in Calabria?]

writers of our own nation, but by writers of the whole Universal Church, by some in general, by others in detail; among whom are Simeon Metaphrastes, Cardinal Baronius, and Nicephorus. Likewise, also, do Euthymius and Sozomen write of him. So also the martyrologues of the Latin, Greek, and Syrian Churches, mention his feast on the thirtieth of September. And as to the historians and other authors who make mention of our Illuminator, who can count them?

Here, therefore, shall we make an end of our poor, insignificant narrative, in honour of our thrice blessed holy Father Gregory the Illuminator; to the glory of Christ our God, who is blessed for ever. Amen.

THE END.

June, 1868.

New Works

IN COURSE OF PUBLICATION

BY

Messrs. RIVINGTON,

WATERLOO PLACE, LONDON;
HIGH STREET, OXFORD; TRINITY STREET, CAMBRIDGE.

Newman's (J. H.) Parochial and Plain Sermons.

Edited by the Rev. W. J. Copeland, Rector of Farnham, Essex. From the Text of the last Editions published by Messrs. Rivington.

Crown 8vo. 8 vols. 5s. each. (*Vols. I. & II. just published.*)

The Divinity of our Lord and Saviour Jesus Christ; being the Bampton Lectures for 1866.

By **Henry Parry Liddon**, M.A., Student of Christ Church, Prebendary of Salisbury, and Examining Chaplain to the Bishop of Salisbury.

Second Edition. Crown 8vo. 5s.

Sketches of the Rites and Customs of the Greco-Russian Church.

By **H. C. Romanoff.** With an Introductory Notice by the Author of "The Heir of Redclyffe."

Crown 8vo. 7s. 6d.

A

A Key to the Knowledge and Use of the
Book of Common Prayer.
By **John Henry Blunt**, M.A.
Small 8vo.   2s. 6d.

Aids to Prayer: a Course of Lectures delivered at Holy Trinity Church, Paddington, on the Sunday mornings in Lent, 1868.
By **Daniel Moore**, M.A., Honorary Chaplain in Ordinary to the Queen, &c.
Crown 8vo.   4s. 6d.

Hymns and Poems for the Sick and Suffering; in connexion with the Service for the Visitation of the Sick. Selected from various Authors.
Edited by **T. V. Fosbery**, M.A., Vicar of St. Giles's, Reading.
This Volume contains 233 separate pieces; of which about 90 are by writers who lived prior to the 18th Century; the rest are Modern, and some of these original.
New and cheaper Edition.   Small 8vo.   3s. 6d.

Flosculi Cheltonienses: a selection from the
Cheltenham College Prize Poems, 1846—1866.
Edited by **C. S. Jerram**, M.A., Trinity College, Oxford, and **Theodore W. James**, M.A., Pembroke College, Oxford.
Crown 8vo.   9s.

Annals of the Bodleian Library, Oxford,
from its Foundation to A.D. 1867; containing an Account of the various collections of printed books and MSS. there preserved; with a brief Preliminary Sketch of the earlier Library of the University.
By **W. D. Macray**, M.A., Assistant in the Library, Chaplain of Magdalen and New Colleges.
8vo.   12s.

Popular Objections to the Book of Common

Prayer Considered, in Four Sermons on the Sunday Lessons in Lent, the Commination Service, and the Athanasian Creed; with a Preface on the existing Lectionary.

By **Edward Meyrick Goulburn**, D.D., Dean of Norwich.

Small 8vo. 2s. 6d.

The Mysteries of Mount Calvary.

By **Antonio de Guevara**.

Being the First Volume of the Ascetic Library, a Series of Translations of Spiritual Works for Devotional Reading from Catholic Sources. Edited by the Rev. **Orby Shipley**, M.A.

Square crown 8vo. 3s. 6d.

The Annotated Book of Common Prayer;

being an Historical, Ritual, and Theological Commentary on the Devotional System of the Church of England.

Edited by **John Henry Blunt**, M.A.

Third Edition, pp. 760, with three Plates. Imperial 8vo, 36s. Large paper Edition, royal 4to, with large margin for Notes, 3l. 3s.

Proceedings at the laying of the First Stone

of Keble College, Oxford, on S. Mark's Day, 1868. With a Design and Plan of the Buildings.

Small 4to. 3s. 6d.

The Dogmatic Faith :

an Inquiry into the Relation subsisting between Revelation and Dogma. Being the Bampton Lectures for 1867.

By **Edward Garbett**, M.A., Incumbent of Christ Church, Surbiton.

8vo. 10s. 6d.

A 2

Vestiarivm Christianvm: the Origin and

Gradual Development of the Dress of Holy Ministry in the Church, as evidenced by Monuments both of Literature and of Art, from the Apostolic Age to the present time.

By the Rev. **Wharton B. Marriott**, M.A., F.S.A. (sometime Fellow of Exeter College, Oxford, and Assistant-Master at Eton), Select Preacher in the University, and Preacher, by licence from the Bishop, in the Diocese of Oxford.

Royal 8vo. 38s.

On Miracles; being the Bampton Lectures

for 1865.

By **J. B. Mozley**, B.D., Vicar of Old Shoreham, late Fellow of Magdalen College, Oxford.

Second Edition. 8vo. 10s. 6d.

The Prayer Book Interleaved.

With Historical Illustrations and Explanatory Notes arranged parallel to the Text, by the Rev. **W. M. Campion**, B.D., Fellow and Tutor of Queens' College and Rector of St. Botolph's, and the Rev. **W. J. Beamont**, M.A., Fellow of Trinity College, Cambridge, and Incumbent of St. Michael's, Cambridge. With a Preface by the **Lord Bishop of Ely.**

Third Edition. Small 8vo. 7s. 6d.

Flowers and Festivals; or, Directions for

the Floral Decorations of Churches. With coloured Illustrations.

By **W. A. Barrett**, of S. Paul's Cathedral, late Clerk of Magdalen College, and Commoner of S. Mary Hall, Oxford.

Square crown 8vo. 5s.

The Case of the Established Church in

Ireland.

By **James Thomas O'Brien**, D.D., Bishop of Ossory, Ferns, and Leighlin.

Third Edition, with an Appendix. 8vo. 2s. 6d.

The Life and Times of S. Gregory the Illuminator, Patron Saint and Founder of the Armenian Church.
By the Rev. **S. C. Malan**, M.A., Vicar of Broadwindsor.

8vo. (*Nearly ready.*)

Sermons on Unity; with an Essay on Religious Societies, and a Lecture on the Life and Times of Wesley.
By **F. C. Massingberd**, M.A., Chancellor of Lincoln.

Crown 8vo. 3s. 6d.

A Fourth Series of Parochial Sermons, preached in a Village Church.
By the Rev. **Charles A. Heurtley**, D.D., Rector of Fenny Compton, Warwickshire, Margaret Professor of Divinity, and Canon of Christ Church, Oxford.

Small 8vo. 5s. 6d.

Daily Devotions; or, Short Morning and Evening Services for the use of a Churchman's Household.
By the Ven. **Charles C. Clerke**, Archdeacon of Oxford.

18mo. 1s.

The Beatitudes of Our Blessed Lord, Considered in Eight Practical Discourses.
By the Rev. **John Peat**, M.A., of St. Peter's College, Cambridge, Vicar of East Grinstead, Sussex.

Small 8vo. 3s. 6d.

Selections from Aristotle's Organon.
Edited by **John R. Magrath**, M.A., Fellow and Tutor of Queen's College, Oxford.

Crown 8vo. 3s. 6d.

Warnings of the Holy Week, &c.;

being a Course of Parochial Lectures for the Week before Easter and the Easter Festivals.

By the Rev. **W. Adams**, M.A., late Vicar of St. Peter's-in-the-East, Oxford, and Fellow of Merton College.

Sixth Edition. Small 8vo. 4*s*. 6*d*.

Curious Myths of the Middle Ages.

By S. **Baring-Gould**, M.A., Author of "Post-Mediæval Preachers," &c. With Illustrations.

First Series. *Second Edition.* Crown 8vo. 7*s*. 6*d*.
Second Series. Crown 8vo. 9*s*. 6*d*.

Household Theology: a Handbook of Religious Information respecting the Holy Bible, the Prayer Book, the Church, the Ministry, Divine Worship, the Creeds, &c. &c.

By **J. H. Blunt**, M.A.

Third Edition. Fcp. 8vo. 3*s*. 6*d*.

Farewell Counsels of a Pastor to his Flock,

on Topics of the Day: Nine Sermons preached at St. John's, Paddington.

By **Edward Meyrick Goulburn**, D.D., Dean of Norwich.

Second Edition. Small 8vo. 4*s*.

Sermons.

By the Rev. **R. S. C. Chermside**, M.A., late Rector of Wilton, and Prebendary of Sarum. With a Preface by the Rev. **G. Rawlinson**, M.A., Camden Professor of Ancient History in the University of Oxford.

Small 8vo. 5*s*.

London Ordination, Advent, 1867;

being Seven Addresses to the Candidates for Holy Orders, in December, 1867.

By **Archibald Campbell, Lord Bishop of London,** and his **Chaplains.**

Together with the Examination Papers.

8vo. 4s.

The London Diocese Book for 1868

(fourth year of issue), under the sanction of the Lord Bishop of London.

Crown 8vo. In wrapper, 1s.

Consoling Thoughts in Sickness.

Edited by **Henry Bailey,** B.D., Warden of St. Augustine's College, Canterbury.

Small 8vo. Large Type. 2s. 6d.

An Illuminated Edition of the Book of

Common Prayer, printed in Red and Black, on fine toned Paper; with Borders and Titles, designed after the manner of the 14th Century by **R. R. Holmes,** F.S.A., and engraved by **O. Jewitt.**

Crown 8vo. White vellum cloth illuminated. 16s.

This Edition of the PRAYER BOOK *may be had in various Bindings for presentation.*

Scripture Acrostics.

By the Author of "The Last Sleep of the Christian Child."

Square 16mo. 1s. 6d. With Key, 2s.

The Key may also be had separately, 6d.

The Sacraments and Sacramental Ordinances
of the Church; being a Plain Exposition of their History, Meaning, and Effects.
By **John Henry Blunt**, M.A.
Small 8vo. 4s. 6d.

Yesterday, To-day, and For Ever:
a Poem in Twelve Books.
By **Edward Henry Bickersteth**, M.A., Incumbent of Christ Church, Hampstead, and Chaplain to the Bishop of Ripon.
Second and Cheaper Edition. Small 8vo. 6s.

The Gate of Paradise: a Dream of Easter
Eve. With Frontispiece.
Square crown 8vo. 6d.

Songs of Joy for the Age of Joy.
By the Rev. **John P. Wright**, B.A.
18mo. 6d.

Queen Bertha and her Times.
By **E. H. Hudson**.
Small 8vo. 5s.

Sermons preached before the University of
Oxford, chiefly during the years 1863—1865.
By **Henry Parry Liddon**, M.A., Student of Christ Church, Prebendary of Salisbury, Examining Chaplain to the Lord Bishop of Salisbury, and lately Select Preacher.
Second Edition. 8vo. 8s.

The Annual Register:

a Review of Public Events at Home and Abroad, for the Year 1867; being the Fifth Volume of an improved Series.
8vo. 18s.

⁎ *The Volumes for 1863, 1864, 1865, and 1866 may be had, price 18s. each.*

The Holy Bible.

With Notes and Introductions.
By Chr. Wordsworth, D.D., Archdeacon of Westminster.

		£	s.	d.
Vol. I. 38s. {	I. Genesis and Exodus. *Second Edit.*	1	1	0
	II. Leviticus, Numbers, Deuteronomy. *Second Edition*	0	18	0
Vol. II. 21s. {	III. Joshua, Judges, Ruth. *Second Edit.*	0	12	0
	IV. The Books of Samuel. *Second Edit.*	0	10	0
Vol. III. 21s. {	V. The Books of Kings, Chronicles, Ezra, Nehemiah, Esther. *Sec. Edit.*	1	1	0
Vol. IV. 34s. {	VI. The Book of Job	0	9	0
	VII. The Book of Psalms	0	15	0
	VIII. Proverbs, Ecclesiastes, Song of Solomon	0	12	0

The Greek Testament.

With Notes and Introductions.
By Chr. Wordsworth, D.D., Archdeacon of Westminster.
2 Vols. Impl. 8vo. 4*l*.

The Parts may be had separately, as follows:—
The Gospels, *6th Edition*, 21s.
The Acts, *5th Edition*, 10s. 6d.
St. Paul's Epistles, *5th Edition*, 31s. 6d.
General Epistles, Revelation, and Indexes, *3rd Edition*, 21s.

Thomas à Kempis, Of the Imitation of Christ:

a carefully revised Translation, elegantly printed with red borders.
16mo. 2s. 6d.

Also a cheap Edition, without the red borders, in Wrapper, 6d.

The Witness of the Old Testament to Christ.

The Boyle Lectures for the Year 1868.

By the Rev. **Stanley Leathes**, M.A., Preacher at St. James', Westminster, and Professor of Hebrew in King's College, London.

8vo. (*In the Press.*)

The Greek Testament.

With a critically revised Text; a Digest of Various Readings; Marginal References to Verbal and Idiomatic Usage; Prolegomena; and a Critical and Exegetical Commentary. For the use of Theological Students and Ministers. By **Henry Alford**, D.D., Dean of Canterbury.

4 Vols. 8vo. 102*s.*

The Volumes are sold separately as follows:—

Vol. I.—The Four Gospels. *Sixth Edition.* 28*s.* (*In the Press.*)
Vol. II.—Acts to II. Corinthians. *Fifth Edition.* 24*s.*
Vol. III.—Galatians to Philemon. *Fourth Edition.* 18*s.*
Vol. IV.—Hebrews to Revelation. *Third Edition.* 32*s.*

The New Testament for English Readers;

containing the Authorized Version, with a revised English Text; Marginal References; and a Critical and Explanatory Commentary. By **Henry Alford**, D.D., Dean of Canterbury.

Now complete in 2 Vols. or 4 Parts, price 54*s.* 6*d.*

Separately,

Vol. 1, Part I.—The three first Gospels, with a Map. *Second Edition.* 12*s.*
Vol. 1, Part II.—St. John and the Acts. 10*s.* 6*d.*
Vol. 2, Part I.—The Epistles of St. Paul, with a Map. 16*s.*
Vol. 2, Part II.—Hebrews to Revelation. 8vo. 16*s.*

Thoughts on Personal Religion;
being a Treatise on the Christian Life in its Two Chief Elements, Devotion and Practice.
By **Edward Meyrick Goulburn**, D.D., Dean of Norwich.
New Edition. Small 8vo. 6s. 6d.

An edition for presentation, Two Volumes, small 8vo. 10s. 6d.
Also, a Cheap Edition. 3s. 6d.

The Greek Testament.
With English Notes, intended for the Upper Forms of Schools, and for Pass-men at the Universities. Abridged from the larger work of the **Dean of Canterbury.**
In one Volume, Crown 8vo. (*In the Press.*)

Vox Ecclesiæ Anglicanæ: a Selection of
Extracts from the Chief Divines of the Church of England on the Main Points of Doctrine and Discipline.
By **George G. Perry**, M.A., Prebendary of Lincoln, Rector of Waddington, Rural Dean, and Proctor for the Diocese of Lincoln.
Small 8vo. (*In the Press.*)

A Key to the Knowledge and Use of the
Bible.
By **John Henry Blunt**, M.A.
Small 8vo. (*In the Press.*)

Manual of Family Devotions, arranged from
the Book of Common Prayer.
By the Hon. **Augustus Duncombe**, D.D., Dean of York.
Printed in red and black. Small 8vo. (*Nearly ready.*)

Family Prayers: compiled from various
sources (chiefly from Bishop Hamilton's Manual), and arranged on the Liturgical Principle.
By **Edward Meyrick Goulburn**, D.D., Dean of Norwich.
New Editions. (*In the Press.*)

Poems.
By **Henry Francis Lyte**, M.A., late Vicar of Lower Brixham, Devon.
New Edition. Small 8vo. (*In the Press.*)

Liber Precum Publicarum Ecclesiæ Anglicanæ.
À **Gulielmo Bright**, A.M., et **Petro Goldsmith Medd**, A.M., Presbyteris, Collegii Universitatis in Acad. Oxon. Sociis, Latine redditus.
In an elegant pocket volume, with all the Rubrics in red.
New Edition. Small 8vo. (*In the Press.*)

Eastern Orthodoxy in the Eighteenth Century;
being a Correspondence between the Greek Patriarchs and the Nonjurors.
Edited, with an Introduction, by the Rev. **George Williams**, B.D., Senior Fellow of King's College, Cambridge.
8vo. (*In the Press.*)

Catechetical Notes and Class Questions,
Literal and Mystical; chiefly on the Earlier Books of Holy Scripture.
By the late Rev. **J. M. Neale**, D.D., Warden of Sackville College, East Grinstead.
Crown 8vo. (*In the Press.*)

Stones of the Temple: a familiar Explanation of the Fabric and Furniture of the Church, with Illustrations, engraved by O. Jewitt.
By the Rev. **Walter Field**, M.A., Vicar of Godmersham.
Post 8vo. (*In Preparation.*)

The Voice of the Good Shepherd to His Lost Sheep; being an Exposition of the former part of the Parable of the Prodigal Son.
By **Robert G. Swayne**, M.A., Rector of St. Edmund's, Salisbury.
Small 8vo. (*In the Press.*)

Selections from Modern French Authors.
With English Notes.
By **Henri Van Laun**, French Master at Cheltenham College.
Part 1.—Honoré de Balzac.
Part 2.—H. Taine.
Crown 8vo. (*In Preparation.*)

Five Years' Church Work in the Kingdom of Hawaii.
By the Right Rev. **Thomas N. Staley**, D.D., Missionary Bishop of Honolulu. With Illustrations.
Crown 8vo. (*In the Press.*)

England and Rome: a Brief Handbook of the Roman Catholic Controversy, for the use of Members of the English Church.
By **H. B. Swete**, M.A., Fellow of Gonville and Caius Coll., Cambridge.
16mo. (*Preparing.*)

From Morning to Evening: a Book for

Invalids. From the French of M. L'Abbé Henri Perreyve. Translated and adapted by an Associate of the Sisterhood of S. John Baptist, Clewer.

Small 8vo. (*In the Press.*)

The Virgin's Lamp: Prayers and Devout

Exercises for English Sisters, chiefly composed and selected by the late Rev. J. M. Neale, D.D., Founder of St. Margaret's, East Grinstead.

Small 8vo. (*In the Press.*)

Perranzabuloe, the lost Church found; or,

the Church of England not a new Church, but Ancient, Apostolical, and Independent, and a Protesting Church Nine Hundred Years before the Reformation.

By the Rev. C. Trelawney Collins, M.A., Rector of Timsbury, Somerset, and late Fellow of Balliol College.

New Edition. Crown 8vo. (*In the Press.*)

Counsels upon Holiness of Life.

Translated from the Spanish of "The Sinner's Guide" by Luis de Granada; forming the second volume of the "Ascetic Library."

Crown 8vo. (*In Preparation.*)

A Summary of Theology and Ecclesiastical

History: a Series of Original Works on all the principal subjects of Theology and Ecclesiastical History.

By Various Writers.

In 8 Vols., 8vo. (*In Preparation.*)

A Glossary of Ecclesiastical Terms; containing Explanations of Terms used in Architecture, Ecclesiology, Hymnology, Law, Ritualism, Theology, Heresies, and Miscellaneous Subjects.

By Various Writers. Edited by the Rev. **Orby Shipley**, M.A. Crown 8vo. *(In Preparation.)*

Devotional Commentary on the Gospel according to S. Matthew.

Translated from **Pasquier Quesnel.**

Crown 8vo. *(In the Press.)*

Catechesis; or, Christian Instruction preparatory to Confirmation and First Communion.

By the Rev. **Charles Wordsworth**, D.C.L., Bishop of St. Andrews.

New and cheaper Edition. Small 8vo. *(In the Press.)*

CATENA CLASSICORUM,
A SERIES OF CLASSICAL AUTHORS,
EDITED BY MEMBERS OF BOTH UNIVERSITIES UNDER THE DIRECTION OF

THE REV. ARTHUR HOLMES, M.A.
FELLOW AND LECTURER OF CLARE COLLEGE, CAMBRIDGE, LECTURER AND LATE FELLOW OF ST. JOHN'S COLLEGE,

AND

THE REV. CHARLES BIGG, M.A.
LATE SENIOR STUDENT AND TUTOR OF CHRIST CHURCH, OXFORD, SECOND CLASSICAL MASTER OF CHELTENHAM COLLEGE.

The following have been already published:—

SOPHOCLIS TRAGOEDIAE, edited by R. C. JEBB, M.A., Fellow and Assistant Tutor of Trinity College, Cambridge.
[Part I.—The Electra. Price 3s. 6d.
[Part II.—The Ajax. Price 3s. 6d.

ARISTOPHANIS COMOEDIAE, edited by W. C. GREEN, M.A., late Fellow of King's College, Cambridge. Classical Lecturer at Queens' College.
[Part I.—The Acharnians and the Knights. Price 4s.
[Part II.—The Clouds. Price 3s. 6d.

JUVENALIS SATIRAE, edited by G. A. SIMCOX, M.A., Fellow and Classical Lecturer of Queen's College, Oxford.
[Thirteen Satires. Price 3s. 6d.

THUCYDIDIS HISTORIA, edited by CHARLES BIGG, M.A., late Senior Student and Tutor of Christ Church, Oxford; Second Classical Master of Cheltenham College.
[Vol. I. Books I. and II. with Introductions. Price 6s.

DEMOSTHENIS ORATIONES PUBLICAE, edited by G. H. HESLOP, M.A., late Fellow and Assistant Tutor of Queen's College, Oxford; Head Master of St. Bees.
[Parts I. and II. The Olynthiacs and the Philippics. Price 4s. 6d.

The following Parts are preparing:—

HOMERI ILIAS, edited by S. H. REYNOLDS, M.A., Fellow and Tutor of Brasenose College, Oxford.
[Vol. I. Books I. to XII.

HERODOTI HISTORIA, edited by H. G. WOODS, M.A., Fellow and Tutor of Trinity College, Oxford.

DEMOSTHENIS ORATIONES PRIVATAE, edited by ARTHUR HOLMES, M.A., Fellow and Lecturer of Clare College, Cambridge.
[Part I. De Corona.

TERENTI COMOEDIAE, edited by T. L. PAPILLON, M.A., Fellow and Classical Lecturer of Merton College, Oxford.

ISOCRATIS ORATIONES, edited by JOHN EDWIN SANDYS, B.A., Fellow and Lecturer of St. John's College, and Lecturer at Jesus College, Cambridge. [Part I.

TACITI HISTORIAE, edited by the Rev. W. H. SIMCOX, M.A., Fellow and Lecturer of Queen's College, Oxford.

HORATI OPERA, edited by J. M. MARSHALL, M.A., Fellow and late Lecturer of Brasenose College, Oxford. One of the Masters in Clifton College.

MARTIALIS EPIGRAMMATA, edited by GEORGE BUTLER, M.A., Principal of Liverpool College; late Fellow of Exeter College, Oxford.

DEMOSTHENIS ORATIONES PUBLICAE, edited by G. H. HESLOP, M.A., late Fellow and Assistant Tutor of Queen's College, Oxford. Head Master of St. Bees.
[Part II. De Falsâ Legatione.

SOPHOCLIS TRAGOEDIAE, edited by R. C. JEBB, M.A., Fellow and Assistant Tutor of Trinity College, Cambridge.
[Part III. The Philoctetes.

PLATONIS PHAEDO, edited by the Rev. ALFRED BARRY, D.D., late Fellow of Trinity College, Cambridge, Principal of King's College, London.

RIVINGTONS,
London, Oxford, and Cambridge.

www.ingramcontent.com/pod-product-compliance
Lightning Source LLC
Chambersburg PA
CBHW020238240426
43672CB00006B/565